LEARNING AND LITERACY OVER TIME

Learning and Literacy over Time addresses two gaps in literacy research—studies offering longitudinal perspectives on learners and the trajectory of their learning lives inside and outside of school, and studies revealing how past experiences with literacy and learning inform future experiences and practices. It does so by bringing together researchers who revisited subjects of their initial research conducted over the past 10–20 years with people they encountered through ethnographic or classroom-based investigations and are the subjects of previous published accounts.

The case studies, drawn from countries in three continents and covering a range of social worlds, offer an original and at times quite emotive interpretation of the effects of long-term social change in the UK, the US, Australia and Canada; the claims and aspirations made by and for certain kinds of educational interventions; how research subjects reflect on and learn from the processes of being co-opted into classroom research as well as how they make sense of school experiences; some of the widespread changes in literacy practices as a result of our move into the digital era; and above all, how academic research can learn from these life stories, raising a number of challenges about methodology and our claims to 'know' the people we research. In many cases the process of revisiting led to important reconceptualizations of the earlier work and a sense of 'seeing with new eyes' what was missed in the past.

Julian Sefton-Green is an independent scholar working in Education and the Cultural and Creative industries. He is currently Principal Research Fellow at the London School of Economics and Political Science, UK.

Jennifer Rowsell is a Professor and Canada Research Chair at Brock University, Canada. She is currently Principal Investigator of a SSHRC-funded study linking literacy with community and the arts, entitled Community Arts Zone.

LEARNING AND LITERACY OVER TIME

Longitudinal Perspectives

*Edited by Julian Sefton-Green
and Jennifer Rowsell*

NEW YORK AND LONDON

First published 2015
by Routledge
711 Third Avenue, New York, NY 10017

and by Routledge
2 Park Square, Milton Park, Abingdon, Oxon, OX14 4RN

Routledge is an imprint of the Taylor & Francis Group, an informa business

© 2015 Taylor & Francis

The right of the editors to be identified as authors of the editorial material, and of the authors for their individual chapters, has been asserted in accordance with sections 77 and 78 of the Copyright, Designs and Patents Act 1988.

All rights reserved. No part of this book may be reprinted or reproduced or utilised in any form or by any electronic, mechanical, or other means, now known or hereafter invented, including photocopying and recording, or in any information storage or retrieval system, without permission in writing from the publishers.

Trademark notice: Product or corporate names may be trademarks or registered trademarks, and are used only for identification and explanation without intent to infringe.

Library of Congress Cataloging in Publication Data
Learning and literacy over time: longitudinal perspectives/edited by Julian Sefton-Green, Jennifer Rowsell.
  pages cm
  Includes bibliographical references and index.
  1. Literacy. 2. Literacy—Longitudinal studies. I. Sefton-Green, Julian.
  LC149.L36 2014
  302.2'244—dc23
  2014013695

ISBN: 978-0-415-73777-7 (hbk)
ISBN: 978-0-415-73778-4 (pbk)
ISBN: 978-1-315-81781-1 (ebk)

Typeset in Bembo and Stone Sans
by Florence Production Ltd, Stoodleigh, Devon, UK

CONTENTS

Acknowledgements	*vii*

1 Introduction: Making Sense of Longitudinal Perspectives on Literacy Learning—A *Revisiting* Approach
Julian Sefton-Green — 1

2 School Literate Repertoires: That was Then, This is Now
Barbara Comber — 16

3 *Fire+Hope* Up: On Revisiting the Process of Revisiting a Literacy-for-Social Action Project
Claudia Mitchell — 32

4 Cultural Studies Went to School and Where Did it End Up?
Julian Sefton-Green — 46

5 Revisiting Children and Families: Temporal Discourse Analysis and the Longitudinal Construction of Meaning
Catherine Compton-Lilly — 61

6 Who Were We Becoming? Revisiting Cultural Production in Room 217
Saskia Stille — 79

vi Contents

7 The Everyday and Faraway: Revisiting *Local Literacies*　　98
　Mary Hamilton

8 Artifacts of Resilience: Enduring Narratives, Texts,
　Practices Across Three Generations　　116
　Kate Pahl and Aliya Khan

9 Reframing Reading Youth Writing　　134
　Michael Hoechsmann and Naomi Lightman

10 A Steadfast Revisit: Keeping with Tradition, in a
　Different Space and Time　　149
　Jennifer Rowsell

11 Drama and the Literacy of Lives in Progress　　164
　Kathleen Gallagher

12 Life in Rhyme: Art, Literacy, and Survival　　183
　Glynda A. Hull and Randolph Young

About the Contributors　　*202*
Index　　*206*

ACKNOWLEDGEMENTS

We would like to thank Jennifer Colautti for her super editing work on draft versions of the chapters. In addition to the authors in this volume, we would also like to thank the following individuals who attended the SSHRC-funded seminar in Toronto 2012 on the theme of Revisiting: Jim Cummins, Will Edwards, Rahat Naqvi, Mary Saudelli, Rob Simon, Jennifer Vadeboncoeur, and Burcu Yaman-Ntelioglou. We would also like to thank Naomi Silverman and Christina Chronister from Routledge for their support and encouragement.

1

INTRODUCTION

Making Sense of Longitudinal Perspectives on Literacy Learning—A *Revisiting* Approach

Julian Sefton-Green

The Challenge

This is an unusual volume about educational research in the current political climate. Bringing together experienced researchers from the US, Canada, the UK and Australia, it does not directly address the problems of schooling in these countries. It does not particularly engage with current debates about classroom management, curriculum policy or effective pedagogy. Yet we think the project of this volume is at the heart of all teachers' and all policy-makers' interests in education.

The contributions collected here all responded to a challenge issued in 2012 when Jennifer Rowsell and I asked established and experienced literacy researchers to find and investigate research subjects they had previously written about—in some cases almost 20 years earlier.[1] The researchers had to find, contact and then reinterview or revisit their initial 'subjects' exploring a number of possible themes. All the researchers would loosely describe themselves within a 'new literacies' frame and we deliberately included researchers who had worked with an expanded understanding of literacy to include print text, media studies, cultural studies, multimodal production, digital story-telling and drama. The researchers had worked in a range of contexts; primary and secondary classrooms, teacher education, and youth and community spaces; some were education specialists, others sociologists of language and learning. We asked researchers to review with the people they found:

- Their current literacy practices, thus seeking to contextualise the researchers' past accounts;
- and/or their current reflections on the kinds of intervention or project you worked with them in the past;

2 Julian Sefton-Green

- and/or how lifecourse experiences may have shifted some of their earlier literacy practice orientations—the travel and traversal (citing Lemke, 2000) of their literacy practices;
- and/or how the current digital regime have may have offered new and different opportunities for those earlier literacy practices;
- and/or how revisiting these research subjects may reveal underlying trends about current literacy practices in general.

In addition, we asked researchers to reflect on the methodological implications of this process, asking: in what ways does the idea of a revisit [2] and of espousing a longitudinal perspective help research in literacy and learning and how might it challenge the status quo in research in our field?

As many of the contributors discuss in their chapters, this was a hard challenge at three levels: first, practically—finding, contacting and reconnecting with individuals; second, emotionally—renewing friendships, relationships, past hopes and dreams; and finally, intellectually—working out what revisiting adds to what was already known or how it destabilises that knowledge. Yet despite these difficulties, which we shall return to throughout the rest of this Introduction, we also want to suggest that this challenge has resulted in a series of interesting insights into the long-term nature of innovative interventions in classrooms, reflections on the value of literacy research, and of the status in general about the nature of findings in educational research.

We want to offer this volume as a contribution to an important set of arguments about the difference that school, and in particular forms of literacy learning, claim to make across and along the lifecourse for individuals. Although we appear to be living through an era where our general understanding about education seems inordinately focused on what happens at school, this volume suggests that such a focus misses a much larger picture. This is then very much a volume about the limits and possibilities of educational research as much as it is about living and learning.

The volume brings together the results of our challenge. The rest of this Introduction outlines some of the key theories and ideas that animated our collective enquiry and which helped set the framework for the processes of revisiting which structure many of the chapters that follow. It unpicks some of the complex methodological questions, which inevitably asserted themselves as authors encountered the revisiting process and then situates the individual chapters as responses to these enquiries.

The Long-term Perspective

At one point in her recent lifelong study of the descendants from the children of Trackton and Roadville, Shirley Brice Heath writes: 'The truth is that some children in families make it and some do not. Neither early language socialization nor earnest envisionment of bright futures can determine those who will and those who will not' (Heath, 2012, p. 104). This bleak assessment comes at the end of a particularly distressing series of life histories and points to the limits of what differences education and educators might claim to make. There clearly comes a point where 'life' or, more strictly, society, takes over and any sense of being able to intervene in life pathways, routes and other learning trajectories is knocked back either by chance or circumstance.

While the empirical challenge of following individuals over extended periods of time and revisiting earlier sites of research is considerable and poses a series of practical challenges, it is also, as Heath noted in her second appendix, possibly a vanishing art and almost certainly a disappearing mode of academic enquiry. However difficult the practicalities of extended enquiry, the real problem it seems to me is not just to collect this data but how to make sense of it.

If longitudinal and revisiting research simply replicates a kind of rarefied common sense about life, what does it tell us? A key question for this book must therefore be what kind of analytic frame, what kind of theory, and what tradition of interpretation can we use to best make sense of the data we might gather? While the stories we tell might seem to have a meaningful resonance and the aura of wisdom accrued through history, it is much more difficult to devise the kind of analytic frame that enables us to turn the weight of experiences into a critical knowledge and more particularly a theory of change. This is because the underlying investigation behind any narrative over time is how to account for historical change (see, for example, MacLeod, 2008; Willis, 1978). We aren't just interested in stories for the sake of them, of lives as gossip or as voyeurism, but because of the way we construct change as insight into contemporary society.

Any proposition to consider longitudinal perspectives on literacy and on learning over time more generally seems to rest on three interlinked areas of enquiry, which contain their own sets of challenges and themes. This Introduction to the book offers a first pass at mapping the kinds of theory, and the kinds of approaches used and applied to the challenge of making sense of qualitative revisiting. It attempts to draw out the theory of change that animates different approaches to this field.

Revisiting

This term is taken from anthropology and strictly speaking describes the process of revisiting an earlier site of research. In many cases the authors collected here had to grapple with how the people they met again dealt with different perspectives in time, how stories from the past are mobilised in the present, and how future aspirations are imagined and enacted in talk. Revisiting offered a double articulation: first the move back into the past, leading to kinds of evaluation of the present, and second a different kind of understanding of how we revisit in day-to-day contemporary interactions.

4 Julian Sefton-Green

Michael Burawoy has written a helpful and comprehensive review of the different types of revisits, as well as analysing the different theoretical and conceptual frames employed across these different approaches (Burawoy, 2003). We have taken the term 'revisit' from his matrix of definitions. In analysing the different kinds of approaches taken to revisiting, Burawoy distinguishes between the constructivist and empiricist. These describe how differences over time can either be attributed to how the researcher constructs his or her research (including drawing on different types of theory) or due to changes in the internal or external context. He then goes on to speculate about seven different types of revisiting. These include a rolling revisit, punctuated revisits, heuristic revisits, archaeological and valedictory revisits, as well as by biographically based and nested revisits. The criteria he uses to define each type vary between approaches taken by the researcher, the kind of data collected, and changes within the research site. From our perspective, I would draw attention to his description of a nested revisit because it contextualises and recontextualises the local site in changing global perspectives. The idea of a punctuated revisit that can explore consistency and change is also generative. The contributors to this volume draw explicitly on several of these models in their individual approaches to revisiting in their chapters.

I suggest, however, that it is the idea of the biographical revisit which is perhaps closest to some of the proposals for this book. In this model, researchers return to individuals rather than to locations. Burawoy cites the work of Richard Sennett who returns to individuals he first studied in *The Hidden Injuries of Class* (co-authored with Jonathan Cobb in 1973) in his later book *The Culture of the New Capitalism* (Sennett, 2007). Sennett consistently investigates the subjectivity of class as it is constructed through work and other forms of labour. Burawoy also cites the classic study *Ain't no Making It* (MacLeod, 2008) where the author returns twice to groups of young people over a thirty-year period.

The questions Burawoy raises are whether researchers bring with them to the revisit different theoretical constructs, which means they then 'see' the material differently. This problem is complicated by how the relationship of the researcher to the research is also likely to be different and this too affects the 'before and after' or 'baseline' assumptions which often underpin this kind of return.

In the idea of a revisit, however, Burawoy offers us an important lens with which we can examine the long-term because he explicitly argues that the idea of 'longitudinality' as it were—of change over time—can be conceptualised through this ethnographic tradition and that this offers a particular and specific contribution to studies of long-term change. He particularly makes the case that we need to acknowledge and develop the role of the reflexive ethnographer in this analysis because the change we are interested in observing is as much a dynamic property of the observer as it is of either of the sites or people we work with over time. However, it is not always clear what this appeal to reflexivity can offer to audiences beyond the academy.

Reflexivity and Co-construction

The problem with an appeal to reflexivity is not that it isn't generative, in that self-awareness on the part of the researcher can add layers of interpretation to the project, but that it can replace knowledge about others with an (at times) self-indulgent solipsism. Again, as Heath implies in her appendices to her recent volume, the autobiography—she uses the term auto-ethnography—becomes the focus of a revisit by default as change within the researcher or at least their 'history' seems to become the object of study. There is even, I would suggest, a small genre of methodological appendices to these extensive studies, which reprises this concern: see, for example, Dimitriadis (2003) and MacLeod (2008).

A key feature across these disparate studies is the way in which the researcher attempts to displace their own reflexivity on to the researched, thus drawing these individuals into the enterprise as joint collaborators. Jay MacLeod recounts how the young men he studied had found out about both the first and second editions of his study, and had both positive and negative responses to it and their perception of what the publication said about their place in the world (and how much money he might have made from his work). Shirley Brice Heath either played back or gave transcripts of her subjects' earlier talk to the individuals concerned both as a mode of sharing but also to elicit subjects' responses. While classic ethnography demands that subjects interpret in their own words (see, for example, discussion by Marcus, 2011) the actions observed by the researcher, this on-going process of reflection and shared memory often bringing out repeated key incidents and/or language use is more a kind of co-construction over time. This is not only a political act trying to bring some equality of attention to the researcher/researched relationship but a way of making of the subjects' reflexivity a matter of interest to the reader, as well as allowing the ethnographer's reflexivity to merge into the background.

A twist to this focus on reflexivity is an attention to how the action of revisiting enforces a change to the forms of narrative of reporting and recounting that conventionally frame research as described by Cortazzi and Jin (2006). The argument is that a renewed focus on the researcher as an actor in his or her research along with the difference that co-constructing events makes to the writing process means that revisiting often produces different kinds of written research. It is no longer tenable to write from a single omniscient perspective as doubt and reflexivity require multiple voices and perspectives. This is certainly the case in this volume with a number of contributors choosing to jointly author their chapters for this volume rather than reprise earlier single author accounts (see the chapters by Hoechsmann and Lightman, Pahl and Khan, and Hull and Young, and the extensive uses of email correspondence by Gallagher).

A recent study by Lissa Soep brings these concerns into the digital era (Soep, 2010). Soep followed the production of a piece of youth radio over an extended period of time—more a long sequence of study than a revisit. She described an interesting process as the subject of her research also blogged about the production independently from Soep's own analysis. Soep argues that this is more than just a kind of co-construction because the subject's own reflections (and reflexivity) have a life of their own beyond her construction of them within her more scholarly narrative. This is a peculiar and original feature of research in the digital age and raises a number of questions about the authority and independence of the academic. It also hints at some interesting and troubling times to come for what it means to be an ethnographer in the digital era. It also suggests the need to develop more creative and inclusive forms of representation than the all-knowing academic narrative. Soep also imagines how changing forms of publication and the ways in which different audiences will access studies and information about the object of research creates, if not another kind of revisit, then a kind of 'co-revisiting,' as yet another new form of longitudinal study. In Soep's study the reflexivity of the researcher becomes yet another actor within a swiftly multiplying web of competing stories.

What 'Theory of Change' over What Period of Time?

As Burawoy noted a number of times in his piece, the key question with any notion of a revisit or even of longitudinal study is how to account for change either in a grand theoretical tradition—as historical change—or in more modest and personal terms. The difficulty here is the relationship between a sense of difference produced by the account of the revisit standing in for an analytic account of change. In his discussion of a multi-sited ethnography, Marcus deploys the term 'para-ethnography' as a way of encompassing 'complex technical systems . . . that are not fully contingent on convention, tradition, and "the past" but rather constitute future-orientated cognitive practices' (Marcus, 2011, p. 31); this is a way of rationalising the use of these wider analytic frames without harming the integrity of the ethnographic process. Shirley Brice Heath intersperses her account of families and individuals with wider historical analysis of migration patterns within the United States and structural changes to the family and the workplace as a result of neoliberal economic reforms. In her study of the white working class, Lois Weis returns to theories of class stratification and the formation of class-based subjectivities as a way of explaining how the young people she encountered in high school have now moved into the labour market and begun families (Weis, 2004).

In that study, Weis draws heavily on macro-social theory, exploring how individuals' aspirations have been tempered by experience and how subjectivities have been formed and re-formed through employment, gender and family. She shows particularly how male and female employment trajectories now offer different life-chance routes and carry changing expectations as the labour market has been transformed by structural change. Heath tells a similar story about the uprooting of community, migration and alienation in the large metropolis. Both writers, in different ways draw heavily on one of the touchstone studies in this genre—namely, Paul Willis's *Learning to Labour* (Willis, 1978).

Weis and Willis interrogate the formation of class-based subjectivities significantly in the context of educational institutions ostensibly aimed at very different projections of the future. Willis does not revisit his lads whereas Weis does return to them over time. This is an interesting contrast because of the temporal dimension either implied or made explicit in these studies of changing subjectivities where the theoretical narrative is determined by an overarching idea about social change. Willis's study is retrospectively problematic because the kind of factory life and the kind of male working-class identity that he argues is being produced by the young men in their resistant behaviour to the school (and thus suggesting that school by default acts as a form of social reproduction) was being destroyed at the same time as he was conducting his study. The identities these young men worked so hard to make for themselves would actually not find the lives to enable them to be 'realised'—or described in a putative revisit. Weis is subtler in her calculations as the design of her study suggests that the time-lag between prospective or anticipated realisation needed to be supported by knowing what was going to happen next.[3] Again, the model of the revisit has to be quite strict in how it can calibrate future (and therefore unknown and unknowable) change.

There is thus an inextricable difficulty in disentangling accounts of change from the way that 'future time' impacts on present or contemporary processes. Our awareness of both past and prospective identities exists in the present and not just as something that can only be accounted for over a period of time. The process of social change is, of course, uneven and this means again that it is difficult to construct a theory of change exclusively on the research evidence of the revisit. I have met some researchers who told me that a longitudinal study could simply be defined by researching the same subject or site on at least three separate occasions. But of course we have no idea about the significance of the actual growth over time or change in between these moments. A revisit in that sense cannot just be defined as simply sampling at another point in time but without the external theory of change it isn't at all clear how we can define the 'longitudinality' of the longitudinal. Heath uses a quotation by George Eliot to express the idea that a fragment of a life—in our terms the moment of research—is an uneven representation of the whole, it is not a fractal; and equally importantly it does not allow us to see its significance in the gradient of travel. As the next section shows, how we conceptualise change over time is important as opposed to the simple measure of time passing and thus offers a range of differing dimensions in the analytic frame used across this book.

In this volume the contributors encounter a range of past experiences, but it is how they construct the meaning of time passing as they grapple with the vicissitudes of life that determine the success of each revisit in terms of what it contributes to the literature about literacy learning.

8 Julian Sefton-Green

Research Questions

In this book we have invited a broad range of researchers to reflect on change over time in respect of broadly conceptualised literacy practices and education. This means that the chapters themselves both address conceptual questions about the nature of revisiting (including discussion of some of these methodological considerations) as well as the original 'content' of the research.

Given that some of the original cases took place prior to the penetration of the Internet and forms of digital culture, it was obvious that any difference the digital makes both to ourselves—as researchers and the kind of knowledge worlds we now inhabit—as well as to the individual's literacy practices, was going to be a central question for enquiry. Indeed, virtually every chapter traces this theme in some form or other. In many cases, the findings at this level are incredibly pragmatic and suggest an extraordinarily easy flow across media and platforms; in others the specificity of the digital is curious and instructive.

However, it is also true that many, but not all, of the chapters return to young people whose literacy practices were very much dominated by the ecology of the school or the family, but whose current literacy practices are now those of independent adults. In some cases we can see people we knew as young children now acting as young parents and so still engaged in the same kinds of literacy practices albeit from an entirely different perspective. In other cases, it has been much more apparent how the forms of literacy we observed in the past were very much bound up with the way that individuals now reflect on the more general category of schooling and therefore the literacy practice is now marked by values associated with formal learning and education. Equally, our studies have now followed young people from classrooms into workplaces and we see these new frames determining current contemporary activity in ways that were quite simply unimaginable 10 to 20 years ago.

Many of these chapters, however, end up focusing on individuals as much as they do on practices and this raises a number of questions for the authors collected here. First of all, as I have already indicated, virtually all of the contributors found the process of revisiting personally uncomfortable and challenging. This is significantly related to each author's expectations but it has had two kinds of effect. The first impact has been on the researchers' confidence about themselves as academics given that the revisiting experience has clearly challenged the security and integrity of the original findings. Many of these chapters contain accounts of a troubled researcher who is now working through some of the values they previously took for granted. Second, there is the issue of the new adult individual that we faced on our return. There is a persistent sense of the researcher touching on matters that typically get left out of classroom research and having to face up to the sorts of social and economic problems that educational research does not usually pretend it can influence. None of the contributors to this volume wanted to avoid this challenge head-on and it speaks to the ethical commitment of many literacy researchers that it seems irresponsible to ignore these wider social difficulties even though it may not be as experts that we have much to offer.

I have already mentioned the relationship between revisiting as a method and as a mode of writing and again it seems clear that many of the researchers collected here found the best way to deal with the revisit was to engage in the kind of new perspective offered by changing the nature of their writing, moving from conventional academic to more shared and mutually produced forms of understanding. Some of the chapters reflect explicitly on the nature of this collaborative process, but it seemed quite natural that the confidence to write *about* another would be replaced but the desire to write *with* them as the certainty of our previous insights become troubled and confused.

Research profiled in this collection also considers the role of place as a part of the revisiting experience. For instance, Glynda Hull cannot document her revisit of Randy without an account of Oakland, California, and Julian Sefton-Green cannot separate Steve's and Clare's stories from where he first met them—Tottenham, London—both places filled with urban disturbances. Place marks time, time marks places, and a strong theme within these chapters has been an emphasis on links between the history of contexts and their associations with revisits. A recurrent theme in the collection is thus the connections people have with places over time. Thinking about longer-term ethnographic accounts, there is a thread that ties place and time to identity mediation. When researchers spend significant periods of time in a place, observations naturally become richer and more grounded in context. Studies such as Barton and Hamilton's account of the literacy habits of adults living in a particular community in Lancaster (Barton & Hamilton, 1998, and revisited here) rely on the role of place on people over time. To conduct longitudinal research, researchers often live, work and exist alongside their participants over sustained periods of time, and a large part of their accounts dealt with the history of places as a part of the research account.

A key challenge for the value of this collection must be the criticism: so what? Critics might suggest that it would be inevitable that returning to many of our subjects would simply mean encountering the complexities of lives beyond the security of the classroom. Here, as editors, we have tried to commission chapters that have explicitly addressed the question of what kind of interpretative lens can make sense of the revisit. While inevitably the research has been extraordinarily interesting for the researcher, we know that this does not necessarily raise concerns for others. We recognise that in some ways the revisit may appear to offer new insights into older problems, just as at the same time it may also be recycling conventional understanding of new problems. All of the authors collected here have grappled with these questions in an attempt to move outside any closed self-centred gaze significantly because the main purposes of literacy research has wider social and political aims beyond the academy. We hope this collection makes the case that for all the complexity and difficulty of engaging in any kind of revisit, such work offers new perspectives and new ways of honestly

10 Julian Sefton-Green

interrogating the nature and purpose of literacy research in education. We believe such perspectives are all the more important at a time when literacy itself is so frequently diminished as a practice in schools around the world.

Outline of the Book

In actual fact, the revisit model is significantly different from chapter to chapter. The book opens with a contribution by Barbara Comber who in some ways conducted one of the most 'classic' revisits in the book. In this chapter, Comber reports on what she learned from recent conversations with two young people who she originally met as part of her research on young people's literacy development in the school years. The young people, Tessa and Cruz, now 20 and 19, were part of two different studies of literacy. Comber first met Tessa in the family home when she was 4 years of age and continued to observe her in the first 4 years of her formal schooling and analyse her literacy development until Tessa turned 10. The object of that study was to identify the connections and disconnections between children's literacy practices at home and in school. Barbara first met Cruz when he was experiencing literacy difficulties in Year 10 of high school. The object of that study was to explore innovative pedagogies that might reconnect young people with school literacy learning and enable future educational trajectories. In revisiting these young people some years later, Comber invited them to talk about the literacy practices in their current lives, to retell their school learning stories from their perspectives and to consider their aspirations for the future. The chapter emphasises the continuously unfolding and unfinished nature of learning, tracing continuities and unexpected discontinuities in these stories.

Claudia Mitchell's contribution is the first of several attempts to revisit youth-based and non-formal learning experiences as it takes up the story of seven young people from two townships in South Africa, who participated in a health-focused literacy project addressing HIV and AIDS awareness from 2001 to 2003. Drawing on Burawoy's (2003) notion of the focused revisit and the various forms this type of work can take, the chapter attempts to shed light on several key questions: What are the various ways that we might think of returning to a site? Is the site the current health and literacy experiences of the individuals we worked with in the first place (and who are now 10 years older), or is the site the health and literacy of fifteen-year-olds growing up now in the age of AIDS in 2012? What is the role of critical autoethnography as a tool for revisiting? How as researchers do we consider various ethical issues, ranging from differing circumstances when we move from working with minors to working with young adults, through to recognising how we ourselves have changed, and to issues related to stirring up memories: can we just drop back into someone's life?

On the surface, Julian Sefton-Green's revisit looks like Barbara Comber's in that it returns to young people he met in classrooms 20 years ago, but

Sefton-Green had a more ongoing, persistent and more interpersonal relationship with the three individuals from his media education classes than simply that of a visiting researcher. This chapter begins the more fluid types of revisiting relationship that characterise several succeeding chapters capturing three individuals, first described in the co–authored book *Cultural Studies Goes to School* (Buckingham & Sefton-Green, 1994)—a book that explored early accounts of media learning in inner city classrooms. Here he describes the subjects' current lives and reflects on emerging findings to do with: being a 'media-educated' person; the question of Tottenham (the locale for the original study) and social mobility (as a consequence of educational success); and the relationship of a single academic subject within a broader perspective about the place of schooling in life more generally.

Catherine Compton-Lilly is similarly flexible in her interpretation of the idea of revisiting inasmuch as her chapter focuses very much on the constructions of temporality in talk but from different moments in time. Compton-Lilly also has an ongoing relationship with a set of families she has worked with and this gives the chapter an opportunity to make sense of the ways that future and present are constructed in talk and mobilised as tropes in discourse. Fifteen years ago, Compton-Lilly was a first-grade teacher conducting her doctoral research project with ten of her first-grade students and their families. Over the next 10 years, she repeatedly returned to the families. As she analysed the data, she became aware of patterns across time. Children and family members recalled some stories over and over again, while others were forgotten. Within and across families, particular ways of talking recurred. Compton-Lilly uses data from this revisiting study to explore temporality—specifically, how meanings and understandings of the past are revised and reworked across time.

Beginning with an overview of the *Re/constructing Literate Identities* study conducted 5 years ago, exploring the experiences of elementary level students who were newcomers to Canada or children of first-generation Canadians, Saskia Stille revisits three key literacy events related to the integration of home languages and digital media into teachers' instructional practice. Expanding the idea of literacy events, defined as situations in which people engage with reading or writing, to include digitally mediated forms of communication, these events comprised new forms of student participation and cultural production in the learning context. Following descriptions of these events, Stille considers what revisiting might offer, to understanding students' digital literacy practices. The chapter concludes that revisiting constitutes a reflexive approach to ethnographic literacy research, allowing an opportunity to notice and account for social and technological change, and its influence upon interpretations and theory development in literacy research.

Unlike the contributions so far, Mary Hamilton's chapter does not stem from any pedagogic relationship. Unlike the authors, who are either researching classrooms, or who were themselves teachers, Hamilton returns to her classic ethnographic study of reading and writing practices, *Local Literacies* (Barton &

12 Julian Sefton-Green

Hamilton, 1998). That study itself was in the process of being reissued as a second edition and from this perspective Hamilton joins authors in this volume who have found revisiting as much a continuous process of reviewing and re-editing. She returns to one individual who occupied a significant role in the original study and the chapter reflects on: social change in the literacy ecology of participants; changes in the outlook and assumptions of researchers themselves; and developments in the theory and methodologies of literacy studies. These are all reframed by the challenges of longitudinal enquiry. The chapter explores new ways to trace the meaning of the local, opening up the nature of place in relationship to wider networks of literacy practices.

The next chapter by Kate Pahl and Aliya Khan begins a sequence of chapters where the act of revisiting has reframed the nature of the academic writing. It revisits the experience of Aliya, who was involved in the original project, *Every object tells a story*, which was conducted in 2006 in Rotherham, in the UK. The chapter explores revisiting collaboratively from the perspective of the researcher and the researched. Here, Aliya reflects on how her literacy experiences, such as reading *Harry Potter*, telling and retelling stories, poems, prayers and everyday sayings, as well as her mother's and grandmother's experiences of literacy have shaped her literate identity over time. This chapter focuses specifically on literacy as instantiated in oral stories, sayings and poems, and recognises the materially and place-based situated nature of literacy practices, drawing on Aliya's insights into her own literacy practices across generations. From this, the chapter articulates a theoretical framework for Aliya's literacy practices, as being instantiated in artefacts of resilience. Resilience as an area for research in the context of literacy practices over time is explored as a possible new area of exploration within revisiting research.

In a similar vein, Michael Hoechsmann invited Naomi Lightman to co-author their experiences of writing for Young People's Press (YPP). They occupied different roles from 10 years previously, one as facilitator and the other as participant. The chapter notes that in the intervening period several things have changed: a) the youth participants (research subjects) have moved out of youth into adulthood; b) the conditions of and for literacy practices have changed thanks to the emergence of participatory practices of Web 2.0; c) the space of youth journalism has changed both in relation to dissemination (limited interest on the part of news media) and production (changing conceptions of 'youth voice' on the part of contemporary youth media organisations and vast new potentials of DIY communication); and, d) both of the authors have a distance from the 'project' that enables some detachment and a critical revisit. The chapter examines the role that the experience of having 'voice' in the high-profile 'young street' section of *The Toronto Star* had on the lives of the young people who wrote for Young People's Press. And, considering the changing conditions of new and digital literacies, it additionally reflects on the potential for 'youth voice' and democratic participation as developed in the era of YPP compared with what is possible in the Web 2.0 era.

Ten years ago, Jennifer Rowsell conducted a research study with a teacher education student, Dorothy, on the development of her teacher identity. In this chapter, she revisits the now primary teacher to become reacquainted with her story. Drawing on life history methods (Goodson & Sikes, 2001), Rowsell reveals how Dorothy negotiates popular trends in teaching and pedagogy with her own iron-clad, committed beliefs about the virtues of her childhood education in Sri Lanka. The chapter signals the importance of revisits as a heuristic to reveal larger patterns such as the resilience of older educational ideologies and discourses in the face of tremendous change and 'innovation.' As well, the chapter throws into relief how revisits are not neat and tidy processes, but instead idiosyncratic and inflected with two stories: the story of the participant and that of the researcher.

Kathleen Gallagher explores the pedagogical value of the collective through revisiting the lives of two women, graduates from a high school drama programme, 15 years after their participation in a research study of their drama classroom. This earlier work explored both the subjectivity of young women in a single-sex school for girls and their engagement with the rites of drama learning. Drama exemplifies a kind of collaborative literacy that can expose important sources of conflict and contestation. Gallagher is interested in pursuing what those ceremonies of collaboration and experiences of conflict have served in the now adult lives of two women. How, if at all, have these women transferred the protean democratic ways of working—features of the temporary culture of the drama classroom—to the wider world? Cultural theorist Richard Sennett (2012) argues that "individualism names a social absence as well as a personal impulse: ritual is absent." Focusing on the pedagogical rituals of listening, classroom social relations, and the practices of critical readings of their worlds, she takes this methodological turn of revisiting as a reflexive practice to further excavate memory as both an engagement with the past and a displacement of certainties that may have unwittingly gathered momentum over time passing.

The final chapter of the collection addresses the very challenging life-world of one our new co-authors, Randy Young, as it continues Glynda Hull's story of a young man she has followed over 15 years, with a larger focus on social movements, institutions and cultures as a backdrop to the revisit. The chapter examines semiotic agency, within the sociohistorical constraints of his life in these times, through sustained and serious engagement with what the authors call, following Paul Willis's (1990) "symbolic creativity" and the creation of a "grounded aesthetics." The authors are especially interested in the exercise of such agency as it intersects with space—material and symbolic, local and global—and with modalities or semiotics—music, print and image—especially for the light these conjunctions shed on the new communicative affordances and demands of a digital and global world. Telling Young's story since meeting him 15 years ago compelled Hull to think deeply about her role as a researcher. A revisiting project has the potential to similarly shift roles, and that was something of the case for Young and her. Although the authors had never lost touch and had, in fact, collaborated around his work during the intervening years, Hull's official request to juxtapose their work together, examining the then and the now, set in motion a new dynamic whereby Young was able to successfully assert his desire to bring his music centre stage, and Hull was able to hear him. As a result, there was a readjustment or realignment of power relations between the researcher and the researched. Insights from the collaboration focus especially on the nature of the needs to engage with symbolic creativity in challenging circumstances.

It is clear from this brief description of contributions to this volume that far from offering answers to classic educational questions about long-term impact, revisiting raises yet more questions. While there is a strong narrative pleasure to this project so that readers can find out what happened to the 'characters' from earlier research, I hope it is already clear that these narratives are as troubling as they imply closure. Indeed, all of the contributors to this volume found the experience of revisiting their research unsettling on a number of levels. It destabilised the project of research in the first place. It very firmly shows how educational interventions can seem overdetermined by social and economic life forces. It undermined the certainty of our ambitions and our younger faith in what might work best. Yet, for all these challenges, the project has positive findings too. It confirms key principles in the broader new literacies approach and shows fundamentally how people find and make meaning in their lives beyond the limited imaginings of schooling. Here, revisiting may point to the need for our understandings of literacy and learning to be an on-going whole-life concern and that if we do not accept such a perspective and reduce literacy learning experiences at school, we deny deep human purpose and agency.

Notes

1. The contributors to this volume all brought their findings to a seminar held in Toronto, November 2012. We would like to thank the Social Science and Humanities Research Council of Canada for funding this event (SSHRC 646–2011–1062. Nos 163534). We want to thank all the attendees at that event.
2. Here we cited Burawoy (2003). See the rest of this chapter for a discussion of this piece.
3. There is the further time-lag, or perhaps time-delay, that is going to exist between the process of research, analysis, writing and publication, but this is a separate methodological perspective.

References

Barton, D. & Hamilton, M. (1998). *Local literacies: Reading and writing in one community.* London, Routledge.

Buckingham, D. & Sefton-Green, J. (1994). *Cultural studies goes to school: Reading and teaching popular media.* London: Taylor & Francis.

A *Revisiting* Approach   **15**

Burawoy, M. (2003). Revisits: An outline of a theory of reflexive ethnography. *American Sociological Review, 68*, 645–679.

Cortazzi, M. & Jin, L. (2006). Asking questions, sharing stories and identity construction: Sociocultural issues in narrative research. In S. Trahar (Ed.), *Narrative research on learning: Comparative and international perspectives* (p. 280). Oxford: Symposium Books.

Dimitriadis, G. (2003). *Friendship, cliques, and gangs: Young black men coming of age in urban America.* New York: Teachers College Press.

Goodson, I. F. & Sikes, P. J. (2001). *Life history research in educational settings: Learning from lives.* Milton Keynes: Open University Press.

Heath, S. B. (2012). *Words at work and play: Three decades in family and community life.* New York: Cambridge University Press.

Lemke, J. (2000). Across the scales of time: Artefacts, activities, and meanings in ecosocial systems. *Mind, Culture and Activity, 7* (4), 273–290.

MacLeod, J. (2008). *Ain't no making it: Aspirations and attainment in a low-income neighbourhood* (3rd ed.). Boulder, CO: Westview.

Marcus, G. E. (2011). Multi-sited ethnography: Five or six things I know about it now. In S. Coleman & P. v. Hellermann (Eds.), *Multi-sited ethnography: Problems and possibilities in the translocation of research methods* (p. 228). New York: Routledge.

Sennett, R. (2007). *The culture of the new capitalism.* New Haven, CT: Yale University Press.

Sennett, R. (2012). *Together: The rituals, pleasures and politics of cooperation.* New Haven, CT and London: Yale University Press.

Sennett, R. & Cobb, J. (1973). *The hidden injuries of class.* New York: Vintage.

Soep, E. (2010). Research methods for web two dot whoah. In P. Thomson & J. Sefton-Green (Eds.), *Researching creative learning: Methods and issues.* London: Routledge.

Weis, L. (2004). *Class reunion: The remaking of the American white working class.* London: Routledge.

Willis, P. E. (1978). *Learning to labour: How working class kids get working class jobs.* Aldershot: Ashgate.

Willis, P. E. (1990). *Common culture: Symbolic work at play in the everyday cultures of the young.* Milton Keynes: Open University Press.

2

SCHOOL LITERATE REPERTOIRES

That was Then, This is Now

Barbara Comber

Introduction

In an author's note to readers at the back of her book, *That was then, this is now* (Hinton, 1998) originally published when she was 22, S. E. Hinton wrote in 2007:

> The difference between the years sixteen and twenty are almost as great as the difference in the years between eleven and sixteen. You learn things. Sometimes hard things. You learn the so-called right thing is not the right thing. You learn there will be roads to choose, some you never believed you would travel.

Hinton tells the story of two boys who grow up as brothers in the same household, who at sixteen begin to engage very differently with their neighbourhoods and to create very different possible futures and identities. They begin to recognise that their frames of reference for being and acting in the world are entirely different than each of them had assumed of the other and that they are going in different directions. I took Hinton's title as a frame for this chapter, and her insights regarding identity shifts during this period of life, as reminders that the initial research I undertook with these young people was done *then* and my revisits were being done *now*, that my assumptions about their literacy learning trajectories may not hold for them or for me or in the context of wider societal and personal change. As I wrote interview questions to seek ethical clearance, I wondered the extent to which they would be generative or indeed whether I was asking the right questions. In any case, below are the 'approved questions,' quite properly focusing on 'literacy.'

- What kinds of reading and writing activities do you participate in during a normal week? In what kinds of places and at what kind of times (e.g. leisure, work, study, friendships, family, etc.)?
- Do you recall being part of the research project? Do you have any comments on the project that you would like to make? What are your memories of learning to read and write at home, in school, other places? Who or what helped you and how?
- Has your approach to reading, writing and communicating more broadly changed as a result of any particular educational life experiences (e.g. speaking a language other than English, undertaking a new job, playing a sport, being a member of a club, etc.)?
- In what ways do new digital technologies impact on your communication, learning, work, relationships, and so on?

When I conducted the initial case studies (Tessa, 1996–2001 and Cruz, 2008–2011), I was working with theories of literacy learning that stressed the situatedness of practice, the politics of literacy, and the potential of inclusive and critical pedagogies. I am still working with those theories, yet I found during the interviews themselves and in analysing the transcripts, that I needed broader theorisations of youth subjectivity to interpret what these young people were saying about their lives, their work, their literacy learning, their reflections on the past and their hopes for the future (McLeod & Yates, 2006; McDonald et al., 2011; Wynn, 2009). I drew from researchers who take an historical, longitudinal perspective on the relationships between social change and people's lives (Brandt, 2001; Heath, 2012; McLeod & Yates, 2006; McLeod & Thomson, 2009; Thomson, 2009).

The two young people who agreed to participate in the 'revisiting project' in 2012 and 2013 are Tessa and Cruz. Both were school students when I met them in the course of my ongoing research in literacy education (Tessa, 1996–2001 and Cruz, 2008–2011), exploring the unequal outcomes of schooling. I first met Tessa when she was attending a preschool in a multicultural western suburb of Adelaide, South Australia. I first met Cruz when he was a Year 10 student and attending a high school in a poor regional town about two hours' drive from Adelaide. Tessa is now 21 and Cruz 20 years of age. Since re-establishing contact, I have interviewed Tessa on four occasions and Cruz once, as well as sharing artefacts and communicating through numerous email exchanges. It was challenging to organise face-to-face meetings as both young people work changing hours and have moved away from their families and the areas where they attended school. I now live in another state.

I first outline the research I originally undertook with Tessa and Cruz when they were at school and summarise the hunches I developed about them *then* as literacy learners at that time. I then discuss what I have learned from revisiting these young people over the last eighteen months—the here-and-*now*. I offer a

18 Barbara Comber

series of illustrative fragments from transcripts of our ongoing conversations in order to show what these young people took up and kept from their schooldays—school legacies for better and for worse. I argue that literacy repertoires learned at school may become integral to life-long learner dispositions. This relationship, however, is not simple or deterministic; rather, these young people demonstrate the active ways in which they make use of selected resources and discourses acquired in their schooldays in their contemporary everyday lives.

Tessa: That was *Then*

I first met Tessa in 1996 when I interviewed her parents in their home. They agreed to Tessa being a case study in the longitudinal *100 Children go to school* and *100 Children turn 10 projects.*[1] The aim was to investigate the connections and disconnections between literacy development prior to school and the first 3 years of schooling. She was one of four case study children I observed closely who were part of a larger cohort of over 100 children in five locations around Australia (Hill et al., 1998; Hill et al., 2002). Tessa attended Riverside Primary School situated in a culturally diverse inner western suburb where half of the children's families were on school card (an indicator of poverty) and over a third of the children spoke English as a second language.

Tessa's parents were of Greek heritage. English was the language of the home while Greek was spoken with the extended family, especially with grandparents. Her mother was a high school teacher and her father an accountant. I began observing Tessa in the context of the preschool when she was 4 years old. Her teachers volunteered that she was precocious in terms of her language and literacy development, and that she frequently self-selected into activities involving literacy-related play.

When I first began watching Tessa in the preschool situation I could readily see how her mother's words, 'Drawing, writing, that's her!' made sense. Tessa was indeed really into books, pencils, computers (e.g. typing her name and that of her little brother, neither of them easy to spell,[2] using MacPaint), playing out scripts and scenarios. She was a star pupil in preschool where she enjoyed high status with her teachers and peers. In observing preschool children, my approach was unobtrusive, yet I believe that even as a four-year-old Tessa was happily aware of my observing her. She recognised and pointed out her name among my messy handwritten field notes. I wrote later that "some children may appear 'ready' for school because they come with a selective repertoire of social and communicative practices upon which school literacy learning is contingent" (Comber, 2000, p. 40). Tessa's ability to enlist assistance and feedback in home and early childhood learning contexts and to display the appropriate participative repertoire for doing school and literacy-related tasks led me to describe her as 'a proactive student in the making.'

At school, Tessa's first teacher, Eleni, was of Greek heritage herself and already knew Tessa's family. Another positive match for Tessa, in terms of cultural and linguistic capital, was Greek being taught as a community language at Riverside. Indeed, Tessa enjoyed many positive connections between home and school. On all measures of literacy in preschool and in the first years of primary school Tessa was well above the norm for her age group. However, by Year 3, according to the standardised tests, her outstanding progress appeared to have slowed somewhat and her enthusiasm for school appeared to wane.

That year I witnessed signs of Tessa's emerging problems with the social demands of schooling, especially with respect to her interactions with more assertive female peers. During a range of literacy tasks assigned for groups or pairs to complete collaboratively, I observed Tessa being ignored, ostracised or criticised by other capable girls. Given her desire to get things right, avoid conflict and to help others, this treatment appeared to be hurtful and alienating.

Tessa's engagement with, and enjoyment of, school visibly diminished—evidenced by her not putting up her hand to contribute, mumbling when she read aloud, sitting at the back, not bringing her work to the mat to share. Her rate of progress on standardised literacy tests plateaued. However, during this same period she assembled new literacy practices with her family and her parents reported that her school-life seemed 'happy enough.' At home she made cards, wrote stories, did still-life drawings, read bedtime stories to her younger brother, collected stationery, ordered books from the Lucky Book Club, read the street directory, collected her parents' expired credit cards and designed competitions using the family computer. Hence her literacy learning repertoire and disposition developed, but her status as a very high achieving student and popular peer began to be less stable.

Cruz: That was *Then*

When he was identified as having literacy difficulties on the Year 9 standardised test of literacy, Cruz's mother gave permission for him to participate in a series of projects concerned with the impact of literacy and numeracy on high school students' learning.[3] He was an extremely willing, aware and articulate participant and eagerly collaborated with the researchers and his teachers.

Along with several of my university co-researchers,[4] I first met Cruz at his regional high school in the early months of his Year 10. He had been, by his own admission, underperforming in most curriculum areas and described himself as having been 'pretty much a troublemaker' throughout Years 8 and 9. Cruz claimed that people 'have always thought I was dumb.' However, he was aware of the consequences of such a label and with his teacher mentor, Alan, he was turning around his school performance.

With concerted efforts of Alan and other teachers, Cruz began to reconnect with his school learning, to improve his grades and his attitude to the point whereby he was elected as school vice captain and went on to successfully complete his schooling. From a student who had been headed for 'slow English,' a 'troublemaker' and who subscribed to stories that he was 'dumb,' Cruz began to see himself differently and to think about options after schooling.

> I really want to get to uni, and I either want to study zoo-keeping or becoming a PE (Physical Education) teacher. I still haven't decided which I want to do yet, because I am thinking zoo-keeping because I really love animals and everything, but I really like teaching, I really love PE and all that.

The repertoires of literate practices that became crucial for academic success at that time included preparing and participating in public speaking on a topic where he had expertise, writing notes for these presentations, negotiating arrangements with collaborating peers and teachers, preparing and presenting PowerPoints, and so on. The support from his mentor teacher ('I used to have to go and see him so I don't walk off and leave school grounds') and his new English teacher ('She's like a teacher I've never had before—happy, jovial and involved') made an incredible difference to Cruz. They enabled him to renegotiate his relationship with schooling and to set specific academic literacy goals. When we last spoke to him in his final school days he was hoping to move to Adelaide with a friend who was starting university.

I now update the literacy learning lives of Tessa and Cruz based on our recent *revisiting* conversations and emails during 2012 and 2013. I foreground the stories they volunteered about their pasts, their presents and their hoped-for futures.

Tessa: This is *Now*—Refusing Assigned Identities

I re-established contact with Tessa through her early childhood school teacher, Eleni, who still lived in the Riverside area, and saw members of Tessa's family at local shops. When I met Tessa as a twenty-year-old young woman, she was at a crucial point in her life. She had recently left the family home and was living with her boyfriend. She had deferred two university degrees and was working as a casual employee for a car hire company, where she dealt directly with customers and their bookings. She expressed a strong desire to get on with aspects of living that were important to her—such as travelling, winning a full-time job, earning money, having her own house and car, spending time with her boyfriend, enjoying music, and so on.

In our first interview, Tessa's account of herself as a literate person and as a learner was overshadowed by her portrayal of her life as a young woman. Regarding her direction as a learner and the timing of her university studies, this was clearly secondary to her broader life project and disrupted expected patterns much to her parents' concern. Tessa stated:

Yeah, it's just sort of telling my parents what I want to do with my life, because they still have this image of me, like the perfect image of what I can do with my life, but I'm going astray, and I don't think they're liking it as much.

Tessa had broken the expected pathway of school to university to professional career. She recognised that her parents were finding this difficult, but she was determined to prioritise her relationship with her partner and their immediate combined and individual well-being over her long-term educational goals. She badly wanted to be a physiotherapist but knew that gaining entry into this program was very competitive and that she didn't have the emotional or financial resources to embark on this new educational phase at this time.

It became clear that she was in the process of refusing some of the positions on offer during her childhood and indeed some of the stories that her teachers, her parents and I had told. Regarding one aspect of literacy, Tessa stated: 'I don't actually do a lot of reading and writing. I hate reading, I don't if you knew that when I was little, but I've never been a fond reader.'

This surprised me as I remembered her mother telling me how Tessa had her own little collection of books and that she loved to read to her younger brother. However, Tessa went on to explain that while she loved writing, especially short stories, and also enjoyed the physical aspects of handwriting, she found reading extended texts difficult. It wasn't that she couldn't read complex texts.

TESSA: I still like drawing but, yeah, no, reading, I've never had the . . . I get bored.
BARBARA: Was it always like that or did it change at a certain point?
TESSA: Not really sure. If I find a good book I can read it in a day. You know, when *Twilight* came out, I read those, that's the only book, the only book series I've ever read.

She reported that after primary school she had never read set novels and coped with assignments by watching the movies. Tessa indicated that the physical stillness and time alone required for reading extended texts precluded her devoting sufficient attention.

TESSA: Like for me all my English projects, all the books we had to read, I passed and got good grades but I watched the movies. I'm more of a visual and I have to be practical.

She reported getting more satisfaction from Facebook interaction, watching movies, listening to music and playing games. While I and her teachers (not to mention the standardised tests) had predicted a great future for Tessa at school and as a reader, none of us had anticipated or recognised what she reported as an antipathy to reading.

Tessa arrived for our second interview with a box of her school and university work, which she had collected from her parents' home to share with me. In high school Tessa reported a range of experiences with teacher responses to her writing that echo many I have heard from other young people.

Tessa: Math was always easy for me. Some of my English teachers liked how I wrote, and other teachers hated it.

Barbara: I want to get that down. Say a bit more about that.

Tessa: Because I had one English teacher in Year 10, and we were asked to write a short story, and he absolutely loved it, he gave me full marks, and then I think the year after or the semester I had a different teacher, and he just, all teachers are different, he just didn't like . . . So with some English teachers I'd get good marks, some I wouldn't, I just wasn't too much of a fan of the reading.

A lot could be said about the implications of Tessa's comments about the impact of teacher judgements on young people's learner identities that teachers may not anticipate or ever know. Suffice it to say that if young people are already fragile in their views of themselves as students, unpredictable negative assessments may be experienced as personal failure.

Earlier I reported that the early signs of Tessa's changing relationship with schooling were visible in primary school. From being seen as a gifted student in early childhood, from Year 3 onwards periods of social exclusion followed her and escalated in high school where she experienced bullying and alienation. She explained: 'I didn't like most of the kids at school, like in Year 8 I'd hang around with the Greek kids, you know, and then after a couple of days they ditched me and then I didn't like them.' She stated: '[I]n Year 12 I hardly spoke to anyone, like I was friends with people and then I just didn't really . . . I only started to really speak to one person throughout Year 12.'

Tessa still managed to successfully complete Year 12 and was offered a place at university. Unsure of what she wanted to do, she decided to follow in her father's footsteps and opted for Commerce. Unfortunately, she did not enjoy this at all and switched to Disability Studies. Although she was doing well in that course, she decided it was not for her and went on to temporarily defer her academic studies. Tessa even brought two of her assignments, for which she received Credits and High Credits, to show me, including ironically a case study of a four-year-old girl. However, other personal experiences, including being violently mugged, contributed to depression with which Tessa was still struggling.

Yet, Tessa had a clear view of her desired future—namely, to become a physiotherapist. She was realistic about how difficult it might be to achieve this goal and that she might need to undertake related courses in community education settings (such as in massage) before reapplying to university. Towards the end of our second interview I asked Tessa to sum up where she thought she was in terms of literacy and learning.

BARBARA: Well let's start with now, you know, I mean where are you in your life as a learner in terms of your literacy, then where do you want it to go.

TESSA: Because at the moment I really don't know where I want to be in life, like whether I just want to settle down, start a family, or whether I want to go straight to study at uni, because my dad, my parents still want me to study and I don't really want to at the moment, but as far as all my literacy and stuff goes, pretty good, like I have no problems with writing, writing formal letters and stuff.

BARBARA: That doesn't hold you back in any way, does it?

TESSA: Nup, no, like I have good spelling and everything up front. People annoy me when they don't do their *theirs* correctly. I guess with my English literacy I could, I correct people a little bit, I correct Justin a lot when he writes things wrong.

In the exchange above Tessa's uncertainty about the big directions in her life, including any future formal learning, is palpable. As she goes on to make clear, in the workplace and in her private life she has a more than an adequate repertoire of literacy practices not only to fulfil her own personal and work needs, but also to help others, including her brothers and partner.

TESSA: Yeah, so I'm always correcting like spelling errors, yeah, and I do that with my brothers as well and stuff, but with my learning at the moment, I was helping Cosmo, like whenever he needs a hand with anything, *Just come over, like because I've done most of the subjects, if you need a hand, I'll give you a hand,* so my learning will be helping him at the moment.

Tessa did not see her literacy learning as her possession or a personal achievement, but reframed it as cultural capital, as a resource that she could make available to others.

TESSA: Yeah. Like at the moment with all my reading and writing, I'm just doing a lot of reading into legal matters for Justin, because we are completely lost for help, like you call the lawyer and they can't help you, so I've just been doing a lot of research for him to see what his rights are, like even when I was getting screwed around at work, I do a lot of research to find out my rights if I was not getting paid enough.

She elaborated that she had gone back to refer to her school Legal Studies notes in order to know where to begin such processes. Her reading and writing was

24 Barbara Comber

powerfully motivated when it came to arguing for hers and her partner's legal and financial rights. She was eager to help her brothers achieve their academic goals. Her literacy practices were employed in order to meet her work, social and familial responsibilities as she saw them. Summing up where she'd like to be in 5 years' time, she explained that she did want to 'be a mum,' but added: 'I don't plan on doing nothing for the rest of my life. I don't want to be a housewife.' For now, simply managing hers and her partner's health and well-being, their relationship, finding work, managing costs on a limited budget and staying positively connected with her family while living independently were her immediate goals.

When young people leave the predictable pathways of schooling and further study and the family home they are confronted by complex institutional systems not designed for them. It is not easy to navigate publicly available information about medical and legal services, and employment rights and conditions. Yet Tessa's literate repertoire was up to such challenges.

Cruz: This is *Now*—Ready for Adventure

I re-established contact with Cruz through his high school mentor and teacher, Alan, who connected us through email. When Cruz returned from overseas he responded quickly to my invitation to meet.

> Yeah, I'm always on my iPhone, yeah. I got the new iPhone5 and I'm just, I'm in love with it . . . iPhone, like yeah, it's all about text messaging, it's probably text messaging and phone calls is how we communicate when we're not around, my partner or my friends.

When we met in 2012, Cruz was confident, warm and friendly. He recalled that the previous research project had been important to him and explained it in the following way: 'I remember it pushing me, being on that really . . . Actually, it helped me push to succeed, because I didn't want to really not only fail myself but fail you guys.'

Like Tessa, he wanted to enjoy life as much as he could right now. Early in our conversation he explained his decision to work at McDonald's:

CRUZ: Well at the moment I'm actually just a manager at McDonald's, but this is, it's more because I enjoy how I can get freedom of time, like I can just get time off whenever I want, and because of that I can go on more holidays, like in three weeks I'm off to go on a cruise.

Since returning from his Contiki tour of Europe, he had already been to far North Queensland, was booked to go to Vanuatu and planned to back-pack in Canada and North America in 2013. Interestingly it was Alan, Cruz's teacher, who had taken him on his first trip interstate and first journey by plane when Cruz was in Year 11, and it was Alan who had helped Cruz to plan his travels to Europe. Now he was hooked on travel and talked enthusiastically about his experiences so far as life changing. It's the phrase 'freedom of time' I want to explore momentarily here. It echoes with Tessa's desire to 'do things' while she is 'young/young.' She too had been excited about the travel she had done while still in school—trips to Italy and Greece, which had opened her eyes to possibilities for other ways of living. Both Tessa and Cruz were eager to enact their lives as independent adults. There was no postponement of adulthood, described in other research (Arnett, 2000, 2007; Silva, 2012); indeed, I found both Tessa and Cruz to be 'conscious and purposeful' (McDonald et al., 2011) of their short-term and long-term goals for future employment and credentials. Cruz's current strategy was to take advantage of the 'decent money' that being 'a high up manager' provided him to save for travels.

Cruz reported that his long-term goal was to become a firefighter and explained that the possibility of adventure was a key attraction. However, he was also interested in working directly with young people.

BARBARA: If I met you again in five years, what would you hope you'd be doing?

CRUZ: I wouldn't mind being a youth worker. If someone said to me *You'll be a youth worker in five years,* I'd be like *I'm glad to be.*

While Cruz acknowledged these careers were very different, he saw both as compatible with his strengths and preferences—at different ends of a spectrum.

CRUZ: But they both have their own advantages about me, like I have a huge adventure side like about me, I love adventure, but I really have a really, really big soft spot for like helping people, and that's another thing why I really love working at McDonald's. It's the satisfaction I get out of the customers. It sounds silly but it's amazing.

Cruz's positive analysis of his experiences indicated that he was able to tell a coherent storyline about his present and the possible future he hoped for. The travel, the working at McDonald's, the possibilities of work as a firefighter or a youth worker made sense to Cruz because they all required a sense of adventure and a love of people. He explained that he really liked working with his young crew.

CRUZ: Well, I do, because at McDonald's we get a lot of people that want to drop out of school, and I'm really against it because I knew that I was close to doing it, and so every time I see it I always like take it, I know I shouldn't but I take it onto myself to actually sit down and talk to them about like:

It's not really the right choice, and like it might be a good idea now because you're getting more money, but like in the future you won't be getting like a lot more money, you'll be stuck doing really bad jobs, and stuff like that.

Cruz's sense of responsibility towards others was clear, as was his desire to work in a field he was passionate about, which he reported learning from his mother and Alan. Observing and listening to Alan and his mother convinced Cruz to persevere and set himself high challenges. In bringing these themes together he reflected on Alan's role in his recent travel experience.

CRUZ: Push yourself to the limits and make nothing a challenge for me, like . . . *(inaudible)* . . . makes sense. Everything I challenge myself to do I won't stop until I can't do this any more. I just get back up and keep trying because I know that's what Alan would want me to do. . . . And it's, yeah, it's pushed me a lot but I've been able to do it and Europe was a big one but I wouldn't have been able to do it without Alan. Like I said to Alan *I wouldn't be able to afford it* and stuff like that, and Alan said *Just try, just try,* and he helped me, he came up with a few saving ways that I managed and I did it.

Several years after Cruz graduated from high school, his former teacher Alan, now a friend, continued to assist Cruz directly with his learning as a young adult, giving him the resilience to tackle significant challenges. Alan also offers Cruz practical assistance with budgeting and planning his travels—complex forms of literacy and numeracy with considerable positive payoffs.

School Literacies: That was *Then* and This is *Now*

Both Tessa and Cruz successfully completed their secondary schooling. Tessa gained entry to university and deferred her studies after the first year. Cruz won an apprenticeship as a tiler, but withdrew when he was exploited financially in his workplace. While Tessa shone in primary school and was identified as a student with high intellectual potential, her high school days had proven lonely and academically mixed. The combination of alienation from her peers and waning interest in academic learning (especially reading extended prose) resulted in low motivation for study, upon which her long-term goals remain contingent. While Cruz's primary and early high schooling saw him identified as a student with literacy and behaviour difficulties, in his last 3 years at high school this trajectory of failure had dramatically turned around. He credited much of this sustained change to experienced teacher and counsellor and now friend, Alan.

In terms of their everyday literacy practices, both organised most communication through the Internet through iPhones and other tablet devices. Both researched extensively online to find information to help them in everyday life, planning leisure and travel, and also to stay connected with friends and family.

Both were highly competent computer users where technology was seamlessly integrated into their everyday working lives. Both mentioned key teachers who had inspired them to believe in themselves as students; both mentioned family members, parents and grandparents who had encouraged them at different stages of schooling. Tessa's Greek heritage was important to her and she spoke English and Greek fluently and knew some Italian. Cruz was hoping to learn Italian (his cultural heritage). Tessa still enjoyed writing short stories, but admitted she hardly ever finished them. Neither reported reading for pleasure.

As a privileged long-term literacy researcher I feel remarkably fortunate to have revisited and learned once again from Tessa and Cruz as young adults, just as they grapple with the intense and challenging processes of learning to live independently: to manage their relationships, their finances, their working lives and indeed their learning lives. Both focused on helping others within their sphere of influence. Both welcomed the possible insights that research can produce. Classroom literacy pedagogy at all levels of education typically emphasises what students can do alone—their reading, their writing, their spelling (for exceptions, see Comber, 2013; Comber & Nixon, 2008). This emphasis on the normative individualised nature of literacy assessment is particularly evident now with the move to audit cultures and high stakes assessment. However, Cruz and Tessa focused on the social and immediate nature of their literacy practices—collaborative processes at work, organising events and travel, communicating with friends and family, and researching to solve life challenges and to plan future pathways. Neither enjoyed, or participated in, the extended reading or writing of prose on their own. Neither at this point was engaged in academic study, though both saw it as a possibility in their futures.

What they had gained from school literacy/learning and from life experiences, thus far, had prepared them well for the work they were currently doing. From his last 3 years at school, Cruz had taken an optimistic and determined disposition about his potential that was sustaining him well as he tackled challenges he hadn't even imagined when I first met him as a fifteen-year-old. His confidence and enthusiasm were contagious. Tessa was handling a range of very complex challenges associated with her partner and his previous relationship, his need for support and to find work. At the same time she was focused on earning money, dealing with depression, maintaining positive family relationships, while still hoping for a university degree and a professional position. Having grown up in a middle-class family and now living on a low and unpredictable income, she is currently engaged in researching what services she and her partner can access in terms of health and legal matters. Both Cruz and Tessa have graduated from their school lives as articulate, perceptive, generous, resilient and independent young adults. In terms of their school literate repertoires, both assembled a range of useful academic practices, which were necessary to successfully complete their schooling (and for higher education if and when they resume their studies) and occasionally relevant to their personal goals, including researching on-line to plan, access recourses and solve problems. Not a large part of how they choose to spend their time now directly relates to literacy tasks from their schooldays, but then why should it? However, it may be that they have appropriated other crucial capabilities as learners, critical dispositions towards texts that allow them to investigate whether they are being treated fairly by people, workplaces and institutions. It was also clear to me that both actively employ their positive repertoires of literate learning practices and educational dispositions to work and play collaboratively. Both were very much devoted to using what they had learned to help themselves and others.

Final Thoughts: Work in Progress

This chapter cannot do justice to these learning lives, which are, of course, still unfolding. Each email or chat with Cruz or Tessa takes me to the ways in which their learning/lives are dynamic and changing. That's life, but as Cruz and Tessa entered new phases of their adult lives different aspects of their dispositions, their resources, their literate practices become visible and, of course, they continue to learn what they need in these contexts. Their lives are indeed works in progress. As a witness I can see that the learner dispositions and literacies that matter are those they take up to enhance their own and their friends' and families' lives. Tessa continues to take an active critical approach to researching her rights at work and her partner's legal rights towards his children. She even gets her old Legal Studies textbooks out to refer to, even though she claims to dislike and to have rejected most academic reading. Literacy practices as taken up and used is very much contingent upon the motivation inherent in the actual work of reading and writing. We do it when we need it, when it helps us to achieve other social goals or personal purposes. Similarly, Tessa instructs her younger brother in various aspects of academic literacy, in order to help him to do well with his studies, even as she puts her own academic career on hold. I am not arguing for a utilitarian approach to literacy education; indeed, my point is that as educators we need to aim high and introduce young people to specific discursive practices (academic, workplace and leisure) so that they can begin to deduce the logics of particular ways with words.

When Cruz's mentor teacher and counsellor, Alan, invited him to join Scaly Survivors it was not only to reconnect Cruz with learning by capitalising on his interest in reptiles, it was an invitation into learning another way of being in school, where he could become an expert, where he could mentor other troubled students, where he could learn to present in public, where he could represent the school, where he could lead others. Alan had identified a potential in Cruz, which was not only fostered by his current experience of schooling, but almost denied. His capacity to be outspoken and outgoing, his already-adult demeanor, his confidence from years of part-time work in the fast-food industry could find no ready outlet in the school uniform and rule-driven day. However, with Alan and his English teacher negotiating the curriculum and brokering a different way of learning at school, Cruz quickly assembled the literacies and learning practices he needed to research reptiles and develop presentations for local community shows and primary school visits. He lost 'the bad guy look.' Without Alan, Cruz would in all likelihood have left school without improving his written literacy and without learning how to make the most of his many assets. Now as a senior manager at McDonald's he mentors other young people who want to drop out of school. He sets standards for appropriate ways to interact with even difficult customers. He demonstrates many of the traits he so valued in Alan. Like Tessa, he is aware of workplace rights and responsibilities, and wants to do what he does as well as he can and to help others to do the same. Like Tessa, he imagines further learning and training and moving into a profession down the track. However, like Tessa he wants to live his life now. Both these young people have a highly developed sense of social responsibility and a strong desire not to postpone their adult lives. Neither prioritise qualifications and educational credentials *before* making serious commitments to partners, travelling or living independently.

As a literacy researcher, my focus in longitudinal studies is to discover the kinds of literate practices made available to different students and what different students make of that. Hence I have always seen pedagogy as negotiated and learning as a joint accomplishment. However, even as I undertook such studies strong normative discourses about development inevitably impacted on what I was able to see and hear, and the interpretations I was able to make. Increasingly, I bring insights from Dorothy Smith's (2005) institutional ethnography to my research in literacy studies. This means attending even more closely to how people accomplish the work of everyday life and what coordinates that work. I also seek out theories that take a complex line on subjectivity, that work against binaries, limited understandings of power, and static versions of identity.

It is too late to do justice to such theories here; however, in closing, for *now*, I want to remind myself of the need to interrogate my own discourses and research repertoires. From Tessa and Cruz I was reminded of the contingency of the effects of schooling and indeed school literacies. I was reminded to be wary of making judgements about 'life pathways.' Tessa and Cruz are making decisions about how they want to, and how they can live, right now. They are narrating their own stories. In order to do this complex work, and now to do it with their partners, and indeed children, they constantly analyse what's right for them for now. Since I drafted this chapter over a year ago their learning lives, of course, have continued to change, both predictably and not. Cruz is now married and has a three-month-old daughter. Tessa is still with her partner who now has rights to access visits with his children with a former partner. Tessa completed her first course in massage. Both are still working in their previous positions—that is, as manager at McDonald's and as part-time administrative assistant with a car hire company. Both have optimistic hopes for the future even as they deal with the

30 Barbara Comber

pragmatic challenges of the responsibilities of the present. They are still learning, sometimes hard things, but they already know how to prioritise family, friendship, fairness and fun.

Notes

1. The projects—Connections between literacy development in the prior to school period and the first year of schooling (1996–1998) and Literacy development in the early years: A longitudinal study from the year prior to school to the first four years of school (1999–2001)—were conducted by Susan Hill, Barbara Comber, Bill Louden, Judith Rivalland and Jo-Anne Reid, and were funded as part of the Federal Government's National Children's Literacy Projects Scheme.
2. Tessa and Cruz are both pseudonyms. Tessa's actual name comprised eight letters.
3. The projects—School to Work – Literacy and Numeracy Innovation Program 2008–*2010*—were conducted by Barbara Comber, Phil Cormack and Lyn Wilkinson, with Jenny Barnett, Di Bills, Marie Brennan, Mike Chartres, Rob Hattam, Rosie Kerin, and John Walsh and were funded by the South Australian State Government's Future SACE Office, DECS, South Australia.
4. Several of my colleagues have also published accounts of Cruz and others are under review. The published papers with Rosie Kerin are listed in the references (Kerin & Comber, 2008a and 2008b). My point here is that Cruz has been the subject of other researchers' attention, each writing their own accounts, which may be quite rare with ethnographic case studies and which I might explore in future papers.

References

Arnett, J. (2000). Emerging adulthood: A theory of development from the late teens through the twenties. *American Psychologist, 55*(5), 469–480.

Arnett, J. (2007). Emerging adulthood: What is it, and what is it good for? *Child Development Perspectives, 1*(2), 68–73.

Brandt, D. (2001). *Literacy in American lives.* New York: Cambridge University Press.

Comber, B. (2000). What *really* counts in early literacy lessons. *Language Arts, 78*(1), 39–49.

Comber, B. (2013). Schools as meeting places: Critical and inclusive literacies in changing school environments. *Language Arts, 90*(5), 361–371.

Comber, B. & Nixon, H. (2008). Spatial literacies, design texts and emergent pedagogies in purposeful literacy curriculum. *Pedagogies, 3*(2), 221–240.

Heath, S. B. (2012). *Words at work and play: Three decades in family and community life.* New York: Cambridge University Press.

Hill, S., Comber, B., Louden, B., Reid, J. & Rivalland, J. (1998). *100 Children go to school: Connections and disconnections in literacy experience prior to school and in the first year of school* (3-volume report). Canberra: Department for Education, Employment, Training and Youth Affairs.

Hill, S., Comber, B., Louden, W., Reid, J. & Rivalland, J. (2002). *100 children turn 10: A longitudinal study of literacy development from the year prior to school to the first four years of school* (2-volume report). Canberra: Department for Education, Science and Training. Available at: www.sapo.org.au/pub/pub364.html

Hinton, S. E. (1998). *That was then, this is now.* New York: Speak, The Penguin Group.

Kerin, R. & Comber, B. (2008a). Assessing the risks and possibilities: Standardised literacy testing at Year 9. *Curriculum Perspectives, 28*(3), 65–70.

Kerin, R. & Comber, B. (2008b). A national English curriculum for all Australian youth: Making it work for teachers and students everywhere. *English in Australia, 43*(3), 21–27.

McDonald, P., Pini, B., Bailey, J. & Price, R. (2011). Young people's aspirations for education, work, family and leisure. *Work, Employment & Society, 25*(1), 68–84.

McLeod, J. & Thomson, R. (2009). *Researching social change*. London: Sage.

McLeod, J. & Yates, L. (2006). *Making modern lives: Subjectivity, schooling and social change*. Albany: State University of New York.

Silva, J. (2012). Constructing adulthood in an age of uncertainty. *American Sociological Review, 77*(4), 505–522.

Smith, D. E. (2005). *Institutional ethnography: A sociology for people*. Oxford: Rowman Altamira.

Thomson, R. (2009). *Unfolding lives: Youth, gender and change*. Bristol: The Policy Press.

Wynn, J. (2009). *Youth health and welfare: The cultural politics of education and wellbeing*. South Melbourne: Oxford University Press.

3

FIRE+HOPE UP

On Revisiting the Process of Revisiting a Literacy-for-Social Action Project

Claudia Mitchell

Introduction

We are used to the conventions of 'based on a true story' in films. Just before the credits roll at the end of the film, the faces, or at least the names, of all the key characters flash on to the screen and we discover what this one or that is now doing, and there is a certain sense of closure—'ah, so that's how they ended up.' It is a little precipitate, of course, since unless the characters are now all dead, they are still becoming. In some ways Burawoy's (2003) notion of the focused revisit is not that different when we as researchers begin to wonder whatever happened to 'our participants.' What does 'whatever happened to X or Y?' have to do with our work? We introduced our grade 8 students to Leonard Cohen's poetry in 1975, or we carried out a study with youth on combating gender violence in 2000, and we wonder what they are doing now, and maybe we even dare to ask what difference this work had made to them. But there are other issues. One of the challenges of social research relates to isolating the features or factors that make a difference (if at all) in an intervention or project. If we attempt to evaluate the influence or impact, the short time frames of many interventionist studies make it likely that we fall into the potential trap of making exaggerated claims, or miss significant outcomes simply because we stopped too soon. In this chapter I focus on a project involving a group of young people mostly between the ages of 14 and 18 from secondary schools in several townships in the Western Cape of South Africa, who participated in an HIV&AIDS-focused literacy project, the Soft Cover project between 2001 and 2003. The connections between literacy and activism here are critical in seeking to shed light on how revisiting might help us to reconceptualize social practices of literacy.

The 'up' in the title '*Fire+Hope* Up' signals a particular type of sociological revisit, inspired by the television series produced by Britain's Granada Television, which followed a group of 14 children first interviewed in 1963 and then filmed at regular seven-year intervals (7 *Plus Seven* was released in 1970, followed by *21 Up* in 1977, *28 Up* in 1984, *35 Up* in 1991, *42 Up* in 1999, *49 Up* in 2005, and *56 Up* in 2012). The series of 'revisits' or 'x years up' that I talk about here began several years after the official end of the project and in the beginning were organized primarily around the phenomenological prompt 'how are you doing?' (really more of a 'where are you now?'). Later, as a result of new funding, I was able to begin to focus more on the question of what difference the project had made in the lives of the youth who participated.[1] In the chapter I offer a chronology of revisiting based on some of the sessions that took place over a period of close to a decade, and in so doing ask a number of questions: What are the various ways that we might think of returning to a site? What is the role of critical autoethnography as a tool for revisiting? How as researchers do we consider various ethical issues, ranging from differing circumstances when we move from working with minors to working with young adults, through to recognizing how we ourselves have changed, and to issues related to what might be referred to as 'stirring up memories'? For example, can we just drop back into someone's life and, if we do, what are the consequences?

Chronology of Revisiting

2003

It is late June, just the beginning of the cool and rainy weather in Cape Town, and my colleague Shannon and I are there for the launch of *"In My Life": Youth Stories and Poems on HIV/AIDS* (Schuster, 2003) a small book of poetry and other writings by the group of 21 youth between the ages of 14 and 18 from four local townships: Khayelitsha, Retreat, Gulu and Atlantis. They have been participating in the activities of the Soft Cover project[2] for the last year and a half, and a writing workshop leading to the publishing of it is the last component of the project. Our funding is pretty much at an end, but there is a certain type of exuberant closure with the launch of the book and the completion of a video documentary. Some of the authors at the book launch say that they have status as 'super stars' in the community with loveLife's agreement to enter into widespread print and distribution of *In My Life*. As Laura, one of the participants from Khayelitsha, comments: 'People in my neighbourhood are always coming up to me and saying, I like your book.' These are the movers and shakers in their community. As part of the Soft Cover project and also part of their community work with the Treatment Action Campaign, these young people have all been highly involved in engaging other youth in HIV peer education. Now it is time to move on. It is almost the end of high school for most of the participants who have all been committed to a project of social activism through the visual and literacy.

34   Claudia Mitchell

2006

It is a cold, wet, windy and thoroughly miserable Cape Town winter day in July of 2006. As my colleague, Shannon, and I make our way on foot through section R of Khayelitsha with Jordie, the former youth worker who helped us to convene the Soft Cover project, a school-based literacy and creative arts-focused HIV&AIDS awareness initiative several years earlier, we wonder who will actually show up for the interviews we plan to conduct with former participants in the project. It is just over 3 years since the launch of their publication, *"In My Life": Youth Stories and Poems on HIV/AIDS* and the release of a short documentary *Fire+Hope* that Shannon has directed and that includes many of the participants from the project speaking about how they see their role as youth activists in addressing HIV&AIDS. Now inspired by the Seven Up,[3] we decide that it would be fascinating to find out what various members of our project are now doing. In the context of a country that is hard hit by HIV and in the context of working with a group of young people who are (or were the last time we had seen them) committed to social activism in relation to HIV prevention and access to treatment, it is no insignificant question to want to know what they are doing even 3 years later. Enter our own version of *Fire+Hope* Up.

We plan to meet up at a café later in the evening with as many of the original 14 youth who can come, but decide that perhaps we might be able to do some of the interviews in the daytime as well. We aren't quite sure who will still be around, especially in the middle of a weekday afternoon when you would think that most nineteen- or twenty-year-olds would probably be in university or training or at work. This day there are four of the original group (sometimes called the Soft Cover group and sometimes referred to as the *Fire+Hope* group) who show up at the house of Gene,[4] one of the group members. They are not at work, they are not studying or in training, and really it turns out that mid-afternoon is a perfect time to meet because they are doing nothing that afternoon or most weekday afternoons. We gather in the small two-room house, which closely resembles all the other small two-room houses of section R of Khayelitsha. We hear many things that afternoon. Some, like Gene, the one whose peers would have voted most likely to succeed in 2003, hasn't actually been able to complete his matric, even though 3 years ago he was on the verge of writing his final exams. Laura[4] feels discouraged. She is still talking about the piece she wrote for *In My Life*, but now that she has part-time work as a cashier in Checkers, a supermarket chain, she can't figure out how she can do any more writing, the one activity that has given her some personal satisfaction. Daniel is working on a building site quite close to Gene's and we go to visit him on his break, but even there we hear the frustration in his voice about having a low paying unskilled job and uncertain hours, and then working out in the rain and wind and cold on this Cape Town winter day. Gene would like to get something going in drama and performance in the community. In the intervening years he has had a chance to participate in an arts-based workshop in Europe, for which he has received funding but is not sure how to go about getting some local activity off the ground. Later in the evening when we go to the café, we meet up with other members of that original group of 14. Some are working, or taking up training, or are attending university. More of the ones who are now working or studying are from Atlantis, the township that always seemed somewhat more prosperous than Khayelitsha. Sheena[4] from Atlantis, for example, is studying to become a social worker. Greg[4] is in a first-year arts program at one of the local universities. Reshma[4] is working in a bank—but then when Gene and Daniel[4] and Laura and others join in, there is a sense that on balance this is a very uncertain time.

2008

It is not such an elaborate meeting this time, and the time Shannon[4] and I spend in Cape Town is spent mostly with Jordie[4] who seems to stay in touch with everyone from the Soft Cover project. Daniel, it turns out, now has a steady job that provides on-the-job training and he apparently is much more hopeful. Things, however, have not been so good for Greg who has had to leave university because of financial difficulties as a result of very tragic events in his family. His older brother was killed a year earlier by a gang member in Atlantis. Their younger sister was going out with this gang member and when the brother tried to intervene, he was killed. Then in the same year, Greg's younger brother was playing in the street in Atlantis when a police car in a high-speed chase struck and killed him. Greg left university and got a job as a mechanic to help out with expenses. Life for Gene too, it seems, has been difficult and he has been involved in drugs and alcohol. He is not working.

2011

It is almost the end of 2011, and close to 10 years after the inception of the Soft Cover project. Four members of the original group plus Jordie, fly from Cape Town to Durban to attend the 'What difference does this make? 10 years later'[5] symposium to talk about the literacy and creative arts project they participated in. Now Sheena is a well-established social worker who is making important contributions to her work in the Department of Social Development. She wants to do more work with girls on the street and in relation to gender violence. A financial settlement to Greg's family as a result of the police cruiser hitting and killing his brother has made it possible for him to go back to university. Gene is still struggling and still has some problems with alcohol and drugs, but he is also part of a theatre group and is very involved in community theatre. But it is Jordie, the former youth worker who is now 33 years old, who expresses great anxiety about the future. He gives a sense of how difficult it is to maintain the idealism he had almost 10 years earlier to make a difference and to establish an IT business.

I mean the reality of the matter is that I need money to live on. And activism is not going to give me this. I mean, not now. Like, here we are fighting for the future, but I'm hungry now, I'm starving now. So I kind of needed a solution to that. So I think for me, for me the change started to happen there, is like, now I'm empowered enough, I understand things and I understand, the vigour that I had to change things, that was not going to happen overnight. It was kind of defeating really when you actually see what you have been working hard for. It didn't make any difference. I mean, just a very small difference, but you would have hoped that people would have understood things the way that you do, and changed things the way you want things to change for all of us. So it's kind of defeating to see, actually, things are getting worse. So all the knowledge, all the education, the workshops, kind of went to waste. It was a drop in the ocean.

(Cited in Walsh, 2012, p. 412)

Revisiting: At What Point in Time?

"Time," as Neale (2010) writes, "is a complex and endlessly fascinating phenomenon, not simply the medium through which we do research, but an important topic of enquiry in its own right" (p. 3). Had we severed contact with the Soft Cover group in June 2003, Shannon and I might have simply had the idea that youth empowerment is quite straightforward and that the kind of literacy-and-creative arts work we were doing with youth is exactly what is needed to engage them in social activism in relation to HIV&AIDS. If we were to look over some of our field notes from the time we would also see this point endorsed in print. If we had gone with our findings from that rainy, wet, cold winter day in 2006, we would have perhaps drawn some other conclusions—and, of course, in the (almost) Ten Years Later conference where we also have the benefit of hindsight of the youth-now-adults, we could reach other conclusions.

When we first completed the Soft Cover project our focus was on HIV awareness and we hoped that the various arts-based activities would contribute to making a space for dialogue about HIV&AIDS. When the group from the Soft Cover project came to the 'What difference does this make?' symposium, many of the other participants in the session were very interested in posing that exact question to them. The answers were fascinating. Sheena, for example, says she remembers really none of the specific activities in which she participated as part of the Soft Cover project; she only remembers the open-endedness of the discussion and indeed, that it is this that she has carried over into her social work practice. Greg recalls that it was in the Soft Cover project that he learned about condoms and credits being alive today to the in-depth discussions about condoms. At 17, he was not publically 'out' as a gay youth, but during the video interviews we did for the *Fire+Hope* documentary he discussed what sexuality meant for him, and the need for a safe space.

I think one of the biggest challenges is this whole thing about sexuality, who you are? When am I ready for sex? Should I do it? Shouldn't I? They've thrown, like, the whole subject of sex in our face and now we have to deal with it. And in between that we still have to find out who we are too, so, it's like, kind of complicated. It just complicates life!

(Taken from *Fire+Hope*)

In a group interview session in 2011, Greg explains the link for him between his identity when in drag and the creative work we did in the Soft Cover project that allowed him to find his own way of self-expression and activism.

I think coming out in drag and being out in drag, is really a tool for expressing myself, and in that way, also showing that it's okay to be yourself and to express yourself in a way that might not be a social norm. . . . where Soft Cover fits into that is that I came to understand that process led to [this expression]. I can see it as a platform, because of the way that we took things . . . [like] the writing about everyday life experience. The Soft Cover Project showed that we can, [and that] it actually means something to some other people. The stories we wrote, other people could relate to. I think that is the biggest thing that I take from the Soft Cover Project is coming to feel comfortable with working with different mediums, and not just thinking that standing on a pedestal and saying a speech is the sum total of activism or doing your bit . . . there is a whole creative process. I am not a painter or poet, but [drag] is my creative outlet.

(Cited in Walsh, 2012, p. 411)

But then this work offers 'high stakes' for the researcher. As members of the research team, Shannon and I were excited to have members of the original Soft Cover group participate in the opening panel of the symposium. When we issued the invitation and made the travel arrangements, we had not been thinking about how the group would feel about being there, or even how we as the researchers would feel. It was really the idea of the reunion itself. Once the introductions have taken place, however, and I am sitting there as the Principal Investigator of the Soft Cover study, I am thinking that this feels like a fishbowl and that it may seem that we have brought in the Soft Cover group to Durban as Exhibit A, 'See what a great project this was and weren't we wonderful to rescue these township youth?' There is a cringe factor or some version of 'tell the people how we helped you.' Of course, it was far from that as this very serious group of young adults contemplate the questions posed to them from the audience. One participant offers a concern about the issues that still exist for youth in relation to HIV&AIDS and the links to poverty. The symposium takes place at a lovely coastal hotel and she offers the view that perhaps the money that has been spent on organizing a 'ten years later' event could be better spent on improving current

38 Claudia Mitchell

conditions for young people. Moreover, as can be seen in Jordie's comments above, the 'ten years later' situation is far from rosy and indeed he expresses a somewhat cynical view, which may have been exacerbated by the event itself.

Conceptual and Methodological Issues

As must be obvious from the sections above, we did not deliberately set out to do a longitudinal study or one where we would be engaging in some sort of revisiting. Even at the time of the first revisiting meeting in 2006 on that cold, wet, winter day in Cape Town, the theme of our field notes was really 'What if we hadn't come back to talk with the group? We would have missed so much.' In a sense, we had fallen into the 'what ever happened to . . . ?' film roll and had assumed perhaps that we had now managed to catch what we would have otherwise missed—but had not fully comprehended the idea that there was going to be more. It was only in 2007–2008 when I applied to the Social Sciences and Humanities Research Council of Canada to carry out a study called 'What difference does this make?' that we could think about a more extensive follow-up. Now that I have embarked upon this work in a more deliberate manner and over a period of time, I want to highlight several key conceptual issues and methodological issues.

What or Who is Being Revisited?

One of the challenges in thinking about this work is to consider literacy and social activism in the context of the shifting landscape of HIV&AIDS and what that might mean in a focused revisiting project. Are we to revisit the original participants in a project (who were 15 or 16 at the time of the Soft Cover project), or are we to revisit the project of youth sexuality over time? In my descriptions of revisiting earlier in this chapter, I focus on the same cast of characters over time: Gene, Laura, Sheena, Greg, Daniel—all of whom were 15 and 16 when we embarked upon the Soft Cover project and who at the time of the last revisit activity were 25 and 26. When the project started, rates of new HIV infections in South Africa were soaring and it is noteworthy that the theme of the International AIDS Conference, which met in 2000 in Durban was 'breaking the silence.' It was clear that there was a need for the participation of young people themselves in taking action, although it was only at the International AIDS Conference held in Barcelona in 2002 that there was even an informal recognition of this, with demonstrators throughout the conference carrying placards with the slogan 'Where are the youth?' In 2002, a diagnosis of AIDS in South Africa was considered a death sentence. With the roll-out of antiretroviral drugs (ARVS) in 2004–2005, the landscape changed, at least in some geographic areas of South Africa where there was greater access to getting tested and improved access to ARVs. But since then new issues and new forms of activism have arisen. While it is beyond the scope of this chapter to trace the history of AIDS activism,[6] it is worth noting that in 2002 the key concerns in South Africa were about awareness of HIV ('breaking the silence') as an issue in itself, and alongside that the concern about access to ARVs. By 2004 the issue at the global level is on harm reduction. In 2006 in South Africa the issues of stigma and getting tested are critical, with the idea that if there is access to treatment, then it makes sense to 'know your status.' The activism among youth changed towards highlighting stigma and getting tested (see also Gibbs, 2009). Clearly, the dynamic agenda of AIDS literacy is something that needs to be factored in.

There are therefore at least three different scenarios of revisiting. If the project of revisiting were about literacy and social action in the context of the lives of the young people who participated in the Soft Cover project 10 years ago, then the various points in time that I have highlighted (2006, 2008, 2011) serve as markers of influence. Perhaps these will stabilize, but if memory studies can inform this work, it may be that how people recall a particular time will continue to change (see, for example, Mitchell and Weber, 1999). In a second scenario that is closely aligned to the first but still separate, one might consider that if the point of the revisiting project is in relation to how literacy and social action shift over the life-span, then one would frame quite differently comments such as Jordie's 'I mean the reality of the matter is that I need money to live on. And activism is not going to give me this. I mean, not now.' In the third scenario the question of revisiting is about revisiting HIV&AIDS among fifteen- and sixteen-year-olds. Revisiting this work from 2002 to 2013 would point to quite different practices over time. The actions of the Soft Cover youth in 2002, for example, were framed within a 'death sentence' discourse, something that is still evident in work in some rural areas of South Africa (see, for example, Mitchell et al., 2011), whereas campaigns and agendas following this have focused on such issues as getting tested, fighting stigma and safer sex practices. In the context of a clearer focus on such 'drivers' of the epidemic as gender and cross-generational relationships, more recent forms of literacy and social action have included such issues as the 'sugar daddy' phenomenon.

Textual Practices of Reading Back

Revisiting, as illuminated by the ten-year Soft Cover study, heralds the emergence of new dimensions of self-study and autoethnography in relation to 'looking in' to our research by 'looking back' (see Pithouse et al., 2009). Drawing on the work of Caroline Ellis (2004, 2009) and others, we might, for example, work back through the claim-making in our own publications. As has been highlighted in the revisiting process, as researchers we sometimes reach different conclusions as a result of time, and something that seemed apparent in 2003—claims about confidence in taking action, for example, seemingly as a result of participating in such a project—are shattered years later. While this may not be unique to the

40 Claudia Mitchell

revisiting process in social research, the idea of studying the writing itself and especially the conclusions that we make over time is critical. In carrying out this work, which is, in some ways, not unlike Jane Miller's "autobiography of the question" project (Miller, 1995), I am struck both by questions of where to begin and where to end. More conventionally, perhaps, such an exercise is left to the struggling doctoral student trying to make sense of a literature review, or to some sort of retrospective of an academic life rather than as a practice that represents the dynamic quality of our own research.

What are the most appropriate strategies for a textual 'reading back'? Here I draw on Stephen Riggins's (1994) idea of socio-semiotic readings based on denotative and connotative meanings. In the process of revisiting the Soft Cover project I encountered at least three layers of data. First there was the fieldwork data (such as transcripts of interviews, video clips and photographs) attached to the various revisits over time. Then there is the archival data made up of conference papers, conference programs, funding proposals, reports, book chapters and journal articles.[7] These accompany such evidence as *Fire+Hope*, the documentary and the various peritextual features such as flyers, the *In My Life* book, and even photos from conferences. These first two are denotative in that they offer artefactual evidence. A third level, which is connotative in nature, refers to the personal meanings that I as the researcher attach to these artefacts, or that are evoked by this work and which are a key feature to the revisiting process but one that is more difficult to represent.

The connotative as most people would agree is a 'mixed bag.' I can look back through a series of photographs taken at the International AIDS Conference in Durban in 2000, which was the inspiration for writing the funding proposal for the Soft Cover project in the first place, and it is easy for me to recall the excitement and hope and spirit of activism. It was the first conference of the IAS that I had attended. It was the first time that the IAS had met in an African country. The history of South Africa is one of activism and in the post-apartheid era the agenda could shift from the liberation struggle to one of keeping people alive in an age of AIDS. When I look at my photographs from the conference, they show scenes of a massive red AIDS ribbon draped around the Durban City Hall and crowds of activists wearing their cause on T-shirts, which, as Moletsane and Lolwana (2012) highlight, is the activist tool for South Africa. I can so clearly see myself as part of the activist project in these photographs since I am present in them, but even in the photographs that I myself took I am somehow there as well. However, as Norquay (1993), hooks (1989) and others highlight in their work on memory, this may be a good example of a certain nostalgia on my part. At the same time, I must force myself to reflect on Jordie's public statement at the Ten Years Later conference: 'So it's kind of defeating to see, actually, things are getting worse. So all the knowledge, all the education, the workshops, kind of went to waste. It was a drop in the ocean.' Indeed, reflecting on what I felt as the 'cringe factor' in bringing together the Ten Years Later group is also an example of the connotative meanings attached to revisiting. The fact that I worried that it would seem like a 'fish bowl' is a critical aspect of this. As I argue elsewhere (Mitchell, 2013), autoethnographic investigations (and I would place revisiting in the middle of this work) may force us to confront images of ourselves that may not put us in the most favorable light.

Some Ethical Considerations

Every study has its own particular ethical concerns and the act of revisiting offers new challenges. One of these is the question of how to write about the adult participants. The published writings coming out of the Soft Cover project included both anonymous references, which drew on pseudonyms (Mitchell, 2006a, b; Mitchell et al., 2007, 2010; Walsh, 2007; Walsh & Mitchell, 2004, 2006; Walsh et al., 2002), as well as writings such as the *In My Life* publication and the *Fire+Hope* documentary where real names were used. Now that it is 10 years later, what is the most appropriate way to represent adult participants in their present situation? Ironically, our Research Ethics Boards (REBs) are primarily concerned about protecting youth participants or participants who are regarded as particularly vulnerable populations. Vulnerability, however, is in and of itself tricky to define. In the case of the Soft Cover participants, all of whom are now adult, it is important to draw attention to the ways that they are making their way in the world as employees and jobseekers, as students, partners and parents. To what extent should we use new pseudonyms for the participants? Is the trail of each participant too easy to follow? Should I continue to screen *Fire+Hope* in public venues now that I know so much more about the participants as adults? And at the same time, and given the reach of the Internet and Google searches, is there any way to prevent the ardent researcher from tracking the participants?

Another ethical issue of revisiting relates to the politics of what might be described as stirring up memories. Jordie's forthright 'kind of went to waste' comments at the Ten Years Later conference might be taken as a feature of his current frustration with making a go of his business after so many years, or it could mean that 'now is enough; the project is over and let's move on.' At the same time, we have never been able to track down some of the original participants at all, a fact that is worrisome given the high rates of HIV and high rates of crime, but perhaps some participants don't want to be found and revisiting projects need to take this into consideration. It is worth noting that in the *7 Up* project, now at *56 Up*, one of the original 14 participants who withdrew from the project has now returned to it. At the same time, as a *Globe and Mail* article from October 14, 2013 reports:

> Now in middle age, many are frustrated about how they have been portrayed. They point out that Apted [the director] arrives for a week every

seven years and, from a week's worth of footage, their lives are then summarized in mere minutes.

(np: www.theglobeandmail.com/arts/television/56-up-a-celebration-of-ordinary-life/article14830996/ (retrieved December 2, 2013))

Conclusions

When does a project end? Will the revisiting continue? These are not questions that are easy to answer. What I have tried to highlight in this chapter are some of the tensions in revisiting the process of revisiting, and particularly in the context of literacy and social action attached to youth and HIV&AIDS, which itself is complex and ever-changing. At the beginning of the chapter I noted that the connections between literacy and activism are critical in deepening an understanding of the social practices of literacy. The ways in which young people spoke differently over time about the activities of the Soft Cover project and about their changing identities in terms of activism suggests that we need to be more nuanced, and more conservative perhaps, in how we frame our findings and the claims that we make as researchers. I have also highlighted some of the complexities in relation to autoethnography and placing ourselves in the middle of this research. It is work that reminds us of the truth factor in social research. If I presented all of the artefactual data alluded to throughout the chapter to another researcher, how would he or she represent the data and the findings? My colleague Shannon Walsh offers a different, though not totally dissimilar narrative in her article "'We grew as we grew': Visual methods, social change and collective learning over time" (Walsh, 2012), a text to which I have deliberately tried to avoid returning as I have been writing this chapter, although we do share some data from the Ten Years Later conference. While we began the work of literacy, meaning-making and AIDS activism at exactly the same point, we entered the project itself at very different points in our careers, so the question of where revisiting this project takes us is itself a component of revisiting. What is critical here are the questions that emerge when we do this kind of work and the reminder of the ways in which the work is never really done. This is something that may fly in the face of REBs who may want us to destroy our data after a certain date. At the same time, if there are new policies and practices related to the storage of electronic data, and to new forms of access, perhaps there can be more regular and even more rigorous forms of revisiting.

Acknowledgements

I gratefully acknowledge Shannon Walsh's participation in the Soft Cover project and the follow-up work. It has been through Shannon's excellent networking skills that it was possible to continue making contact with the various youth participants. I also acknowledge the Social Sciences and Humanities Research

Council of Canada for its financial support for the study 'What difference does this make? Studying youth as knowledge producers' (2008–2011), which made the revisiting possible. I would also like to thank the Canadian Society for International Health for its support for the Soft Cover project in the first place. Finally, I would like to thank the Soft Cover participants themselves for their inspiration and enthusiasm.

Notes

1. What difference does this make? Studying youth as knowledge producers (2008–2011). Social Science and Humanities Research Council of Canada.
2. The Soft Cover project was an HIV/AIDS Small Grants Canadian Society for International Health project (2002–2004) headed up by Claudia Mitchell and funded through the then Canadian International Development Agency (CIDA) and ICAD. As a partnership between McGill University and the Centre for the Book in Cape Town, the project had as its overall goal the idea of studying the ways in which youth expression using the visual, the arts and the literary could be a vehicle for community-based activism in addressing HIV&AIDS. Its activities included a conference called 'Getting the Word Out' (March, 2002), which included youth as co-researcher/presenters, a book-making activity, the production of a video documentary, and a writers' workshop that drew together HIV&AIDS education and creative writing.
3. The series was originally part of *The World in Action* and was directed by Paul Almond. Michael Apted, his assistant, was the one who proposed to visit the children every seven years, with the idea of exploring the links between class and life success in Britain. Apted is now the series director.
4. All names of participants are pseudonyms.
5. The conference, organized through the JL Dube Chair of the Centre for Visual Methodologies for Social Change, UKZN, the James McGill Professorship of McGill University, and the HIV&AIDS Chair in Education, Nelson Mandela Metropolitan University held December 4–6, 2011 near Durban, brought together arts-based researchers focusing on HIV&AIDS from Canada and South Africa.
6. There are several excellent works: Nattrass (2007).
7. Mitchell, C. (2002). Risky spaces: Youth, negotiation and HIV in South Africa. 9th Annual Canadian Conference on International Health, Ottawa, Ontario, October 27–30; Mitchell, C. (2003). In my life: New perspectives on young adult literature in South Africa. Children's Literature Conference. University of Potschestrom, September 30–October 2; Mitchell, C., & Walsh, S. (2004). Re-representing the data: Life stories of young township women taking about their experiences of HIV and AIDS. Annual conference of the American Educational Research Association. San Diego, April 11–15; Mitchell, C., Walsh, S., & Larkin, J. (2003). Hidden from view: on methodologies for unravelling young women's talk about body, sexuality and HIV/AIDS prevention. A paper presented to Sex & Secrecy Conference, Johannesburg, South Africa, June 22–25; Mitchell, C., & Larkin, J. (2002). Gendering HIV/AIDS in a globalized world: implications for prevention programs for youth. A paper presentation at The 14th International Congress on Women's Health Issues, Victoria, BC, June 15–18; Mitchell, C., & Larkin, J. (2002). Transnationalism and AIDS prevention: Reframing gender. A paper presented to the Gendered Worlds 8th International Interdisciplinary Congress on Women (IICW), Makere University, Kampala, Uganda, July 21–26; Mitchell, C., Smith, A., & Walsh, S. (2002). South African youth culture and youth participation in HIV prevention. A poster presentation at the XIV International AIDS Conference,

Barcelona, Spain, July 7–12; Mitchell, C., Walsh, S., & Smith, A. (2002). Youth participation and the gendered discourse of HIV/AIDS. A paper presented to Invitational Conference on HIV/AIDS and South African schools. School of Education, University of Natal, April 8–10.

References

Burawoy, M. (2003). Revisits: An outline of a theory of reflexive ethnography. *American Sociological Review*, *38*, 645–679.

Ellis, C. (2004). *The ethnographic I—A methodological novel about autoethnography*. Oxford: Altamira Press.

Ellis, C. (2009). *Revision—Autoethnographic reflections on life and work*.Walnut Creek, CA: Left Coast Press.

Gibbs, A. (2009). Understanding the HIV epidemic in South Africa. In C. Mitchell & K. Pithouse (Eds.), *Teaching and HIV&AIDS* (pp. 49–67). Northlands: Macmillan.

hooks, b. (1989). Choosing the margins as a space for radical openness. *Framework*, *36*, 15–23.

Miller, J. (1995). Trick or treat? The autobiography of the question. *English Quarterly*, *27*(3), 22–26.

Mitchell, C. (2006a). "In my life": Youth stories and poems on HIV/AIDS: Towards a new literacy in the age of AIDS. *Changing English*, *13*(3), 355–368.

Mitchell, C. (2006b). Visual arts-based methodologies in research as social change. In T. Marcus & A. Hofmaenner (Eds.), *Shifting the boundaries of knowledge* (pp. 227–241). Pietermartizburg: UKZN Press.

Mitchell, C. (2013). Oil rights/rites: Autoethnography as a tool for drilling. In T. Strong-Wilson, C. Mitchell, S. Allnutt & K. Pithouse-Morgan (Eds.), *Productive remembering and social agency* (pp. 123–138). Rotterdam: Sense.

Mitchell, C. & Weber, S. (1999). *Reinventing ourselves as teachers: Beyond nostalgia*. London and New York: The Falmer Press.

Mitchell, C., Walsh, S. & Weber, S. (2007). Behind the lens: Reflexivity and video documentary. In G. Knowles & A. Cole (Eds.), *The art of visual inquiry* (pp. 281–294). Halifax: Backalong Press.

Mitchell, C., Strong-Wilson, T., Pithouse, K. & Allnutt, S. (Eds.). (2011). *Memory and pedagogy*. London and New York: Routledge.

Mitchell, C., Stuart, J. Delange, N. Moletsane, R., Buthelezi, T., Larkin, J. & Flicker, S. (2010). What difference does this make? Studying South African youth as knowledge producers in the age of AIDS. In C. Higgins & B. Norton (Eds.), *Language and HIV/AIDS* (pp. 214–232). Toronto: Multilingual Matters.

Moletsane, R. & Lolwana, P. (2012). Wearing our hearts on our sleeves: The t-shirt and the South African activist agenda. In R. Moletsane, C. Mitchell & A. Smith (Eds.), *Was it something I wore? Dress, identity, materiality*. Cape Town: HSRC Press.

Nattrass, N. (2007). *Mortal Combat: AIDS denialism and the struggle for antiretrovirals in South Africa*. University of Kwa Zulu-Natal Press.

Neale, B. (2010). Foreword: Young lives and imagined futures. In M. Winterton, G. Crow & B. Morgan-Brett (Eds.), *Young lives and imagined futures: Insights from archived data* (Timescapes Working Paper Series No.6).

Norquay, N. (1993). The other side of difference: Memory work in the mainstream. *Qualitative Studies in Education*, *6*(3), 241–251.

Pithouse, K., Mitchell, C. & Moletsane, R. (Eds.). (2009). *Making connections: Self-study and social action*. New York: Peter Lang.

Riggins, S. (1994). Fieldwork in the living room: An autoethnographic essay. In S. Riggins (Ed.) *The socialness of things: Essays in the socio-semiotics of objects*. Berlin: Mouton de Gruyter.

Schuster A. (Ed.). (2003). *"In my life": Youth stories and poems on HIV and AIDS*. Cape Town: Centre for the Book.

Walsh, S. (2007). Power, race and agency: Facing the truth and visual methodology. In N. DeLange, C. Mitchell & J. Stuart (Eds.), *Putting people in the picture*. Rotterdam: Sense.

Walsh, S. (2012). "We grew as we grew": Visual methods, social change and collective learning over time. *South African Journal of Education*, *32*(4), 406–415.

Walsh, S. (Director) & Mitchell, C. (Producer) (2003). *Fire + Hope*. Montreal: Taffeta Productions.

Walsh, S. & Mitchell, C. (2004). Artfully engaged: Youth, gender and AIDS activism. In A. Cole, J. Neilsen, G. Knowles & T. Luciani (Eds.), *Provoked by art* (pp. 191–202). Halifax: Backalong Books.

Walsh, S. & Mitchell, C. (2006). "I'm too young to die" Danger, desire and masculinity in the neighbourhood. *Gender and Development*, *14*(1), 57–68.

Walsh, S., Mitchell, C. & Smith, A. (2002) The *Soft Cover* project: Youth participation in HIV/AIDS prevention. *Agenda*, *53*, 106–112.

4

CULTURAL STUDIES WENT TO SCHOOL AND WHERE DID IT END UP?

Julian Sefton-Green

The Backstory by Way of Introduction

In 1986 I started teaching English at Northumberland Park Community School in Tottenham. The school is directly behind the football stadium—the local club Tottenham Hotspur FC is by far and away the most famous business in the area. Tottenham will play a key role in my account, so by way of context I need to say that it is one of the most deprived areas in the United Kingdom with a very socially mixed population and high unemployment. Just before I began teaching there had been riots in the local housing estate, Broadwater Farm, and unusually for England this had resulted in the death of a police officer. This made the area notorious and in the eighties that event was one of the key markers of poor relationships between the police and black communities. The area itself is a curious mixture of beautiful but decayed Georgian buildings and more brutal social housing. In 2011 the death of yet another black man by the police in Tottenham provoked large-scale rioting, which spread across London and two other major cities in the UK. In some ways, and I say this also because of visits I have made as a result of an on-going research project, the area has not changed greatly in the last 25 years.

Although I began as a teacher of English, by the time I left the school in 1992, I was a full-time teacher of media studies. The subject, media studies, was being developed for public examination at that time and I played my part in the process of curriculum development. A few years after I began teaching I became involved in a range of classroom research projects around the development of media studies and media education along with my friend and collaborator, David Buckingham. David led a series of initiatives at the Institute of Education in London and I worked with him closely on a number of these (see Buckingham, 1990). In 1994,

Cultural Studies Went to School **47**

just a few years after I left the school, we published a book called *Cultural Studies Goes to School* (Buckingham & Sefton-Green, 1994). This book still remains one of the most detailed accounts of classroom practice in media learning.

Most of the book consists of a series of case studies from my classrooms examining a series of young people making and reflecting on media and the differences between media studies and English. It is very much rooted in new literacy paradigms—indeed, it was published in Allan Luke's *Critical Perspectives on Literacy and Education* series. One key theme is the importance of reading and writing forms of popular culture usually proscribed by the school. We were interested in how young people brought significant resources and levels of informal scholarship to their reading of comics, magazines, TV series and films. We were also interested in the nature and meaning of the pleasures and significance they derived from appropriating and identifying with these texts. Coming out of what was then known as the 'new audience studies', the book explored the intersection of active meaning-making as part of an audience with a neo-Vygotskian theory of learning, which prized the social, and the added value of the academic discipline of media studies to everyday literacy practices.

My passion developing the new subject, media studies, meant that my classrooms were often seen as more unusual and perhaps 'alternative' spaces at the school. I ran the school magazine and aspired to make media studies itself a new, innovative and a self-validating curriculum offer. Coupled with production based, group-work pedagogies, I tried to offer the subject, as it was then emerging as an academic discipline, as cutting-edge, radical and personal.

My recollection of school culture was (filtered through the romantic hue of memory) warm, diverse, lively and energetic. There were perhaps no more than 5 per cent of young people from middle-class homes—often with politically committed parents—and the young people mainly came either from what was then the remnants of a blue-collar working class and the often aspirational but discriminated against migrant populations. Relationships between staff and students were, on the whole, open, warm and trusting. In some respects, school and the adults found there were more motivating and enthusiastic than some young people found at home. Many of the young people who appeared on the pages of *Cultural Studies Goes to School* worked with me over 5 or 6 years. In the various guises and roles (including form teacher, subject teacher or as a pastoral leader) I knew them, I saw them change and grow over their school career.

Since I left the school I have kept in touch with several students—most of whom I worked with teaching them media studies A-level (when they were 17/18 years old) and who appeared in the 1994 book. When Facebook first started, a number of ex-pupils 'friended' me and we have exchanged small family catch-up kinds of correspondence. I have had several e-mails asking if I was the person who taught at Northumberland Park with comments on how I was remembered as a teacher. I have worked with one of the students, Steve, on and off in the last 10 years, employing him as a media arts tutor in the out-of-school centre

48 Julian Sefton-Green

where I worked and also co-authoring a couple of chapters with him, particularly around new technologies and collaborative learning (see O'Hear & Sefton-Green, 2004a, 2004b).

It was partly this ad hoc series of connections that made me want to investigate some of the premises from *Cultural Studies Goes to School* more systematically. The book had argued that engaging with popular culture in a disciplined and especially a production-based fashion enabled both a quality of learning and a socio-political kind of understanding. We weren't suggesting simply that validating and investigating pleasures were meaningful as an end in themselves but that, as an educational project, such activities contributed to young people's efficacy, the development of their sociological imagination and their political identities. We did suggest that media learning could thus act as a lever for engagement in further and other kinds of study as much as an end in itself. These are, of course, ambitious goals and also they open up very speculative areas of enquiry. How could we ever know what kind of difference studying cultural studies in education might make to an individual's life journey?

Reconnecting Rather than Revisiting

I ended up conducting three separate interviews with three very different now not-so-young people. For what it's worth, I have also reached out to three more of my ex-students, all of whom were very friendly on Facebook, very positive about staying in touch but when push came to shove, it seemed that they didn't want to follow up my invitation to reflect on what happened to them since they left school. This is obviously fair enough. With one of them—whose Facebook status read that she was widowed and whom I deduced had experienced quite a lot of challenges in life—I made a series of arrangements to meet but these always broke down. My hunch was that reconnecting with an old teacher forces a kind of reflection about the person you were going to be when there appeared to be more possibilities in life. However, if the realities of your life don't quite match up, then I think meeting with ex-teachers and reviewing where you are now and what you might have been, could be a more painful experience.

I met up with Michael in a local restaurant. In the 1994 book he had insisted on being called Ponyboy, after the S. E. Hinton book, *The Outsiders*. He was very much a fan and exhibited serious fan commitments and allegiances; see Henry Jenkins's work (Jenkins, 1992, 2006) in terms of fan culture. He was obsessed with various kinds of films and early computer games and I spent a long time in the 1994 book discussing a short novel he had produced called *Plaz, The Investigations* (see also Sefton-Green, 1993). I had analysed it in terms of hyper-masculine identity work. I recalled spending many lunchtimes with a rather lonely and awkward young man who would come and talk to me enthusiastically about his passions. He is from a Greek-Cypriot family and his written English was never terribly good, but this never seemed to hold back his enthusiasm.

The second interviewee was Clare. She was one of the co-authors of a feminist parody magazine, *Slutmopolitan*, in the 1994 book. She was a quiet, very hard-working girl who was also active in running a magazine at school. She perhaps did best academically of all of the students and went on to study media studies at the University of East London, then one of the leading institutions to offer this subject in the UK. I recall she had been terribly passionate about media and media studies activities. I met up with Clare in a restaurant outside of London in a dormitory village where she now lives.

The third interviewee was my friend Steve. He too went on to study media studies at university, but on a more production-based course, at Bournemouth, also at that time one of the leading institutions in this field. He too was one of my most enthusiastic students and was particularly interested in digital technologies as they were beginning to emerge at the time when I taught him. I saw Steve at his home.

In discussion with all three of them we reflected on their memories and recollections of studying media at school. For Michael this only took place at the lower level, at GCSE (for fourteen-/fifteen-year-olds) and for the other two additionally at A-level (the examination for seventeen-/eighteen-year-olds). They had all at some stages been in my English classroom, so differences between media studies and English as two kinds academic literacy practices also threaded through our discussions. When we met up—it is difficult to describe them as more formal interviews—we talked additionally about the distinctiveness of media studies in relationship to schooling in general and then we talked about their subsequent education, employment and other significant life-course events. We talked a lot about what media they enjoy now and their sense of themselves as what it might mean to be 'media educated'. We also talked more generally about other people they were still in touch with, including some of those who had been in touch with me, partly out of gossip and familiarity but also as a way of distinguishing themselves from their peers. Indeed, as the conversations continued this mode of talk became a key heuristic for me; how they explicitly and implicitly contrasted themselves and their lives with peers, and how such distinctions derived from positions they were claiming as a result of being educated. This analysis draws on the work of Bourdieu (1984; and see also for an English version Bennett et al., 2009), exploring how marking cultural distinctions is a key way of signifying membership of social class—a key function of what it means to be educated (Albright & Luke, 2008). I return to this analytical lens below.

Two of the three, Michael and Steve, still live in Tottenham. Only Clare has children—they are all in their late thirties. Steve is severely physically disabled and this has affected his capacity to determine where he lives and obviously his family circumstances. Steve has an impressive life in the media in some respects. He has made a few films and has run a series of businesses initially doing Web design in the nineties and most recently developing natural language applications.

He has worked as a technology journalist. He had tried to hold down positions as an editor in several production companies but this ambition never materialised. Work, however successful, has been fairly serial.

Michael has been un- and under-employed ever since leaving school. I suspect he experienced several bouts of depression. He is passionate about martial arts (he was never allowed by his father to do this when he was younger) and teaches this alongside working as a bouncer on the doors to nightclubs. He seems to have a series of jobs in the public sector at a low-level administrative grade. He did a vocational course in computers and has always been interested in technology but paradoxically (given his fraught relationship with writing as a second language), his work seemed to involve forms of clerking.

Clare was very disappointed by university and racked up huge debts leading to her being declared bankrupt. Although she tried junior positions in the media, she ended up working in the civil service at a relatively senior level. She now has three small children—she married a childhood sweetheart from the neighbourhood—and is very involved as a mother in local primary schools.

All of these stories are quite sobering in a number of ways. They immediately raised a series of questions about the possible trajectories of working-class youth from impoverished neighbourhoods—especially poignant given the political insistence on education as *the* route to social mobility. These are more macro-sociological issues then normally pertain to studies of the literacy classroom. Questions about their attitude to the media and the current modes of consumption and what it means to them to consider themselves as media-educated people[1] are inextricably intertwined with these larger social questions.

The slight oddities of my method talking with somebody (me) who had clearly been important at some stage of their lives and who is obviously heavily implicated in some of the questions I was asking, coupled with the intensely personally reflective focus to the discussion, make these themes difficult to disentangle—a point made by Clare: 'You kind of have a sense that your teacher might have expected you to do something and then you think and I've got to tell them how much I have cocked up.'

However, in some ways I was also revisiting ambitions about how working in this subject enabled certain kinds of personal development and possibly I was one of the few people who might know what questions to ask. Clare, it should be added, had read the 1994 book, *Cultural Studies Goes to School*, and we also talked about her interpretation of herself in this volume.

The remainder of this piece will therefore be organised thematically around emerging findings to do with being a 'media-educated' person; the question of Tottenham and social mobility; and the relationship of single subjects within a broader perspective about the place of schooling in life more generally. Each of these themes requires specific analytic frames.

Being Media Educated

In their comparative anthropological account of what it means to be educated, Levinson et al. (1996, p. 21) advocate what they call an 'historical ethnographic' approach in order to analyse how the cultural identity of an 'educated person' is produced, exploring practices and identities, which are then reproduced and resisted. Drawing on a rereading of classic cultural studies theory from the Birmingham Centre for Cultural Studies and social reproduction theory as remediated by Bourdieu, they suggest a form of enquiry that situated the study of subjectivities and identities at the heart of a socially progressive project to study education.

While our project in the 1980s and 90s was interested in media learning as an enquiry into learning in the classroom and dealt with questions of identity and subjectivity, it had little sense of what that might mean over time. What might someone who was media educated, as it were, look like and how might they construct themselves as an educated person in this field as per the frame as suggested by Levinson et al.?

These interviews suggested three interlinked ways of performing being media educated. The first relates to markers of taste and distinction in the Bourdieusian sense (Bourdieu, 1984). Judgements and comments about current media consumption, which positioned the speaker as knowing and an informed 'literate' consumer (or, in Steve's case, as an actor), were asserted with confidence and enthusiasm. Michael, for example, was particularly keen to tell me all about his current reading habits (due in part to his purchase of a Kindle) and how he was reading cyberpunk novels like *Necromancer*. Both he and the other two interviewees were also keen to tell me what they didn't like viewing or reading and how this marked them out in some ways as different from their peers. Clare talked pejoratively about a school-friend's poor taste in watching TV shows, 'tripe' as she put it, whereas she emphasised her selectivity. She has old classic TV shows for her oldest child (*Trumpton* and *Bagpuss*) and didn't like him watching Americanised manga, like *Pokémon* or *Ben 10*. Steve is not only a film-maker and a keen digital geek, but intriguingly he talked about reading as now being his most meaningful kind of cultural consumption. In the retrospective light of his negative comments about the value of studying English—made in the original study and which he recalled without my prompting—we both thought this was pretty funny.

All three were self-conscious—perhaps even reflexive—about their media tastes and what this said about them. Typically, they marked themselves out as being different from their friends and peers, and in different ways they tried to claim membership of an elite. The characteristics of this elite group are a capacity not to be 'taken in' by the media and to possess a completely self-contained point of view where the individual can stand aside from the mass of society. Clare says that she 'is suspicious of most media' and talked about how she 'Look[s] at films

52 Julian Sefton-Green

in a critical way and think what relevance they might have, even when I watch things like *Ice Age*, [I] think what relevance it has.'

For Steve, this perspective is central to his identity and his career:

> I have always loved the media . . . in terms of the, you know, 'inside baseball' . . . I mean, I always watch the *X Factor* and I watch it, obviously from a media lens. I watch it thinking, 'Is that bit manufactured? How is that going to play in tomorrow's headlines?' But I love that game, yeah, that PR game . . . whatever you want to call it . . . and what social media and all that shit, and the way I have handled my career as a journalist, as a modern-day journalist. I am *so* aware that I am the brand, the whole person sort of thing and that is what's taken care of my career, so that is sort of, like media skills, like image and how you spin things and all that shit . . . with social media that applies to the brand more . . . I don't know whether that is a digital thing or a middle-class thing but that is how I have looked after my career.

While Ponyboy was in general critical of the media in a generalised conspiracy theory kind of way, he wasn't as explicit in this respect as the other two.

In the original study and in a subsequent volume (Buckingham et al., 1995) we were very interested in what the idea of critical consciousness might mean in practice as opposed to its display within and for academic purposes. Here we can see accounts of a day-to-day critical awareness, but it is additionally framed in terms of markers of social class distinction—'how I am not like the other people I grew up with.' In some ways these comments describe Bourdieu's classic middle-class 'distanciation' but they also suggest a very particular way in which the experiences of being media educated can produce the tools and 'data' that constitute such a process.

In later work, David Buckingham (1998, 2003) developed this line of thinking, further questioning what it means to develop criticality in radical pedagogy and how such aspirations frequently underpinned some of the political ambitions for the development of media studies as an academic subject. He identified a curious feature whereby the demonstration of radical critique actually was most manifest in the cynical and satirical uses of media studies by frequently middle-class students who used their knowledge as a way of enacting class status and therefore the relationship between the supercilious outsider and the avant-garde radical critic often took on the same form and language. Steve and Clare elided the critical power of the margins with this assertion of their own social difference.

This leads us to the second element of defining what it might mean to be media educated: namely, how the students saw themselves as products of a media education and having experienced what was, and to some extent still is, an unusual and unorthodox set of qualifications. Clare admitted that she was embarrassed to tell people she had studied media studies at university and both she and Steve

Cultural Studies Went to School **53**

joked about its status as an academic pariah subject due to its presence in the popular press as an object of derision. On the other hand, they spoke fondly and positively about the experiences of learning media at school, and both Clare and Steve talked about practical work they had completed and the meaning of these projects for them at the time. They both talked explicitly about the meaningfulness of this type of learning experience. Both of these two recalled assignments from nearly 20 years ago, and the pleasures and vitality of the classroom experience— although it should also be admitted that this was in most cases expressed as alternative to their recollections of other more mainstream subjects and experiences. There is thus an underlying ambivalence about having formally studied the media and what this means to themselves and others.

Unlike Clare, Steve is proud of having graduated from Bournemouth and of being a media studies graduate. He sees this as an example of how cutting-edge he is and this brings us to the third dimension of what it might mean to be media educated: as a member of the digital generation. All of these ex-students talked about their current immersion in all forms of digital culture. They all offered accounts of their first computers and how they were early adopters of digital culture. For Ponyboy, this was about gaming, for Steve getting into digital editing early—even ahead of his university—and for Clare, similarly about doing early desktop publishing— far ahead of projects at university. However, unlike Steve, she recognised that the desire to go to university was poorly informed in terms of where or how she could have built on her practical production expertise.

All three of them are clearly active digital consumers and in some ways digital activists and citizens. Clare is active on Mumsnet[2] and talked interestingly about its range of political views and how, although its middle-class actors stifle opinion, it is a varied and rich source of information about everything, including the Greek debt crisis. Steve is a techno–journalist and active blogger, and even Ponyboy was working on how to set himself up as a games commentator following games-fan channels. They all had stories of friends (both high and low academic achievers) who had to some extent ridden the wave of computerisation so that not only their lives but the lives of their peers have been opened up by opportunities as computer coders (high level in banks) and systems engineers (at lower levels).

This sense of themselves as being part of the digital generation is intriguing given that widespread Internet adoption and penetration of digital culture effectively post-dated their learning with me. I wonder whether studying media studies acted as an early way of legitimating a more scholarly and critical interest in leisure pursuits and forms of popular culture? It must be an unusual historical moment in the history of literacy that an early grounding in rather marginal and excluded literacy forms (media studies) could be recuperated as early training in such mainstream developments (digital culture).

These digital habits and histories are indistinguishable from more general aspects of what it means to be media educated. They all suggested that their digital activities

54 Julian Sefton-Green

and interests stemmed from the earlier media learning experiences. Whether this sense of personal efficacy is a feature of the digital age—that is, something we all claim whether it is objectively true or not—or whether it genuinely is something that could be traced to the critical understanding of the media might deserve further investigation. As expressed, it appears to exemplify some of the democratic aspirations behind participating in digital culture—representing as it does explicit indicators of being digitally literate (Jenkins et al., 2007).

Of course, all of their responses to these questions are problematic in as much as they might have construed these conversations as in some ways as a continuation of the teacher–students' relationship and were thus trying to show me what 'good students' they still were. This methodological caveat aside, it did seem that they all possessed a distinctive sense of what being media educated might mean and how this might position them in some ways as different from their peers and friends. It also seems to be a form of reflexivity that is pretty central to their current identities.

Straight outta Tottenham

The use of markers of taste to indicate the judgement of an educated person was perhaps most acute and problematic in references to Tottenham. All three talked about their ability or inability to escape (and this is their formulation) this iconic neighbourhood. In recent years place and place-making have become an important theme for literacy education both as an avenue into the identity work that underpins some of the ambition behind much literacy education and as a way of supporting an awareness and understanding of the social in people's lives (Comber et al., 2007). It should also be noted that there has been an equal focus on non-spaces (Auge, 2009) and virtual ones (Coyne, 2010; Leander et al., 2010) as a kind of inverse to this emphasis on actual place. In these interviews, Tottenham also became a cipher for social mobility (one of the key discourses about the purposes of education in contemporary British society) as well as a way of reflecting on social justice, ethnicity and multiculturalism. In her study of the discourses of identity and place, Taylor suggests that we discursively imbue certain places in our lives with a bundle of symbolic powers, and this process was apparent in these interviews (Taylor, 2009).

Clare was the only one of these three who no longer lived in Tottenham and her friends from school had likewise 'emigrated' north through the more edge-city suburbs into the commuter towns and villages that surround London. While she talked nostalgically about what she missed, she also commented that telling other people that she came from Tottenham always drew a surprised response. She did not wax lyrical about lost communities but talked about the nitty-gritty of living on a housing estate and her recollections of crime. More tellingly, given that Clare is white, is her attitude towards where she now lives. While she likes her children being in the local village school and she is busy with the PTA (Parent-

Teacher Association), she is acutely aware that her children will not possess the same kind of street resilience that she has and neither will they experience the same kind of mixing with people from other ethnic and social backgrounds. She talked about her brother who she said was racist and she repeatedly contrasted her experience with her best friends who weren't allowed to play on the street, back in the day. Ponyboy was very clear that he regarded his inability to leave Tottenham as a key marker of his failure as a person. He repeatedly described his neighbourhood as 'shit'. For him it wasn't just the intrinsic qualities of the neighbourhood that were the issue, but his inability to move on. Place for him is not a marker of comfort or homeliness but a reminder of failure and lack of movement.

For Steve, Tottenham was always used adjectivally as in 'a Tottenham boy' and as a descriptor of people. He talked about being cautious taking up invitations to renew friendships from 'bad boys' who had lived around the corner from him and at the same time suggested that if various friends had lived in other neighbourhoods their life courses would have been simpler. He was also critical of the way that people from Tottenham are not going to be able to turn up punctually 99 per cent of the time (when we were talking about going to work) and that, unlike himself, his peers were likely to have lower expectations and lower achievement horizons.

All three of them (like myself) reflected on the meaning of Facebook connections and how they maintained contact with people from their past—especially those from Tottenham. Curiosity about what people were doing was mixed with a sense of still needing to control how they presented themselves, and Steve in particular guarded his 'reputation' carefully and strategically. He explicitly and repeatedly related this social process to his learnt understanding of how the media constructed and controlled the presentation of identity in a digitally mediated world.

While for Ponyboy and Clare, Tottenham was a way of measuring the travel of social mobility (both negatively and positively), for Steve it seemed to stand for more existential qualities as it went to the heart of what he had become (as a professional person) and could thus stand as a metric for analysing other less successful peers. However, for Clare and Steve, in contradistinction to Ponyboy, Tottenham also stood as a way of understanding contemporary British society. They were both sensitive to the talents and lost opportunities of their peers and how their present understanding of social injustice, as exemplified by Tottenham, affected and pulled the strings of their own and others' life chances.

Subjects, Subjectivity and Education as Fate

This final section explores how the three individuals conceptualised the role of schooling in general and where, if possible, they could disentangle the effect of one subject (media studies) from other wider social processes. While literacy or cultural educators have a clear sense of what their subject contributes distinctively to understanding, skills and knowledge, I was struck by how people rework their experience of education as an aggregate and not necessarily with reference to the disciplinary distinctions that preoccupy educators. To an extent, I was guided here by what the interviewees chose to remember, and although I asked the questions I was struck by the quality of significant remembering that seems to apply to the narratives we construct about our educational formation (for analysis of the role remembering narratives in educational research, see Bathmaker and Harnett, 2010; Goodson et al., 2012, as well as feminist approaches by Nava, 1992 and Walkerdine, 1997).

Ironically, given that I clearly feel Ponyboy has not achieved his potential (whatever that means), I was struck by how positive and affectionate he was towards his memories of school. While I may feel that school (and me) had let him down, he repeatedly said it was a good school, that he didn't feel angry or let down by his education, and that school 'doesn't prepare you for work' anyway. While he admitted that he didn't think school had helped him that much and that 'by this stage I would have thought I would have had everything sorted', he didn't necessarily blame school for his current position. Indeed, I was struck by how he attributed agency to others, himself, his family and wider social determinants as if school could have no possible effect. In some senses he appeared to believe that personality is fate—that nothing could really have changed the way he is, and that rather than seeing school as in some way a constituting process in itself, it did the best it could.

Paradoxically, Steve also partly echoed this sentiment. He talked about how some of his peers 'lacked certain social skills', 'that they were unable to turn up on time' and so on. These behaviours and personality attributes can be attributed to Tottenham—'society and capitalism may have given [an individual by name] a bad deal'—but fundamentally he echoed Ponyboy in attributing success and achievement to inherent and intrinsic personal qualities. As he talked about his peers and what they were now doing, his view was that the ones who have succeeded would have succeeded in any case (and vice versa); that 'X was always a bit of a geek', that 'Y was always reliable', and so on. The implication of this discourse is that the same applies to him, that his achievement and success are due to his abilities and his will. School and the influence of particular subjects within it are therefore subordinate to these determinations. He remembered his experiences of various learning experiences as retrospectively calibrating the strategies that ensured his success. For example, he remembered doing a research essay in English that was in practice a genre study and therefore really a piece of media studies work thus identifying and marking out the young scholar who was already developing approaches and skills he would use in later life.

Steve now possesses a professionalised and theorised understanding of pedagogy and an explicit understanding of educational philosophy (at one point he talked about learning-by-doing/constructivism with me) so that on several occasions he talked about the work we did in media studies as being 'tangible' and 'relevant'. He had a clear sense not just of the pleasures that it afforded but how learning in this way contributed to a more effective and meaningful education in general. Here he saw how the syllabus we developed was as much about the capacity to do 100 per cent coursework as it was about the content.[3] A key issue, however, is the sense of agency and independence that it fostered. He recalled what it meant to work in this way and how this foreshadowed later production work. How integral these processes are to the content of the academic subject or whether they indicate more generic educational strategies is open to question. On the other hand, Clare made it clear that it was the content of the projects that was as important as the process. She said of the *Slutmopolitan* exercise:

> We weren't just doing things for fun, is that what you mean? No I think even at the time we realised the value of it . . . I think . . . We knew at the time what we were doing was a piss-take at the time and we could see how it was relevant to the media around us anyway. But I don't think it was just me. I think we all got a sense of that.

She didn't distinguish as much between an aggregated notion of schooling and subject specific activities and experiences. For her, the subject was about being individually identified as a good student, as a success, and this is a point she made when talking about reading the original book:

> Seeing yourself in text is just weird anyway . . . you look back and you think, 'God that was really bad.' That's 'cos you've moved on and you know what you could achieve now. It's also an element of pride that somebody was interested in what you are doing because generally, most people passed through school life and they are ignored. They are . . . you know teachers forget their names. . . . That's life.

Indeed, part of her story about university and why it didn't really work for her is also about a lack of individual attention and a lack of specific guidance. Her account of being ignored in a larger institution without the personal one-to-one relationships, which characterised her schooling may have told a story about her own unreadiness as much as it did about the way that tertiary education didn't engage with her expectations. In this sense, Steve's access to greater cultural capital not only allowed him to generalise about learning and schooling, but also enabled him to review his educational experiences as a resource that he could deploy strategically and retrospectively, whereas for Clare classroom activities and schooling appeared more individualised and are interpreted more personally. Quite possibly Ponyboy's more passive and almost disinterested appraisal of school as a distant and irrelevant process reflects his position even further along this interpretative continuum than Clare's.

Conclusion

The whole experience of revisiting the earlier intellectual project and of reconnecting with these individuals in different circumstances has been—and I think it was for them too—an absorbing and quite unsettling experience. While I have suggested that there are a number of ways in which this revisit can shed light on the earlier project in terms of the identity work being involved in being 'media educated', it is also a sobering corrective to some of those early ambitions. However, the continuing sense of these individuals' sense of maintaining critical distance is encouraging, especially in relationship to new forms of participation in digital culture. Perhaps not unsurprisingly questions about social mobility, of the relationship of an individual to the neighbourhood where they grew up, the tentacles of poverty and social reproduction have certainly set limits to some of the optimism expressed in the earlier publication.

On the other hand, it seems plausible to suggest that some of the after-effects of this kind of cultural studies education are perceptible both to me, and the individuals themselves. The quality and nature of a reflexive mode of media consumption, of participating in digital culture and of having experienced a qualitatively different kind of curriculum from their peers seems to have been an important part of their current identities. Steve is clearly the most knowing about claims made for learning and education in general. The application of these understandings to his own experiences gave him a different position from which he can review its effects. At different times during these interviews, Clare and Ponyboy offered similar kinds of reflexivity. However, the fact of the matter is that education in general has worked best on one level for Steve and that it is very clear that however successful Clare and Ponyboy were at different stages at school and indeed beyond that, such knowledge and understanding have more self-knowing than instrumental benefits—not that an instrumental outcome is, of course, the only purpose to schooling.

There is no doubt that the discourses we draw on to make sense of our education are affected not only by wider social processes and public debate but the kind of language that our earlier experiences enabled us to use. This is clear in the case of Clare and Steve where it seems to me that the qualities of a production-based curriculum reflecting on their own position as members of an audience and of actively being engaged in critical and creative ways does seem to have, what I, following Soep (2010), have termed, an 'after-effect'. Developing an analytic frame to make sense of these very broad life-course experiences is not straightforward. At times I imagine there was a therapeutic dimension to my revisits and that the value of these interviews may well be important for the individuals themselves as they, and we, struggle to rationalise our place in the world in the light of school—clearly an institution that casts its shadow in all sorts of ways for a very long time after we have left.

Notes

1. I draw on Levinson et al. (1996) using this term and see the following section.
2. Available at: www.mumsnet.com
3. As Steve himself knew, this is politically contentious, with successive governments trying to change coursework assessment in the English system to terminal examinations.

References

Albright, J. & Luke, A. (Eds.). (2008). *Pierre Bourdieu and literacy education*. London: Routledge.

Auge, M. (2009). *Non-places: Introduction to an anthropology of supermodernity*. London: Verso Books.

Bathmaker, A.-M. & Harnett, P. (Eds.). (2010). *Exploring learning, identity and power through life history and narrative research*. London: Routledge.

Bennett, T., Savage, M., Silva, E. B., Warde, A., Gayo-Cal, M. & Wright, D. (2009). *Culture, class, distinction*. London: Routledge.

Bourdieu, P. (1984). *Distinction: A social critique of the judgement of taste* (R. Nice, trans.). London: Routledge.

Buckingham, D. (1990). *Watching media learning: Making sense of media education*. London: Falmer Press.

Buckingham, D. (Ed.). (1998). *Teaching popular culture: Beyond radical pedagogy*. London: University College London Press.

Buckingham, D. (2003). *Media education: Literacy, learning and contemporary culture*. Cambridge: Polity Press.

Buckingham, D., Grahame, J. & Sefton-Green, J. (1995). *Making media: Learning from media production*. London: English & Media Centre.

Buckingham, D. & Sefton-Green, J. (1994). *Cultural studies goes to school: Reading and teaching popular media*. London: Taylor & Francis.

Comber, B., Nixon, H. & Reid, J. (2007). Literacies in place: Teaching environmental communications. Primary English Teaching Association. Retrieved from http://eprints.qut.edu.au/38572

Coyne, R. (2010). *The tuning of place: Sociable spaces and pervasive digital media*. Boston, MA: The MIT Press.

Goodson, I. F., Loveless, A. M. & Stephens, D. (2012). *Explorations in narrative research*. Sense Publishers.

Jenkins, H. (1992). *Textual poachers: Television fans and participatory culture*. London: Routledge.

Jenkins, H. (2006). *Convergence culture: Where old and new media collide*. New York: New York University Press.

Jenkins, H., Clinton, K., Purushotma, R., Robinson, A. & Weigel, M. (2007). Confronting the challenges of participatory culture: Media education for the 21st century. Retrieved from: http://digitallearning.macfound.org/atf/cf/%7B7E45C7E0-A3E0-4B89-AC9C-E807E1B0AE4E%7D/JENKINS_WHITE_PAPER.PDF

Leander, K., Phillips, N. & Headrick Taylor, K. (2010). The changing social spaces of learning: Mapping new mobilities. *Review of Research in Education, 34*, 329–394.

Levinson, B., Foley, D. & Holland, D. (1996). *Cultural production of the educated person: Critical ethnographies of schooling and local practice*. New York: State University of New York Press.

60 Julian Sefton-Green

Nava, M. (1992). *Changing cultures: Feminism, youth and consumerism*. London: Sage Publications.

O'Hear, S. & Sefton-Green, J. (2004a). Creative 'communities': How technology mediates social worlds. In D. Miell & K. Littleton (Eds.), *Collaborative creativity: Contemporary perspectives*. London: Free Association Press.

O'Hear, S. & Sefton-Green, J. (2004b). Style, genre and technology: The strange case of youth culture online. In I. Snyder & C. Beavis (Eds.), *Doing literacy online: Teaching, learning and playing in an electronic world*. Cresskill, NJ: The Hampton Press.

Sefton-Green, J. (1993). Untidy, depressing and violent: A boy's own story. In D. Buckingham (Ed.), *Reading audiences: Young people and the media*. Manchester: Manchester University Press.

Soep, E. (2010). Research methods for web two dot whoah. In P. Thomson & J. Sefton-Green (Eds.), *Researching creative learning: Methods and issues*. London: Routledge.

Taylor, S. (2009). *Narratives of identity and place*. London: Routledge.

Walkerdine, V. (1997). *Daddy's girl: Young girls and popular culture*. Palgrave Macmillan.

5

REVISITING CHILDREN AND FAMILIES

Temporal Discourse Analysis and the Longitudinal Construction of Meaning

Catherine Compton-Lilly

Introduction

> MS. JOHNSON: Their parents aren't helping them. I mean, in this neighborhood alone you would not believe the late night hours these kids are outside. (Grade 1)
>
> MS. JOHNSON: I don't think a lot of them are doing too well at all. 'Cause a lot of them, I mean their parents, are never at home. They don't do anything with them. (Grade 5)
>
> DAVID'S OLDER SISTER: Yeah, because of their parents. (Grade 5)
>
> MS. JOHNSON: They don't get it from home. Parents don't read with them. (Grade 8)
>
> DAVID: Parents play a big role in that case and it's just like teachers and everything plays a big role. But it's just the little things that you wouldn't think that would set a child back. (Grade 11)

Across a decade, David, his mother, and his sister rearticulated a deficit discourse about parents in their low-income urban community. They blamed poor parenting for the challenges faced by many children. This discourse was not only repeated but it also circulated among participants. It was first articulated when David was in first-grade by his mother, later repeated by his older sister, and eventually revoiced by David when he was in high school. These recurring discourses were revealed as part of a *revisiting* study.

Educators have found the prefix 're-' particularly useful. *Rethinking Schools* (1986–present), a progressive school journal, has used 're-' to invite educators to reconsider existing policies and practices with an eye toward equity and social justice. The goal is to invite educators to rethink what they do and how well their students are served. Remediation and re-mediation have contrasting meanings in educational circles. While remediation focuses on helping students to catch up with their peers and entails providing instruction that will directly influence achievement, 're-mediation' involves the reorganization of learning contexts, social relationships, and learning artifacts to create classrooms that respond to diversity (Gutierrez et al., 2009). I titled my second book *Re-Reading Families*. This text, a sequel to *Reading Families*, presented my re-reading of the children and their families following a four-year absence and my return to revisit and re-examine their literacy learning across time. In this current edited volume, we again draw on 're-' to capture our return, our reunion with participants, and our revisiting of previously collected data in light of new experiences. While the term 'visit' invokes colloquial images of a cozy kitchen and cup of tea, the 're' suggests temporality related to return and reunion. 'Visit' also suggests a place, an arrival, and ultimately a departure.

In this chapter, I present data collected during a series of revisits; I focus particularly on temporal dimensions of revisiting. In previous writing (Compton-Lilly, 2014), I have referred to this analysis as temporal discourse analysis. Specifically, I analyze discourses across time to highlight time as a constitutive dimension of experience that people use to conceptualize their encounters with literacy, schooling, and identity. Temporal discourse analysis provides insights into how people make sense of their experiences across and within time and can be used to examine discourses over long or short periods of time—a ten-year school trajectory or a forty-five-minute class period. Researchers applying temporal discourse analysis attend to the temporal language used by participants (e.g. 'Last week,' 'when I was four,' 'when my mom was little,' 'When I grow up') while also documenting how participants draw on larger social histories (e.g. 'Dr. King said . . .'; 'Frederick Douglas lived nearby') to make sense of their own experiences. Temporal discourse patterns are also evident as discourses and stories are repeated, revised, and revisited across time and as people draw upon the past and possible futures to construct meanings in the present.

To illustrate temporal discourse analysis techniques, I draw on the case of David, a bi-racial African American/European American student from a low-income urban community. When I began the research, David was a student in my first-grade classroom. When I last visited David, he had left school during eleventh-grade. While there are many ways I could tell David's story, I focus on how David, his mother, his sister, and I used time to understand his school trajectory and describe David as an emerging young adult.

Temporal Discourse Analysis

Like many qualitative researchers, I routinely use grounded coding and constant comparison methods (Strauss & Corbin, 1990) to analyze data sets that include numerous interviews, audio-recorded classroom interactions, field notes, and discussions of artifacts. For the longitudinal study that included David and his family (Compton-Lilly, 2003, 2007, 2012), data was collected when David was in grades 1, 5, 8, and 11. During the first phase of the study, I coded data across the ten families. Although much was gained through this cross-case analysis, when I revisited the families when David was in fifth-grade, I coded the data for each case separately in order to highlight the particular experiences and insights of each family. In the third phases I returned to cross-case coding and in the final phase, I again analyzed each case separately. I considered this movement between cross-case analysis and individual case analysis to be a methodological strength of the study and I was initially pleased with the process and its results.

However, by focusing on the themes that emerged at particular points in time, traditional coding processes prevented me from recognizing and attending to longitudinal patterns across the phases of the study. Sorting data into categories at particular points in time obfuscated longitudinal patterns. As I collected multiple phases of data and became a longitudinal researcher, I often found myself re-reading the original transcripts. More and more often I would encounter segments of data as I was transcribing and would find myself digging through stacks of old transcripts looking for a similar discourse or story. It was through my continuing re-reading of the raw data from across the study phases that long-term temporal patterns became visible. I heard David and his mother using similar, and in some cases, identical language across phases of the project. Particular discourses recurred and participants repeated stories that they had told before. In addition, I became increasingly aware of temporal expectations related to literacy and schooling, and the challenges that some students faced in meeting these benchmarks.

These realizations drew my attention to the temporal language used by participants. During the third phase of the project, when I had been working with David and his mother for 8 years, I focused on a small set of codes related to time (e.g. 'change,' 'future,' 'now and then'). While some of these codes were identified during the initial phases of the project, I neither recognized their temporal nature nor their longitudinal significance. Once I recognized these codes as temporal codes, I began to consciously attend to participants' explicit use of temporal language (e.g. 'now,' 'then,' 'someday,' 'next week,' 'after,' 'fast'). I also began to recognize how participants recursively and selectively drew on events and experiences across time, repeatedly returning to some stories while neglecting and forgetting others, and framing some stories as examples of larger patterns. This required me to systematically revisit the raw data to seek stories and discourses that recurred across the study, comparing the various tellings of particular accounts, and attending to what remained and what was discarded. Some books and literacy practices were repeatedly described at multiple interviews while others were forgotten. Some discourses used identical words and phrases and could be tracked across time by using the search function on my computer. Other discourses varied in wording and were identified only through close

64 Catherine Compton-Lilly

re-readings of the data. The meanings that David and his mother constructed over time were not simple, linear, or chronological; they suggested that participants (including myself) judiciously drew on past events as we made sense of literacy, schooling, and ourselves. In fact, this longitudinal analysis is itself explicitly temporal, in that segments of data collected during later phases of the project gained significance when viewed in relation to earlier data. A story told in phase one attained significance if and when it is repeated across a ten-year period. Recollections of the past as well as perceived possibilities for the future converged as David identified and reidentified himself relative to school expectations, literacy practices, and potential identities.

In this chapter, I illustrate five temporal manifestations of discourse that became visible through my analysis of data from this ten-year study (Compton-Lilly, 2003, 2007, 2012).

1. The language that people use to situate themselves within time.
2. References to the pace of schooling and the timelines that operate in schools.
3. Comments and practices that reflect long social histories.
4. Repeated discourses over time.
5. Repeated stories over time.

Before exploring these five dimensions of temporal discourse analysis, I briefly describe the research project.

A Brief Summary of the Ten-Year Study

In the full longitudinal study, I followed seven children from my first-grade class through grade 11. All of the children, with the exception of David who is African American/European American, are African American. Each phase of the study included interviews with David and his mother, David's writing samples, and reading assessments. In the first phase of the project, when I was David's teacher, I also collected a rich set of classroom writing samples. During the final phase of the project, funding from the Spencer Foundation enabled me to visit the students at school and interview their teachers. These school visits and interviews did not occur for David as he was no longer attending school in spring of the year when the school visits and teacher interviews were scheduled. In grade 11, David completed writing samples, audiotapes, drawings, and photographs.

When I taught the students, they were all attending Rosa Parks Elementary School where 97 percent of the students qualified for free or reduced-price lunch. The school was located in the northeastern United States in a city that continues to struggle with unemployment, substandard housing, a lack of quality physical and mental health care services, the closing of local libraries, gang violence, and a proliferation of illegal businesses, including drug trafficking. While this

Revisiting Children and Families **65**

description might suggest a sad and decrepit community, the residents of this community, including David's mother, consistently demonstrated high levels of resilience, agency, and hope for their children. Seven of the original ten families remained in the study through all four phases and continued to attend schools in the district.

Temporal Manifestations of Discourse

In this section, I draw on David's case to illustrate five temporal manifestations that were identified through my longitudinal research. I do not claim that these five lenses capture all aspects of temporality. I offer these as starting points for thinking about how time operates across time. While the examples below occurred within a longitudinal project, I argue that these manifestations of time also occur across short-term studies.

The Language that People Use to Situate Themselves within Time

Below, I present an example of how participants used temporal language to situate themselves within time. Specifically, I explore *now and then* discourses that were used to refer to safety and Catholic schools. In the final example, David draws on these discourses to convince his mother that he should enlist in the military.

When David was in fifth-grade his mother compared the challenges David faced with her own experiences growing up. Ms. Johnson and I are the same age; she referenced our shared temporal lens as she described the peer pressure experienced by her children. '[It's not] like it was when we [Ms. Johnson and the researcher] were growing up. Nothing like it . . . Peer pressure, you know everything that they have out here, like the drugs the alcohol you know the dress styles.'

She continued, saying, 'Especially now days. Remember there's *a lot* of temptations out here. Mmm-hmm, you can see it every day.' At an interview later that year she connected these social changes to her children's safety. She described the dangers of playing outside and recalled David's older sister having witnessed the stabbing of a classmate who was getting off a school bus.

> In the day and age we grew up in, you didn't have to worry about being outside playing. There was nothing like it is nowadays. I mean, people just come by and shoot you, bang you're gone . . . I watch my 15-year-old. He'll watch behind himself, you know, and that's not the way it should be but that's the day and age they are coming up in. I mean it's bad out here . . . I mean, my daughter, went to [middle school]. She didn't even get off her school bus the day that little girl got stabbed, you know, and (turning towards

66 Catherine Compton-Lilly

her daughter who is sitting nearby) [you had] to sit there and watching this happened to another student your age. I mean, it has an impact.

David's sister chimed in, saying, 'Sometimes I be wondering when they [the little children] be playing outside if she's going to get shot today or if something's going to happen him. That is how it is over here.' In both Ms. Johnson's words and his sister's, now is a dangerous time. And as his mother notes, we have to '*live each day to the fullest* because we're not, we don't know if we are going to be here tomorrow. We don't know if we are going to be here this afternoon.'

Now and then discourses were also applied to schooling as Ms. Johnson described the Catholic school she worked in as different from those she attended as a child.

> I went to Catholic and I had a *Catholic* education. Oh, I'll never forget it. But now-a-days they're not into it. First of all, Catholic schools, the children are not taught by the Sisters. It's all lay people now. It is not like it was so I mean, naw, it's no different [from the public schools].

When in the eleventh-grade, David draws on his mother's discourses related to safety and schooling to convince her that he should join the military. His mother was opposed to this plan stating, 'With the world the way it is. Don't you [dare], oh my God. You can't do that.' David argued that by going into the military, he could get a better education and travel the world. He referenced discourses about safety presented above:

> [If you enter the military] you don't have to worry about being on the streets and everything. Like sometimes it's like worse for you to walk home and stuff . . . They got all these gang bangers and all that stuff . . . That's why I probably go into the army cause you like doing like computers and all that stuff. And not just learning about education in schools, like history and stuff and math and stuff. You can learn about all that stuff in the army like the stuff that's happening in the world.

In short, David argues that the local community has become so dangerous that enlisting in the military makes sense because at least there you can learn about 'stuff that's happening in the world.'

Now and then discourses are used to make sense of the lived present in relation to an envisioned past. While these discourses may or may not represent accurate accounts of the past, they act as a basis for comparison to which the present can be understood. Temporal language situates people and their sense-making processes within time-frames that reference past experiences, present realities, and offer future possibilities. They allow us to glimpse at how meanings are constructed over time, revisited, and applied to new situations.

The Pace of Schooling and Temporal Language

David's story of schooling is consistently marked with language related to the pace of schooling and his ability to meet school expectations, get good grades, and be promoted to the next grade level. His general trajectory involved a slow start, improvement, grades going up and down, being on the honor roll, and eventually leaving school.

In some ways, David's trajectory mirrors that of his mother. During David's first-grade year, Ms. Johnson reported that when she first learned to read, 'It was a little hard at first.' Her words echoed her own story when she recalled David's first experiences with learning to read.

> When he was first starting to read and he couldn't sound out a word he used to get very frustrated. Yeah, he would cry and that. I don't know it. I don't know it. And he'd get to the point where he didn't even want to try.

By grade 5, David recounted his slow start, saying, 'I used to have Bs and Cs, now I got As and Bs.' He explained that at first 'It was hard but second-grade it was like I was going to be retained.'

David recognized markers beyond grades that indicated school success or failure. He was aware that some students moved quickly through assigned texts while others did not. 'Some kids were behind in *James and the Giant Peach*. Some kids was on page 100 . . . some other kids was on page 160.' He proudly reported that he was further ahead than most of his peers. David was aware of the role testing played in school achievement. When I asked about students who do not do well on tests, he reported that 'they flunk' and explained, 'They got to do the grade over again and they got to do the test again.'

In eighth-grade, David's mother reported, 'All last year nothing but honor roll.' The following year, David was placed in honors classes. Despite being on honor roll, David and his mother remained watchful. Expectations for keeping pace were especially apparent as David and Ms. Johnson discussed the new State Reading Assessment that was implemented as part of 'No Child Left Behind.' David had scored a '2' on the test indicating that he was below the State Benchmark. In response, his mother took action, 'So I talked with his counselor and she's got him in a tutoring program Tuesdays and Thursdays after school for this test . . . which I thought would help him to do better on it [the test] this year.' Both David and his mother monitored progress relative to benchmarks, test scores, and grades, which in turn reflected their actions in the present.

David implicated teachers as playing a role in student success in school. He described his best teachers as helping students to keep pace with instruction, '[They] give us help on what we need help on, [answers] questions and he goes over what we have done before we take a test and stuff.' His least favorite teachers

68 Catherine Compton-Lilly

'give us tests without going over some of the stuff that's not on it. They'll give us half the stuff that we do in class and then half the stuff we didn't do.'

By September of grade 11, David reported that his grades had slid significantly. He made a thumbs-down motion and explained 'Last year was a throw away year . . . It was a pretty bad year.' David remained optimistic about the current year, reporting 'I'm good now' and '[I] know what I got to do now.' However, in December I visited David's school and learned that David was rarely attending school. When I spoke with David, he reported 'I was late' and missed the bus. David had been taken out of his honors classes due to missing too much school during the prior year, and was finding the regular classes to be too easy. At our final interview at the end of grade 11, David reflected back on his school experiences:

> School, I just think, you know it's like ups and downs but I think like [it's] a setback. Like everybody has their one setback and I think this is it. But I know what I gotta do but I just gonna do it. . . I talked to my mom last night about it and next year I'm going to go take all [my] classes and I think I'm going to end up taking night classes too.

Despite his poor attendance, David assured me that he would not drop out of school. 'It's not nothing about not dropping out or nothing because I know you drop out if you don't have a high school diploma, I don't definitely think I want a G.E.D.' He reported that he always 'kind of assumed' that he was going to get his high school diploma and mentioned his grandma, saying that he hoped 'she gets to see me walk across the stage for my diploma.'

The temporal language indicates more than when things happen (e.g. 'at first,' 'all last year,' 'before we take a test'). Temporal language can reference success or not keeping up (e.g. 'some kids were behind) and the consequences for falling behind (e.g. 'be retained,' 'do the grade over'). A related set of temporal markers highlight explanations and regrets related to time (e.g. 'I was late,' 'a setback,' 'a throw-away year'). A final set of temporal markers reference the future and possibilities (e.g. 'do better on it this year,' 'I know what I gotta do,' 'she gets to see me walk'). These discourses are produced in relation to the official temporal expectations related to passing tests, keeping up with peers, meeting school expectations, and not being retained. They are markers that David, his mother, and his peers draw on as they assess their abilities and identities as students.

Comments and Practices that Reflect Long Social Histories

Larger social histories related to literacy and schooling were also invoked throughout the interviews. Perhaps the most closely referenced historical story is related to the plight of African American people growing up in the South prior to the 1960s. As Ms. Johnson explained: 'Well, I've known a lot of people who

Revisiting Children and Families **69**

come from the South and they actually quit school to take care of home, you know, working at home, farming, that type of thing, and they never finished school.'

This discussion gains significance when we understand that this is the story of David's father. Ms. Johnson reported:

He [David's father] never finished school. He only went far as seventh grade. He is from way down South and he had to go to work. His father died at a very young age. And he had to kind of help his mom support the family . . . Needless to say, I do all the paperwork in the house, pay all the bills, read all the mail but I help him too and he's doing pretty well. I mean, he doesn't read the big words but he's doing pretty well. He can get by.

David's father died of cancer the summer following the first year of interviews. While David regularly spoke of his father, it was not clear whether he realized that his father struggled with reading. Drawing on larger social history related to the denial of schooling and literacy learning opportunities for some people, echoed discourses voiced by this family that associated literacy with survival that were recounted throughout the interviews. During the first year of interviews, she connects literacy with survival.

MS. JOHNSON: Everything that he will ever do in life he has to read. I mean, there is reading in no matter what you do. You fill out an application for a job you have to read. You have to read the paper. I mean, everything you do, I mean, especially if you have a job that requires that. I mean you have to read to understand. And then if you can't read then you miss out on a lot. You know I mean a lot of the history like I'm saying he would never know about. (Grade 1)

DAVID'S OLDER SISTER: If you can't read you, you've got a *big* problem. I mean, you have to read. You got to read in order to get any place you want to go. (Grade 5)

DAVID: So, well those who don't want to, they just don't care to read. They think that in that earlier life they don't have to read in order to get a job. Just like McDonald's. They don't got to read. All they got to do is cook and stuff and all that so they figure they get a job at McDonald's, they think they're going to be good to go but they're not. (Grade 8)

In this family, the language around reading literally invokes survival (e.g. 'everything that he will ever do in life,' 'you miss out on a lot,' 'in order to get any place,' 'you got to read'). For David, being able to read is necessary in order to move beyond a job at McDonald's. It is a discourse of possibility that echoes Ms. Johnson's account of the significance of reading. The historical situations that resulted in David's father's inability to read necessitated Ms. Johnson having to complete all the family paperwork. Ms. Johnson wants more for her children and she describes literacy as a key to their futures. Like the deficit discourses about parents presented earlier, this discourse is first articulated by Ms. Johnson, then David's older sister, and finally 8 years into the study by David himself.

Repeated Discourses over Time

Reading for survival is a discourse grounded in both family history and in larger social history, and like the discourses related to poor parenting it is also a recurring discourse across this data set. Another recurring discourse reflected the prediction that David would grow up to be rich and successful.

At the very first interview when David was 6 years old, his mother described him as being good with money. Ms. Johnson had high hopes for David:

> He wants to be a fireman, the policeman, those kinds of things now. But I see him being some kind of a business person. He is very good with money. Any time he gets money he never spends all his money. He always holds back on his money and he can tell you just how much he has and how much he is spending. He is very good.

As Ms. Johnson spoke, I could hear David's voice in the background telling me how much money he currently has saved.

When David was in grade 5, his mother described the jobs he worked over the summer:

> He made money like [there was] no tomorrow over the summer. Mowing lawns, doing different things for the neighbors. He makes good money. He really does. Cleans up the floor over here. He's really smart, takes after his dad a lot.

By the end of fifth-grade, David was helping his mother with her newly formed catering company. Ms. Johnson described him as a 'money maker' while his sister teased him saying, 'I'm just afraid that he is going to make too much money.'

By eighth-grade, Ms. Johnson reported that David told her when he's 'rich and famous he's going to buy me a mansion.' While as described below, David is still ossilating between his dreams of being a police officer, a fireman, a football player or a businessman, he highlighted his strong work ethic and his interest in making money:

> If I make it to the pros, mama, I'm going to pick up, dang any number of jobs. I'm going to be working full-time. See if I play football, I'm going to have me a night job as a cop or if I'm allowed [as] a firefighter.

Revisiting Children and Families **71**

By high school, David was catering events at the baseball park. He enjoyed working and received an award for being the most 'ambitious' employee. His mother reported that David wanted to own his own business and teased that eventually 'He wants to buy his momma a big mansion.' David joked with me about making 'a couple million [dollars]' after he finished school. While getting to school was a challenge, David reported 'I love to work' and explained 'If there's one thing I could do in life like on a very constant basis like a lot is work.' David reported that he was the person the bosses would regularly call to cover a shift. He says that he is looking for a second job, 'a recreational job' where he would be 'working with some kids.'

In a paper entitled 'What I Want to Be' written in eleventh-grade, David wrote, 'What want to be when I grow up is a successful man.' Interestingly, in this paper success was no longer defined in terms of getting rich; David now wants to 'finish school,' be 'a good role model,' 'help the needy,' and 'make a difference in the world.' For David, the story of success is repeated and rearticulated. While early versions focus on getting rich, in David's later accounts he highlights being a good person. Perhaps this is due to a 'cooling out' of dreams first described by Clark (1960) or to the educational 'setbacks' that David experienced in school. While the definitions of success change, discourses related to David as successful were consistently articulated across the study.

Repeated Stories over Time

While there is a thin line between repeated discourses and repeated stories, repeated stories involved particular events that were referenced, described, and retold at various points in time across the study. David and his family members told and retold two prominent stories. The first study involved David and his brother watching police shows with his father and David's dream of becoming a policeman. The second story involved a retelling of David's overnight trip to Massachusetts when he was in fourth-grade.

The Police Story

When Ms. Johnson first told the police story, her initial telling featured David's older brother. David was in grade 1.

> There is a lot of police pictures on now-a-days, you know, and all of that kind of stuff. My 11-year-old son likes the *Rescue 911*. And he's used quite a few of the things on that show.

Curious, I asked what he might have *used* from the television show. Ms. Johnson replied, 'CPR, he's seen it done so many times [on the show], now he thinks

72 Catherine Compton-Lilly

he can do it. He likes to practice on David.' We both laughed unaware of the role that police work would play in David's evolving dreams.

At age six, Ms. Johnson explained, 'he's at the stage where it's policemen, firemen' that interest him. David explained that the police can drive faster than either the ambulance or the fire trucks. When asked if police officers need to learn to read, he noted that they need to read 'police's books,' which he described as being about guns, knives, and bats.

By fifth-grade, David was particularly excited about being a crossing guard at the school. He tells me he wants 'to make sure kids walk in the halls [and] take off their hats in the morning.' His mother reports that David loves being on the safety patrol, 'He's at the top. He is one of the crossing guards . . . He is just doing so well.' David was particularly drawn to the uniform and the trappings related to police work. David explained, 'I want to be a policeman 'cause they got a lot of cool stuff and then they got the car that goes fast, the police car.' Earlier in the interview he reported that he was 'always going to have a bullet-proof vest on.' As the interview ended, he showed me his safety patrol badge and confidently noted, 'I want to be a policeman or the president of the United States.'

In grade 8, David offered the most complete version of the police story. 'If it weren't for some of these drill cops, I would do it, take the detective's test right after my first year for my skills. I [would] go to the shooting range' [makes gun noises that sound like an automatic weapon].

David's mother is listening to his account; she chimes in, saying 'The thing is, nobody respects the police.' David agreed:

> Yep, soon as they [the police] go down the street they [the criminals are] doing the same things again. I got a trick for that. I could set up cameras. I'm going to make a protest about that. I'm going to have my research by setting up cameras on all the major drug places and some of the finer places [where] they buy their clothes.

David explained that he did not want a desk job:

> As a cop you maybe if you sitting there . . . you got a desk or an office and you stay there all day and you got a person who, um, deals with like bank checks . . .You got to do a lot of research for all that stuff.

He would rather be like the detectives he watched on TV. In particular, he mentioned the TV series *In the Heat of the Night,* a series that aired over a decade before this interview occurred. David explained: 'I used to watch that a whole lot with my dad. [I] probably watch it like once a week now. I don't got my dad to watch with [any more].'

By high school, David was still interested in police work despite his difficulties in school. He explained:

Revisiting Children and Families **73**

I want to be a fireman or a policeman because I like to help people and I just want to be a hero . . . [I want to be a] policeman, 'cause I want to clean up the streets. Because it's real bad out here. Yeah. It's not, it's not good for you can walk outside, and you see fights and shootings and stuff, that's just not good.

David's story about being a policeman is connected to his memories of watching TV with his dad and his brother. He misses his father and continues to watch these old shows. Echoing his mother's concerns about safety in the community, David wanted to catch criminals, be a hero, and clean up the streets.

The Massachusetts Story

When I visited David when he was in fifth-grade he excitedly described the class trip he took in fourth-grade to visit a farm in Massachusetts. He described how his class had to save '$2,700, and we made it by ourselves. We sold candy bars and wreaths.' During their visit, the students worked on the farm for four days and two nights. David's account was filled with exciting details:

We got up at six o'clock in the morning.
I never fed the pigs [before]. It was huge pigs, hogs, they was hogs.
There was only one horse. It was not a riding horse. There was a work horse, I think, and we, fed it. 'Cause he's nice and we did a lot of things with the horse. I took the horse, twenty pictures and, um, I took about five or six pictures of him.
Our socks got wet every day.

David also described the journey down on the bus: 'It wasn't a school bus, though. They got TV . . . And they got a bathroom.'

The most complete version of the story was captured in a writing sample that David completed in fifth-grade (Box 5.1). In this account, David tells a sequential account that opened with him preparing for the trip and ended with his interest in going again.

At future interviews, David often spoke about this fourth-grade teacher, Ms. Gardner, who organized the trip and traveled with the class. David recalled singing in her class and the wonderful stories that she shared with her students. David knew that I was friends with Ms. Gardner and often asked me if I had seen her. Ms. Johnson fondly reminisced about Ms. Gardner, describing her as a teacher who 'goes above, way above and beyond.' In high school, David described Ms. Gardner as one of his 'favorite teachers.'

David's experiences on the farm also contributed to his sense of who he was and what he knew. In the following example, David claimed his experience on

74 Catherine Compton-Lilly

BOX 5.1 David's Farm Story (Grade 5)

Write a story about something that happened at school.

Once I went to Massachusites in the fourth-grade with my teacher and class. First I had to pack at home then I had to get on the bus then I gave my mom a hug and kiss and then I left. We had to raise 27 hundred dollars to go so we did and when we got there I had to go to my bonk [bunk]. Also I met the farmer because we were on a farm we had to milk cows and feed the animals.

So then we had a brake we went to go get lunch our chef was a great cooker. We had free time that's when we played games like kickball and soccer. These people on the farm were Nat and David and Ben. Ben was the farmer it was fun I hope to go again sometime this year.

Sincerely,
David J.

---

the farm as contributing to a degree of his expertise as he challenged some of George Bush's policies:

> During George Bush's term, I think like the farming stuff they talk about some of that stuff is left out. Because I don't know a lot about farming but I've been on a working farm and everything. I mean, a lot of stuff is like, but it is a few things that is like different [from what they say].

In these accounts, David's memories of this remarkable trip were not only caught up with his recurring memories of a favorite teacher but are also taken on as an identity positioning and a degree of expertise related to farming. References to the farm trip and/or Ms. Gardner recurred during every phase of the study and were consistently identified as high points in David's educational experiences.

Some stories were retold, revisited, and re-referenced across the study. David's dream of becoming a police officer and his visit to the farm were repeatedly presented as important stories in his life. They tell us something about David—who he is, and what he believes about the world and about himself. Both of these stories are caught up in relationships with significant people—his father, a favorite teacher. In their retelling, they reveal what David wants to share with me, his positioning of self to his former first-grade teacher and the identity that he chooses to reveal.

Conclusions

Data from David's case study provides an opportunity to explore meaning and identity construction across time. The temporal discourse analysis of accounts provided by David and his family over a ten-year-period offer insight into how David and his family situated themselves and their experiences within time, how David assessed his school success, and his construction of identity narratives across time.

David and his family situated themselves within time through their use of temporal language (e.g. *now and then* discourses) and the ways they drew upon larger social histories to make sense of their worlds. Their use of *now and then* discourses involved comparing the dangers of their local community with a remembered version of the past. Larger social histories related to opportunities for schooling and literacy that were denied to David's father fed into Ms. Johnson's discourses relating reading to survival. In both cases, we see families drawing on shared knowledge of the past to negotiate and make sense of their experiences in the present.

This longitudinal analysis reveals novel insights as I track the discourses that circulate among family members and across communities. Temporal discourse analysis allows an examination of how meanings are constructed and how cultural models (Gee, 2007) of the world are exchanged within families and across communities. In the full collective case study involving all seven families, discourses can not only be tracked over time, but across families as they circulate within communities. It might be argued that the circulation of discourses and cultural models is one means for the continuation and reconfiguration of *culture* as communities take up existing meanings in relation to new situations and circumstances.

Temporal discourse analysis reminds educators that students do not arrive in classrooms as empty slates. Even young children bring ways of understanding the world that are deeply rooted in the experiences of family members and in larger social histories. Teachers are not merely teaching in the present, they are inevitably engaging with the past as students bring familial and social histories to classrooms. Thus, teachers must recognize, respect, and learn about these histories as they prepare to enter communities, and work with children and families.

Temporal discourse analysis also reveals how people make sense of their own abilities and competencies in relation to schooling (e.g. grades, test scores, being promoted to the next grade). Success in school is closely tied to meeting officially recognized temporal benchmarks. These discourses were rearticulated across the study as David and his mother commented on his ability to meet these expectations and his teachers' efforts to support him in meeting these goals. Failure to meet these benchmarks reflected negatively on David and his abilities.

David's ability to meet temporal benchmarks of schooling informed how he made sense of himself as a student. David was exploring whether or not he was the kind of person who could be successful in school. Being a successful student entails an affinity with others who are recognized as belonging in academic settings and ultimately the professions that are contingent on academic prowess. Temporal discourse analysis of the words of David and his mother reveal mixed positionings relative to schooling and literacy, ranging from honor role to a 'throw-away year.'

Longitudinal analysis of school proficiency reveals setback and possibilities. Based on David's story, it appears that success in school is both fluid and potentially recursive. Success can be reclaimed as well as lost, and educators play a role in these negotiations. As David described, teachers can help students to be successful or they can allow them to stumble. Notably, these efforts entail more from teachers than just teaching literacy concepts and strategies. Educators must work to nurture acceptance of students into the intellectual work of schools. This entails acceptance of broad and fluid ways of being literate and invitations for students to participate in stimulating and challenging intellectual pursuits. Possibilities for student success are compromised when success entails narrow, testable, and inflexible goals that fail to recognize the intelligence and capabilities of students.

Temporal discourse analysis invites researchers and educators to revisit specific discourses and stories over time. When particular discourses and stories recur, we note the longitudinal significance of these accounts. We witness shifts in meaning making as speakers highlight various facets of stories across time or consistency as particular details are repeated or forgotten. We glimpse identity claims and positionings in the stories that are told.

When teachers become aware of repeated discourses and stories across time, they are alerted to what matters to students. What do students take up, and how do they use stories to present themselves and interpret their worlds? Stories reveal not only what students value and believe, but also provide clues to conceivable futures that students envision. Perhaps this is the most significant lesson to be gained from temporal discourses analysis—the importance of listening to students, valuing their stories, and seeking ways to support students in moving forward toward their goals. Schooling should be about creating possibilities, not a longitudinal process of cutting off options.

Temporal discourse analysis also offers possibilities for researchers. Conceivably, revisiting studies could simply report *what happened next* in the lives of participants. Temporal discourse analysis invites researchers to focus on change and interrogate how experiences contribute to lives, selves, and understandings of the world. By exploring language across time, we gain clues about long-term processes of identity, meaning making, and culture. When applied to longitudinal data, temporal discourse analysis invites researchers to avoid the dangers of short-term approaches that might describe and interpret particular literacy practices and proficiencies without attending to how these practices are situated within longer streams of events. To explore the purposes of education and what it means to be educated or to be literate, we must understand how learning and schooling unfold and

Revisiting Children and Families **77**

how experiences culminate. In short, inequity, discrimination, and school failure are not short-term processes. They occur over years and require methods that recognize their long-term nature. Revisiting studies invite the long-term processing of data, and temporal discourse analysis is one available tool.

Clearly, temporal discourse analysis is a tool that can be useful in making sense of school experiences of students. However, temporal discourse analysis, like all analytic frameworks, also presents a set of limits. In particular, temporal discourses analysis, particularly as presented in this chapter, decontextualizes language in ways that could violate the ethnographic intentions of the original research. In this chapter, I purposefully selected samples of data from David's case to illustrate five dimensions of temporal discourse analysis. I revealed little about David, the complete study, or the situations from which the data samples were collected. Instead of providing that contextual information in the current chapter, I have directed the reader to other texts (Compton-Lilly, 2003, 2007, 2012, 2014). In short, I have failed to provide a sense of the spaces in which the data was collected as well as the spaces inhabited by the participants. I have not provided a complete description of the people involved, particularly in terms of their agency and resilience. Finally, I have neglected to attend to the ways larger social and political constraints have acted on this family and other families in this study; poverty, the lack of community resources, under-resourced schools, challenges with employment and healthcare have not been examined. This is a perennial problem with discourse analysis—by focusing on discourse and texts, do we lose attention to the world? The solution is in the thoughtful and contextualized use of discourse analysis techniques alongside nuanced accounts of people's lives.

I argue that temporal discourse analysis provides an important analytical tool for exploring longitudinal meaning making and identity construction. The 're-' in revisiting involves not just re-encountering participants from past studies, it also requires the revisiting of data and exploring how words and experiences are used and made sense of at different points in time. Notably, this revisiting of language can be unsettling to researchers as our past interpretations are called into question and our own biases and positionalities are revealed not only to our readers but also to ourselves. Regardless, while analysis of people's experiences at particular points in time can reveal important insights about people's worlds, analysis of data over long periods of time is significant in that longitudinal accounts can complicate, contextualize, extend, and challenge earlier accounts.

References

Clark, B.R. (1960). The "cooling-out" function in higher education. *Journal of Sociology,* 65(6), 569–576.

Compton-Lilly, C. (2003). *Reading families: The literate lives of urban children.* New York: Teachers College Press.

Compton-Lilly, C. (2007). *Re-Reading families: The literate lives of urban children, four years later.* New York: Teachers College Press.

Compton-Lilly, C. (2012). *Reading time: The literate lives of urban secondary students and their families*. New York: Teachers College Press.

Compton-Lilly, C. (2014). Temporal discourse analysis. In P. Albers, T. Holbrook, & A. Flint (Eds.), *New methods in literacy research*. New York: Routledge.

Gee, J.P. (2007). *Social linguistics and literacies: Ideology in discourses* (3rd ed.). London: Taylor & Francis.

Gutierrez, K.D., Morales, P.Z. & Martinez, D.C. (2009). Re-mediating literacy, culture, difference, and learning for students from nondominant communities. *Review of Research in Education, 33*, 212–245.

Rethinking Schools (1986–present). Available at: www.rethinkingschools.org/index.shtml on 12/10/2013.

Strauss, A. & Corbin, J. (1990). *The basics of qualitative research: Grounded theory procedures and techniques*. Newbury Park, CA: Sage Publications.

6

WHO WERE WE BECOMING?

Revisiting Cultural Production in Room 217

Saskia Stille

Introduction

To reflect upon contemporary changes relating to the use of digital media in education, this chapter draws on ethnographic data gathered during a school–university research collaboration and follow-up interviews with one teacher and several students 3 years after the project was completed. Exploring several significant literacy events (Heath, 1983) across the timespan of the project and beyond, the chapter articulates the limits of fixing affective, embodied events as static moments in time. Rather, these events can be seen as constituting critical becomings, performances of bodies and selves *in motion*, and on their way to *becoming other*. This revisit was not a one-time activity, nor did it focus on empirical data alone; rather, the return was situated in an extended engagement with fieldwork and a continuous process of interrogating the theoretical perspectives with which these data were analyzed and understood. Ongoing dialogue between both observation-theory and researcher-participants comprises what Burawoy (2003) calls a rolling revisit, the continuous re/shaping of understandings that emerges at the intersection of embodiment, location, and habitus of the researcher and the researched (p. 669).

Beginning with an overview of the *Re/constructing Literate Identities* study conducted 5 years ago for my doctoral research, the chapter revisits three key literacy events related to the integration of home languages and digital media into teachers' instructional practice. Expanding the idea of literacy events, defined as situations in which people engage with reading or writing, to include digitally mediated forms of communication, these events comprised new forms of student participation and cultural production in the learning context. Following descriptions of these events, the chapter considers what revisiting might offer to

80 Saskia Stille

understand students' digital literacy practices in school. The chapter concludes that revisiting constitutes a reflexive approach to ethnographic literacy research, allowing an opportunity to notice and account for social and technological change, and its influence upon interpretations and theory development.

The *Re/constructing Literate Identities* Study

The school–university research collaboration took place 5 years ago in a multilingual, multicultural school in a large Canadian city. Specifically, the research explored the experiences of elementary-level students who were newcomers to Canada or children of first-generation Canadians. Many of these children faced the dual challenge of mastering a new language and acquiring the literacy skills necessary to set them on a positive trajectory for curriculum learning. The purpose of the project was to explore the educational significance of engaging students in digital literacy activities that drew upon their cultural and linguistic resources, diverse histories, and multiple modes of representation in classroom-based learning. To meet the objectives of the project, I, as part of a team of university-based researchers, worked collaboratively with teachers and students to assist them in using digital technology for reading and writing activities, and to encourage students to recognize and draw upon their home languages and cultural knowledge as resources for learning, as described below (Stille, 2011a, b, 2012; Stille & Cummins, 2013). The research component of the study documented students' perceptions and feelings about the process of getting engaged with literacy in this way, and teachers' observations about the effects of the project on students' self-efficacy and literacy accomplishments. The research design started from a basic initial plan that evolved as I entered the field and began to work with and get to know the teachers and students. Together, we determined the goals of our collaboration and created pedagogic activities based on our mutual needs and interests.

The Research Setting

Englishtown Public School[1] is one of three schools in a mostly South Asian community in a large urban center. It is an elementary school serving 2,000 students from kindergarten to fifth-grade. The school district website reports that Englishtown's student population "represents 47 countries." The website also reports that 97 percent of the students speak a language other than English at home, and that 30 percent of the students were born outside of Canada. The school is located in one of the top receiver communities in Canada for new immigrants. According to statistics from the city, the community has a mobility rate 15 percent higher than the city average. These statistics also suggest that most families in the community live on an income 48 percent below the city average, and spend over 30 percent of their income on housing. The neighborhood itself is composed of a cluster of high-rise apartment buildings that are the residences for members of the community, and there are no single-family dwellings in the school catchment area. At the time of the project, the local community center and the public library had been closed for two-and-a-half years for renovation, and there was one small playground in the neighborhood for preschool children. Beside the school is a small shopping mall, anchored by a national discount department store, a dollar store, two banks, and a bowling alley. The other shops in the mall are small independent clothing, housewares, and dry goods stores. Other shops and restaurants in the area include an Afghani kebab restaurant, several samosa shops, and South Asian groceries and bakeries, as well as a franchise coffee shop and a franchise chicken restaurant.

My fieldwork at Englishtown began in March 2009, and continued to October 2010. I worked with 3 teachers and 46 students in 5 classes, including a split fourth-/fifth-grade English as a Second Language (ESL) class, a split fourth-/fifth-grade English for Literacy Development (ELD) class, a fourth-grade and a fifth-grade Newcomer class, and a third-grade class.[2] All of the children and/or their families had immigrated to Canada, and they used a diversity of home languages, including Urdu, Pashto, Dari, Punjabi, Arabic, Tamil, and Turkish. The children ranged from 8 to 11 years of age. The students in the ESL/ELD and Newcomer classes were all in the process of acquiring English proficiency, and many were at the beginning stages of learning and using English. All of the participating teachers were experienced, having taught for 10 years or more. The ESL/ELD and Newcomer teachers had specialist qualifications for second language teaching, and they also supported the school's language assessment and newcomer orientation programs. The third-grade teacher described having a strong social justice focus to his teaching practice, and he had previous experience as an Outdoor Education teacher.

Our work took place over three school terms, with every new term involving a different teaching context, different students, and different pedagogic activities. Each collaboration built upon what we learned in the last, entailing a cumulative progression and refinement of our processes and understandings. As a strategy to support students' literacy engagement, the teachers and I integrated digital tools and resources into curriculum learning activities. Specifically, we used Google Earth, digital storytelling software, PowerPoint, and iMovie, and students created a variety of digital and print media texts, including stories, poetry, letters, presentations, and short documentary films. As a further strategy, we drew on students' home language(s) and lived experience as resources for our literacy work. For example, students' home languages provided a scaffold for lexical development, and supported pre-writing activities and the writing process. Using their home languages, many students were able to write stories that were quantitatively longer than they would have been in English and their stories were qualitatively much richer and more representative of their ideas than text that they could have written in English at this stage in their learning. Moreover, when we began to ask for and expect students to demonstrate their conceptual and curriculum knowledge using the full range of their linguistic repertoires, and across new modes and domains, students rose to this expectation. The teachers observed that students invested themselves into their literacy work, which supported them in accomplishing literacy activities at a high level of accomplishment.

We found that incorporating students' home languages and digital technology tools into reading and writing activities intersected powerfully to influence the language practices of the classroom. Significantly, these practices opened curriculum and pedagogy to connect with students' lives. The many digital texts that students made in the context of the project became representational resources through which the students created and communicated narratives of themselves and their experience. These artefacts constituted what we called digital 'identity texts,' which Cummins and Early (2011) describe as products of students' creative work that reflect their identities in a positive light. Furthermore, the processes involved in creating these texts afforded the opportunity for improvisation: agentive moves through which the students could shift dominant narratives and re/figure representations of the social world to illuminate their interests, concerns, or social conditions, and communicate these experiences to others. As one example, the students wrote digital dual-language books about families and communities. Asad, a nine-year-old boy in fourth-grade, wrote a story called 'My Journey to Canada.' Asad wrote his story in English and in Urdu, and when it came time to present his story, he asked if he could present the story in English and in Pashto. Asad wanted to feature all the languages that he felt confident using, and though he could not write in Pashto, he wanted to incorporate his Pashto oral language abilities into his presentation. A sample page from Asad's story can be seen in Figure 6.1.

Making space for and connecting with students' language practices demonstrated to students that school was a context where their language knowledge was a welcome and needed contribution to learning and to the school community. Students were seen as having valuable knowledge to share, and their linguistic competences were constructed as legitimate language and literacy practices in the school.

Returning to 'The Field'

Deciding to revisit my fieldwork in the *Re/constructing Literate Identities* study, I immediately wondered about the boundaries that I drew in my interpretation of where 'the field' was: when it started and ended, where we began and finished. These boundaries marked the time and place of the study, yet begin to blur when applied to the understandings and relationships that developed through the collaborative, ethnographic work. Initially, the research site consisted of the classrooms where I worked with the students and their teachers; however, it quickly became evident to me that understanding students' language and literacy

FIGURE 6.1 Sample Page from Student's Digital Dual-language Storybook

practices in school would require situating these practices within the broader community context. In addition to my work in the school, I started to get to know students' families and become involved in the community. Spending an extended period of time in the field is part of what gives ethnographic research its validity (Denzin & Lincoln, 2005; Heath & Street, 2008), which often entails developing deep and lasting relationships with participants. My experience was no different in that my relationships with the teachers and some students' families have continued to this day, several years after the study was completed. We maintain communication and I often visit the school community, participating in events or helping with other projects. I can no longer easily distinguish what I knew then from what I know now about the school, the teachers' instructional practices, and the students' trajectories—my understandings have become entangled.

The intersubjective and negotiated nature of this knowledge, and of knowledge production in ethnographic work, therefore presents a challenge for unravelling current and former insights and interpretations. Burawoy (2003) writes that this dilemma is an issue for ethnographic revisits, to separate "the external world from the researcher's own shifting involvement with that same world, all the while recognizing that the two are not independent" (p. 646). The nature of collaborative, ethnographic research is such that the researcher's exit from the field occurs slowly, over an extended amount of time. Throughout this period of winding down, in my experience, the researcher continues, however inadvertently, to 'gather' data and make interpretations. My revisit therefore entailed an on-going process and the continuous development of knowledge about the research site over the past 5 years: deepening, refining, and changing meanings over time. As a means of interrupting settled understandings, this "rolling revisit" (Burawoy, 2003) has been a generative strategy for reflexivity in the research process, an opportunity to compare old and new theories and experiences for a more contingent, situated, and temporal perspective on students and school-based literacy practices in a social context that is increasingly digitally mediated.

Digital Literacy as Cultural Production

Employing the term 'cultural production' to reflect on students' digital literacy events, I aim to foreground changing literacy practices, particularly the ways in which current uses of digital media are rooted in notions of community involvement and integration into cultural processes, involving abilities that are developed in and through social contexts and collaboration (Alvermann, 2008; Erstad et al., 2007; Hull & Katz, 2006; Jenkins et al., 2006; Jewitt, 2008; Sefton-Green, 2006; Vasudevan, 2010). Cultural products are representational resources through which individuals create a narrative of experience, developed with and in social space. Articulating the implications of this sociality, Hall (1981; Hall & du Gay, 1996) draws attention to cultural production as a contradictory space, a site with no guarantees, wherein meanings are socially produced. Attaching interpretations of literacy to the idea of cultural production suggests to me that texts (broadly defined) should not appear "as if they contained within themselves, from the moment of their origin, some fixed and unchanging meaning or value" (Hall, 1981, p. 237). Though meaning is generated when production 'stops,' this stop is neither fixed nor final, but arbitrary and contingent: cultural production is a constitutive process (Hall & du Gay, 1996).

The prevalence of technology in the social and educational context is changing literacy practices. These practices entail new skills for reading, finding information, authenticating information, manipulating, linking, and recontextualizing information in a social, multimodal environment. Teaching students these '21st century literacy skills' is not just a technical process; it is connected to conceptualizations of the learner and the purposes of learning. Digital literacy can serve as an 'amplifier' of student voice, particularly because technology tools can facilitate production of powerful, multimodal identity texts and creative work that can be shared with audiences locally and across new social networks and domains. These resources can assist students in becoming co-producers of knowledge in the classroom as they create content, position themselves, and contribute to reshaping educational discourses (Morrell et al., 2013; Toohey et al., 2012). Reflecting upon these processes over the course of the study, my attention turned to the students' digital texts and their production, and changes in the texts' meaning and value over time. As cultural products, these texts do not represent the world; rather, they articulate conditions through which we live in and through, representations that do not stand outside of context, relation, history, and change.

To reflect upon these considerations, I share three illustrative segments from digital video recordings of classroom literacy activities recorded during the project. I chose these particular data because, to me, they are literacy events that are illustrative of the changes that I observed over the course of the study and beyond. Moreover, these data constitute critical "becomings" (Leander & Rowe, 2006) that materialize the dynamic relations among literacy practice, social space, and subjectivity in a field that is always in motion. This perspective is my point of departure for thinking about the changes that occurred during and since the study, and for reflecting upon my developing understanding of the relationship between digital literacy practices and students' identities in the educational context.

'Our Community is Special'

Introducing digital technology tools into school-based reading and writing activities, the teachers and I focused on the products of students' work initially. Our aim was to assist students to create digital texts, and to showcase their creations to parents and other teachers and students at the school. In the third-grade class, the social studies curriculum topic of urban and rural communities provided a rich content-area focus for our work. We used an inquiry-based approach to the topic, and began by gathering and reading books from the school library about communities, community resources, and land use. To connect with the students' experiences, we used Google Earth to view images of communities around the world, especially in countries where the students had immigrated from. Students also conducted research about the local community. Using a digital video camera, students interviewed one another and their parents. They wrote interview questions such as 'Where were you born?' and 'What do you like about our community?' and recorded and analyzed responses.

The students summarized the attributes of the school community and shared their findings with the whole class. They identified access to nature as an important issue in their community. As one student described, 'our community is special'—in particular, the land use in the community was primarily devoted to high-rise residential housing. Students and their families had few places to explore the natural environment or engage in outdoor recreation. One of the students' notable findings was that many families had a great deal of experience in farming and agriculture in their home countries. Students described growing dates and pomegranates; they told of taking care of chickens, and sifting rice by hand with their mothers. One student described the banana trees that grew on her family farm in Sri Lanka, explaining: 'three children can fit under a banana leaf. When it rains, we use it as an umbrella.' Another student shared his favorite memory of gardening, when his uncle would lift him high up on to his shoulders

86 Saskia Stille

to pick apples. The students' families had few opportunities to draw upon their knowledge and experience in farming and agriculture in their new Canadian home. For instance, one mother explained: 'Surrounding our house we had tea and pepper, and around our house we planted vegetables and flowers. . . . Here we can't grow anything.'

To address the disjuncture between students' experiences in these different contexts, we decided to create a school garden, and to create a digital film to document and share the experience of doing this work. The setting for the garden was one of several courtyards at the school. Caretakers were not permitted to take care of these spaces, and the school courtyards were unused, overgrown with weeds and littered with garbage. We set a goal of transforming one of these courtyards into a garden in order to create a space within the school that students and teachers could use and where they could relate to the natural environment. The students documented the creation of the garden using digital film and photography. We used iMovie software to produce the digital film from this footage. The content of the film is composed of three major components: the students doing research about their school community, the steps we undertook in the creation of the garden, and direct and indirect interviews with the students, teacher, and parents.

The students and teacher were involved in every stage of creating the film. The students decided what events to film, they held the camera, and conducted interviews with one another. They also chose which footage of themselves to include in the film, selecting clips and adding voiceover narration of the scenes if they wished. Finally, the teacher and I assembled these clips into the final product, constructing a narrative to run through the film and connect the clips into a whole. We used techniques such as the insertion of subtitles to assist the audience in understanding transitions to new topics or cuts, and the teacher added a montage of still images taken over the course of the project at the end of the film, which plays to music while the credits role. Figure 6.2 is a screen shot from the iMovie software used to create the film, which was called *Remaking the Ground on Which They Stand: Room 217 Makes a School Garden (12 min)*.

A core theme running through the film was the children's perception that, through their work, they were making a difference in the world. This theme can be illustrated by the following quote from one student: 'We are making a garden because we want to make the world a better place.' Now teens in middle school, the students I interviewed for the purposes of this chapter described what seemed to be issues common to most young people at their age—concerns about school grades, friendships, parents, and what they want to be when they grow up. When I watch the film now, I see the children both as they once were, and as they are now. I hear the students' recorded words as full of possibility, and simultaneously as heavy with the burden of promises yet to be fulfilled. The film itself provides a generative opportunity to compare the students, in current space and time, with their representations from an earlier point in time. Rather than look for what has stayed the same, I was interested in what was different, both for them and

FIGURE 6.2 Screen Shot from iMovie Software Used to Create the Film *Remaking the Ground on Which They Stand: Room 217 Makes a School Garden (12 min)*

for me. I now bring to my interpretation of the film a changed set of theoretical perspectives. In particular, with the distance of time, it is more apparent that viewing the film somehow fails to bring to life the experience of the recorded events as embodied, affective, situated, and temporal acts, from which the students had moved beyond.

The digital film, as a cultural product, exists in a state of continuous negotiation and transaction, involving a "double movement of containment and resistance" (Hall, 1981, p. 228). Leander and Rowe (2006) write that representing relations between multimodal texts and bodies is difficult, even as we build from theorists who have developed rich means of understanding social interaction. Literacy performances are challenging to represent and seem insufficient when frozen as moments in time and space, seemingly more fixed and structured than the lived experience of these performances would suggest. Whereas interpretations of students' performances captured on digital recordings may resonate, the digital recordings "only partially and inadequately capture the vibrant life and dynamism" (p. 431). These considerations prompted me to reanalyze the digital video data in the study, and I decided to focus my attention not on the products of students' digital literacy activities, but on the processes of their production.

'That's What the Worms Eat!'

Throughout the project, I had seen evidence of students' changing forms of participation in the classroom and in curriculum learning activities. However, my previous focus on the products of student work did not adequately represent these changes. I sought a means to assemble evidence, beyond my own observations, of these changes. Reviewing many of the hours of raw digital video footage recorded by the students, the teacher, and/or me during our inquiry process, I focused on the roles, interactions, and processes involved in literacy and curriculum learning activities. The figures below are still images from the video data that illustrate the changing forms of student participation that emerged over the course of the project. Shifting from passive to active users of digital technology tools in the classroom, the students changed from objects to subjects of educational discourse.

Figure 6.3 is a still image from a video recorded at the beginning of the project. The video recorded the teacher showing students how to use Google images on a classroom computer. In this video, which is representative of other events during the project, it is apparent that I am holding the camera and the teacher is using the computer—the expert adults dominating the use of technology in the classroom. The students cooperate with this arrangement, trying to avoid looking at the camera. As seen in Figure 6.3, at times they steal a glance at the camera, admitting its presence and affirming the camera as recorder and me as producer of the story of what is taking place. By contrast, as evidenced in a representative video segment recorded several months later, the students took over as users of the digital camera and other technology tools. They demonstrated developing capacity to produce media content and become active participants in constructing knowledge in the classroom. Such use of digital media comprises a core literacy

FIGURE 6.3 Still Image from Raw Video Data, Showing Technology Use in the Classroom at the Beginning of the Project

FIGURE 6.4 Still Image from Raw Video Data, Showing Students 'Taking Over' as Users of the Technology in the Classroom

practice and civic resource to be an active participant in contemporary society (Morrell et al., 2013). A still image from this video is included as Figure 6.4.

In this video, a student is holding the camera, and first, just one student is sharing his knowledge of garden composting. Soon five other students join in, and together they explain the role of worms in the composting process, each one adding to the discussion and reciting in chorus together at the end: 'That's what the worms eat!' When the students became active participants in the use, direction, and documentation of events, they performed entirely differently from how they did at the beginning of the project. While the students took over as the documenters and recorders of their learning, the teacher remained silent, looking on from the background.

In revisiting the raw video data, I began to see the digital camera as a representational resource through which the students had articulated a narrative of experience. Across the data, students moved from being objects/*produced by* to being subjects/*producers of* representation. Moreover, these data inspired me to seek alternatives to binary constructions of students as either 'engaged' with digital literacy or not. I began to think of digital literacy engagement as complex and dynamic, present in emergent to developed degrees, and related to situated practice and social context. Thinking of digital literacy engagement as not only a factor or outcome of learning, but as an activity and a social practice, I considered conditions that contributed to creating a context of possibility for digital literacy engagement. In particular, I considered the idea of cultural production as a means to frame students' literacy work, and to shift my thinking from what digital literacy *is* to what digital literacy *does* in the classroom context. Unlike autonomous models of literacy skills development and the accompanying focus on standards-based literacy assessment, engaging students in digital media production might prepare them for increasingly public roles as digital media makers and community participants (Buckingham, 2003; Ito et al., 2013; Jenkins et al., 2006; Sefton-Green, 2006).

'I Always Used to Think that it's Hopeless, Because I'm Just a Child'

Revisiting the raw video data brought my attention to the many events and activities we had filmed that I initially thought were tangential to the research data. For example, the students began initiating, creating, and sharing creative works, including rap songs, dramatic performances, poetry, and narrative writing. Every time someone in the class made one of these creations, the students or the teacher immediately requested that we turn on the camera and 'get this on film.' These creations were filled with the students' sensibilities and motivations, their understandings of what constituted important to document or record. From these activities, I learned that integrating the use of digital technologies in the classroom is not just a technical activity. Rather, it is a process that actively reconstructs dominant epistemologies of literacy teaching and learning away from education as cultural reproduction to education as cultural production. Figure 6.5 is a still image from a video recording of one such moment, when a student, Saamini, stands in front of the class to share a poem that she was inspired to write, called 'The Sun.' Below is the transcript of this recording, which illustrates how the students and teacher appropriated the language and practices of a filmmaker.

FIGURE 6.5 Still Image from a Video Recording of Saamini Presenting her Poem to the Class, and a Classmate Clapping her Arms Together as a Filmmaker's Slate

MOHAMMED: Slate ready? Slate?
SEVERAL CHILDREN: OK. Ready!
SASKIA: Who wants to say quiet on the set?
AHMED: Quiet on the set. Camera rolling?
MOHAMMED: Rolling.
TEACHER: And take 2.
SASKIA: Ready? Wait.
CHILD: Take 1. [child claps arms together as a slate]
SAAMINI: I wrote a poem about the sun comes. The sun . . . [erupts in laughter]
SEVERAL CHILDREN: Cut!
TEACHER: Camera keep rolling. Take 2, take 3! [child makes slate action again]
SEVERAL CHILDREN: Action, action!
SAAMINI: I wrote a poem about the sun comes. The clouds open. There is something yellow coming out. Everybody . . . [erupts in laughter]
SEVERAL CHILDREN: Cut, cut!
TEACHER: Take 3.

Another segment from the raw video data documents a musical performance by a group of students. The students had written a rap song about a relaxation and anger management strategy that they had recently learned, called 'Take a BOP [breath of peace].' In the midst of telling me about this song, the teacher suggested that the students perform and record the song with the digital video camera. The students eagerly suggested that they make up a dance to accompany their performance. We recorded the performance, and this recording was later remixed into a digital film that the students created. Figure 6.6 is a still image from the digital video recording of the students performing their rap song.

The students overlaid the video of the rap song with a voiceover by one of the students, in which she explains:

> I always used to think that it's hopeless, because I'm just a child, and whenever a child has an idea adults don't really listen to it. They just ignore that person, that child, and that child can really help make a difference. So I thought to myself, I'm going to stand up for myself and make a difference.

Revisiting these two video excerpts and others within the raw video data with a theoretical perspective that focused on the processes rather than on the products of students' work, I saw that the students had taken over as users of the digital camera and other technology tools in the classroom. They had become active participants in the use, direction, and documentation of events, using the gaze of the camera to their benefit, and taking advantage of the opportunity to showcase their knowledge, to be the center of attention, and to play with the affordances

FIGURE 6.6 Still Image from a Digital Video Recording of Students Performing a Rap Song

of the camera in their learning process. With intentionality, they delivered what and how they wished to be read.

Remembering Nomadically

My approach to revisiting comprised several forms: returning to the research site many times over a period of 5 years, reinterviewing several of the participants involved in the initial study, and reanalyzing video data. Conceiving, as Burawoy (2003) suggests, ethnography *as* revisit, these multiple returns to the field generated reflexivity. The ability of ethnography to understand and portray knowledge of the social world is contingent—observations of the social world are not objective, but situated in between the observer and the observed. Moreover, research representations are never transparent, and the research story will never be completely "right" (Kennedy, 2011, p. 384). This failure of representation highlights the role of the researcher as meaning maker. Meanings are not inherent, but produced through the forces, affects, and temporality of experience circulating with and in embodied subjectivities and social space (for example, Ahmed, 2004; Britzman, 2003; Gallagher, 2008). These social and affective dimensions of experience suggest reasons to doubt the capacity for ethnographic research to 'draw close' to its objects (Lather, 2007). Relationships, histories and trajectories of participation between and among researchers and participants influence both the practice and findings of research. Meeting the limits of this knowing entails the need for reflexive understanding of the researcher's own participation in the ongoing circulation of power and knowledge. This reflexivity is important because ethnographers do more than observe circumstances, contexts, and relationships; they play a part in them (Vidich & Lyman, 2003).

When the same researcher returns to a familiar field site, memory plays a significant, yet under theorized role (Burawoy, 2003, p. 671). I mentioned above my challenge in disentangling my current and former understandings, which I can find a way to theorize by drawing on what Braidotti (2011) calls "nomadic theory." Nomadic theory moves away from the dominant model of subjectivity for ontology "that privileges change and motion over stability" (p. 29). Rather than attempt to understand students and their literacy practices either as they were then or as they are now, I can look back on the past and what was *to come*. Offering the idea of *becoming* rather than being, this notion of subjectivity concerns desire for transformation, highlighting the moments of change that empower alternatives to the way things are (or were). Braidotti writes, "the job of remembering is the capacity to engender the kinds of conditions and relations that can empower creative alternatives . . . it is a purely pragmatic matter, not a normative measure or an ideological injunction" (p. 33). A nomadic remembering comprises an ontological theory of desire, an attraction to change and a *becoming other* that works on a time sequence that is "neither linear nor sequential because processes of becoming are not predicated upon a stable, centralized Self. . . the processes rather rest on a non-unitary, multi-layered, dynamic subject attached to multiple communities"(p. 34). Inspired by the philosophical creativity of Braidotti's nomadic theory, my understanding of revisiting comprises continuity between past, present, and future. Grosz (2005) describes a concept of time that is useful to me in this regard. This conceptualization is open to the movement of time in multiple directions: "one virtual, one actual, one open to anticipation and unknowable future, the other onto reminiscence and the past, functioning simultaneously as present and as the past of that present" (p. 4). From this perspective, students and their digital literacy practices, then and now, are always in motion.

Remembering nomadically acknowledges complexity and instability as central concepts, particularly in the constitution of social subjects. Braidotti (2005) writes that this understanding emphasizes "the productive aspects of the dislocation and recasting of identities" (p. 178). Rather than focus on coherent subjects and single stories of past research, remembering nomadically emphasizes the generative power of multiple states and stories of transition. Theorized from this perspective, revisiting might offer an opportunity to look again at representations of people and communities in research. Taking not only a second but also a long glance, we might notice identities or perspectives that had been flattened in the construction of a coherent research narrative. A nomadic perspective acknowledges multiple, differentiated subject positions and differentiated becomings. Going beyond the need for unity and sameness, people and communities can be seen instead as moving with the discourses and practices of others in a related but non-dialectical manner, bound "by acknowledgement of the shared need to negotiate processes of sustainable transformations with multiple others" (p. 53).

94 Saskia Stille

Taken together, these ideas assist me to acknowledge the challenge of fixing students' identities, particularly when working to understand shifts and changes in the digital literacy practices in the school community that I revisited. The mobility of literacy practices within and across the students' social context is underscored by the impossibility of revisiting the classrooms that contained my initial work. The classrooms were no longer intact locations in space or time (Leander et al., 2010). Not only had the students moved on to middle school, but the teachers were assigned to different grades or teaching assignments, and the school itself was renovated to meet the needs of the growing community and alleviate pressures of overcrowding. Despite my previous work documenting literacy practices within this locale, the practices were always, already, on the move. The classroom, created by and in social space, had unfolded through activity and was positioned in a "nexus of relations" (p. 336) to other locales. So *where* was I to revisit? Rather than focus on the "geographies that increasingly haunt our past and current imagination" (p. 335), I revisited instead three affectively charged intersections among bodies and selves in motion. Revisiting assisted me to understand moving configurations, highlighting multiple, heterogeneous stories of the research that made new connections and understandings possible. It was only through the passage of time and the increasing visibility of the forces of social and technological change, including the viability of digital resources for opening new networks and forms of participation that I could look again at the data and see what else might have been happening as students created their digital texts. The sociality of students' digital literacy practices was ever more apparent to me, and I could identify how they had shifted from being produced by to being producers of digital culture.

Conclusion

To inform commitments and considerations in literacy research, revisiting offers the opportunity to reflect on how understanding the literacy practices of people and communities involves documenting and interpreting literacy events as not only localized practices, but also how these practices meet up with the broader social context, a context that includes the passage of time. Understandings and representations of literacy events and practices, while constituted at a particular moment, nonetheless might shift along with the passage of time and the accompanying change of circumstances, conditions, or theories. In analyzing the research initially, my representations of the students, teachers, and school-based literacy events focused on the products of students' digital literacy work. However, I later reflected that these representations should not be assumed to contain some fixed or unchanging meaning or value; rather these representations were contingent, part of an ongoing production of meaning. Students from non-dominant or minoritized language backgrounds have often been constituted or constructed through dominant regimes of representation that are normalized by and within schools. Therefore, I was moved to consider my ethical responsibility to represent the students' identifications and practices as potential, as unfinished, and in process. I interrogated my researcher constructions to search for a more indeterminate and contingent understanding of the relations among social space, practice, and subjectivity.

Acknowledging my "constructed relation" (Burawoy, 2003) to the data from my doctoral research, I revisited the study with a different theoretical perspective. This perspective assisted me to look beyond the products of students' digital work to see the processes of their production. Looking again and looking differently at the data enabled me to articulate material and symbolic changes in the students' use of technology in school, including new forms of student participation in the learning process. However, it was not only my perspectives that had changed; the research site and participants had moved on and grown. Holding in productive tension both change in understanding and material change, my revisit illuminated the becoming of the students' subjectivities in the process of our work and beyond. Revisiting as reflexive ethnography has therefore assisted me to consider not just the field of my research as it exists in the current moment, but also where it sits in relation to the past and future, recognizing the contingency of my understandings of students' literacy practices in relation to how things are, how they were, and how they might be.

Notes

1. Englishtown Public School is a pseudonym. All names have been changed to protect confidentiality.
2. In this school district, English for Literacy Development (ELD) classes are for emergent bilingual students with limited prior schooling, and Newcomer classes are for newly arrived emergent bilingual students who have been in the country for six months or less.

References

Ahmed, S. (2004). *The cultural politics of emotion.* Edinburgh: Edinburgh University Press.

Alvermann, D. (2008). Why bother theorizing adolescents' online literacies for classroom practice and research?, *Journal of Adolescent & Adult Literacy, 52*(1), 8–19.

Braidotti, R. (2011). *Nomadic theory: The portable Rosi Braidotti.* New York: Columbia University Press.

Britzman, D.P. (2003). *Practice makes practice: A critical study of learning to teach.* Albany, NY: SUNY Press.

Buckingham, D. (2003). Media education and the end of the critical consumer. *Harvard Educational Review, 73*(3), 309–327.

Burawoy, M. (2003). Revisits: An outline of a theory of reflexive ethnography. *American Sociological Review, 68,* 645–679.

Cummins, J. & Early, M. (Eds.). (2011). *Identity texts: The collaborative creation of power in multilingual schools.* Stoke-on-Trent: Trentham Books.

Denzin, N.K. & Lincoln, Y.S. (Eds.). (2005). *The Sage handbook of qualitative research.* Thousand Oaks, CA: Sage Publications.

Erstad, O., Gilje, O. & de Lange, T. (2007). Re-mixing multimodal resources: Multiliteracies and digital production in Norwegian media education. *Learning, Media and Technology, 32*(2), 183–198.

Gallagher, K. (2008). *The methodological dilemma: Creative, critical and collaborative approaches to qualitative research.* New York: Routledge.

Grosz, E. (2005). *Time travels: Feminism, nature, power.* Durham, NC: Duke University Press.

Hall, S. (1981). Encoding/decoding. In S. Hall, D. Hobson, A. Lowe & P. Willis (Eds.), *Culture, media, language* (pp. 128–139). London: Routledge.

Hall, S. & du Gay, P. (Eds.). (1996). *Questions of cultural identity.* Thousand Oaks, CA: Sage Publications.

Heath, S.B. (1983). *Ways with words: Language, life and work in communities and classrooms.* Cambridge: Cambridge University Press.

Heath, S.B. & Street, B.V. (2008). *On ethnography: Approaches to language and literacy research.* New York: Teachers College Press.

Hull, G.A. & Katz, M. (2006). Crafting an agentive self: Case studies of digital storytelling. *Research in the Teaching of English, 41*(1), 43–81.

Ito, M., Guriérrez, K., Livingstone, S., Penuel, B., Rhodes, J., Salen, K., Schor, J., Sefton-Green, J. & Watkins, S. Craig (2013). *Connected learning: An agenda for research and design.* Digital Media and Learning Research Hub.

Jenkins, H., Clinton, K., Purushotma, R., Robison, A.J. & Weigel, M. (2006). *Confronting the challenges of participatory culture: Media Education for the 21st Century.* Chicago: MacArthur Foundation.

Jewitt, C. (2008). *Technology, literacy and learning: A multimodal approach.* New York: Routledge.

Kennedy, R.M. (2011). Toward a cosmopolitan curriculum of forgiveness. *Curriculum Inquiry, 43*(1), 373–393.

Lather, P.A. (2007). *Getting lost.* New York: SUNY Press.

Leander, K. & Rowe, D.W. (2006). Mapping literacy spaces in motion: A rhizomatic analysis of a classroom literacy performance. *Reading Research Quarterly, 41*(4), 428–460.

Leander, K., Phillips, N.C. & Taylor, K.C. (2010). The changing social spaces of learning: Mapping new mobilities. *Review of Research in Education, 34,* 329–394.

Morrell, E., Duenas, R., Garcia, V. & Lopez, J. (2013). *Critical media pedagogy: Teaching for achievement in city schools.* New York: Teachers College Press.

Sefton-Green, J. (2006). Youth, technology, and media cultures. *Review of Research in Education, 30,* 279–306.

Stille, S. (2011a). Ethical readings of student texts: Attending to the process and production of identity in classroom-based literacy research. *Language & Literacy, 13*(2), 66–79.

Stille, S. (2011b). Framing representations: Documentary filmmaking as research inquiry. *Journal of Curriculum and Pedagogy, 8*(2), 101–108.

Stille, S. (2012). Re/making the ground on which they stand: Making a school garden with culturally and linguistically diverse students. *Bilingual Basics: TESOL Newsletter, 13*(1).

Stille, S. & Cummins, J. (2013). Foundation for learning: Engaging plurilingual students' linguistic repertoires in the elementary classroom. *TESOL Quarterly, 47*(3), 630–638.

Toohey, K., Dagenais, D. & Schulze, E. (2012). Second language learners making video in three contexts. *Language and Literacy, 14*(2), 75–96.

Vasudevan, L. (2010). Literacies in a participatory, multimodal world: The arts and aesthetics of web 2.0. *Language Arts, 88*(1), 43–50.

Vidich, A.J. & Lyman, S.M. (2003). Qualitative methods: Their history in sociology and anthropology. In N. Denzin & Y. Lincoln (Eds.), *The landscape of qualitative research: Theories and issues* (2nd ed., pp. 55–130). Thousand Oaks, CA: Sage.

7

THE EVERYDAY AND FARAWAY

Revisiting *Local Literacies*

Mary Hamilton

The *Local Literacies* Project

The project I have revisited was carried out in the early 1990s and reported in a book called *Local Literacies* (Barton & Hamilton, 1998). The project was a 3 year ethnographic study of individuals living in one neighborhood of the town in the North West of England in which I lived, and still live. The study was a situated account of the uses and meanings of reading and writing in this particular community. It linked data and theory, and developed new (for the time) theoretical concepts that would enable us to extrapolate our findings beyond the specific context to the wider world of literacy practices. It was self-consciously interdisciplinary, with reference points in Heath (1983) (education and the ethnography of communication); Street (1984) (anthropology); Scribner and Cole (1981) (cross-cultural psychology) and Graff (1987) (social history).

The book offered a framework in the form of six propositions elaborating the idea that literacies are part of social practices, which are observable in literacy events and are patterned by social institutions and power relationships. This approach lifted the research gaze beyond texts themselves to what people do with literacy, with whom, where and how. It viewed literacies as historically situated and purposefully embedded in broader social goals and cultural practices as well as in the wider routines, choices and preferences associated with communication practices. Literacy practices change and new ones are frequently acquired through processes of informal learning. It asserted the importance of change through the processes of informal learning and sense making. It showed that varying characteristics of literacy practices in different domains of social life could be mapped according to different aspects or elements, which help distinguish between what we called 'vernacular' and 'institutional' literacies.

The aim of writing *Local Literacies* was to produce an account that would be of value to others in at least three ways: they could draw upon the data, the theory underlying the study and the methodology employed. The data were first presented in the form of individual profiles of four very different people. These profiles were followed by a series of thematic chapters drawing on a wider range of research data. We made the qualitative methodology explicit as a set of steps for collecting, analysing and writing up the data. Such explicitness was relatively rare at the time but we wanted to provide a practical methodology, which could be drawn upon and developed by other researchers, and at the same time could be used by students doing projects.

Local Literacies developed the idea of 'collaborative ethnography,' which involved sharing the interpretation of the findings with participants and even inviting them to write their own profiles for the book. In other respects, however, we worked within a traditional paradigm of ethnography in that we chose a bounded local context for carrying out the fieldwork. We were certainly interested in collective literacy events and how these linked with issues beyond the immediate locality (such as housing and taxation). We also documented the visual environment and community resources for reading and writing, but our analysis of these was embryonic and the strongest focus remained on the lives and perceptions of individuals.

Why Revisit *Local Literacies*?

Local Literacies has been reissued as a Routledge Classic (Barton & Hamilton, 2012), and for this new edition of the book David Barton and I researched and wrote a new contextual chapter, reflecting on the original project in the light of changes that have taken place in this particular location and in the field of literacy studies since we carried it out. We noted both continuities and changes in the built environment of Lancaster, and the institutions and resources available to support literacies. These reflect population changes, a difficult economic climate combined with big increases in the price of real estate. However, we went on to say that the most striking change has been in *communication practices* themselves, which are signalled but not plainly visible in the physical environment. This change is found

> in the fast broadband coverage, complete mobile phone coverage and the amount of personal technology which people have access to. In the original study we came across 2 computers in the neighbourhood, one in the local community centre and the other in the house of a man who saw himself as a writer. Both were used by local people wanting to make simple adverts and print them off. There was no world wide web and no Google. Computers and computing were largely restricted to workplaces, as older adults recall (Hamilton, 2012). Laptops were heavy and expensive. Mobile

100 Mary Hamilton

phones were just beginning to become fashionable and text messaging was just taking off in the late 1990s.

Now, most people in Lancaster and across the UK have the internet at home and most people have a mobile phone with them throughout the day (Ofcom, 2011). Furthermore, all the main institutions affecting the city have an internet presence.

People's vernacular practices around literacy have changed profoundly in a relatively short space of time due to this new technological environment. We also speculated about whether continuous access to virtual worlds and the connected sites of the Internet might be changing people's sense of Lancaster as a bounded locality and themselves as citizens within it.

Our reflection on our original study also confirmed that not only have aspects of the research site changed, but that as researchers we have also changed, and the theory and methodologies of literacy studies have substantially moved on since the original study. The problematics of the field are now different. The meanings of literacy itself have changed with the rapid proliferation of digital media, highlighting the need for a stronger focus on the embedded nature of print literacy alongside other media, on how literacy is distributed across time and place, and a more careful focus on the complexity of the social and power relationships of literacy use and learning. Such changes prompted the unsettling thought that were we to explore local literacies today, our starting points and the design of the study might look very different.

The invitation to take part in the *Revisit Project* was therefore timely, and prompted me to extend the reflections and the contextual information we had assembled for the book by following up on one of the participants from the original project.

Aims and Research Questions

The overall aim posed by the revisiting project team was: How can a longitudinal perspective help with the understanding of literacy? This aim was anchored to references to Shirley Heath's new book (2012), in which she revisits *Ways with Words*, an article by the sociologist Michael Burawoy (2003) on revisits and reflexive ethnography, and Jay Lemke's (2000) discussion of time scales. I noted Heath's finding that "families multiplied and spintered, redistributed and redefined themselves over 30 years" and I was particularly taken by Burawoy's question in relation to his own ethnographic work in a factory that no longer existed in that place: "How might I revisit [my research site] today . . . if I cannot find it where I left it?" (p. 674).

Specific questions we were asked to pursue with participants were:

* How do you feel about having taken part in the original local literacies research project?

- Have your literacy practices changed since we interviewed you in 1992?
- How has the change toward computer-based reading and writing affected you?
- Do you see literacy differently now as a result of your life experiences?

The reflections and analysis of contemporary concerns in Lancaster offered in the updated version of *Local Literacies* (Barton & Hamilton, 2012) prompted some additional questions, which guided my choice of who to follow up.

(a) How does literacy (print and online) relate to *civic participation*—specifically engagement with public agendas, institutions and services? How do people engage in voluntary ways as citizens? What attempts are being made by local government and other agencies to engage people as citizens and how are these efforts communicated online and offline?
(b) How is people's *sense of place* mediated by representations of their locality. Specifically, how is Lancaster represented on- and off-line? How are virtual representations of the Lancaster area changing how people construe their locality?
(c) What *methodologies* are now most appropriate to the study of reading, writing and communication, more broadly in a new era of digital media and connected localities? How can we integrate the study of flows of texts and practices in a multimodal environment?

Why Shirley? Themes for the Interview

The core people we interviewed in 1992 were already mature adults at that time and they are now 20 years older. For a while, we kept in touch in a sporadic way with some of the people who took part in the study, but unlike some of the other studies reported in this book, *Local Literacies* had no developmental aim and was not linked to a particular institution, and over time we fell out of contact with them. For my revisit, I selected Shirley Bowker,[1] one of the four people we profiled in the book and one of the younger participants at the time (35 years old). We had identified her as a key member of the community, a great networker who was probably on her way to becoming active in formal local politics. I thought that because she had a semi-public local profile she might be easier to track down than other participants. As it turned out, this assumption proved incorrect and it was only through personal contacts that I managed to find her again.

I was interested in Shirley's community and local political involvements. To a greater extent than some of the other original participants she offered a window beyond personal and family literacy practices out to the civic and wider community domain and the ways in which literacy is involved at the interface of private lives with public services and agencies. How had her involvements changed? Did she become a local politician? And if so, how did she feel about that and what had that meant for her literacy practices?

In preparing for the interview I went back to the original notes and themes we had put together and decided to use these as a starting point for the interviews as they offered immediate points for comparison. For Shirley, the themes were:

1. Ruling passions fighting injustice/community action.
2. Change.
3. Dyslexia and home–school relationship.
4. Community figure and networks.
5. The family—closeness and roles.

To remind Shirley about the project and how she had presented her younger self to us, I listed these themes in my invitation letter to her, as well as sending her extracts from the pen-sketch she had written about herself (see Box 7.1). I took a copy of the book to give her and in the interview I pointed out the illustration of a page from the residents' newsletter she had written and about which David and I later wrote an article (Hamilton & Barton, 1999).

Summaries and quotes from the interview with Shirley are included throughout the rest of this chapter.

Findings: What's Changed for Shirley?

Like our revisit to the *Local Literacies* site more generally, my revisit with Shirley revealed both change and continuity.

In some respects, Shirley's life has changed radically. Soon after we interviewed her in the original project, she moved to a different neighbourhood where property is cheaper, in order to be able to buy her own home outright. She now lives in the house she bought in Morecambe, a town that adjoins Lancaster and is a twenty-minute drive from the centre. Morecambe has its own distinct identity and population that contrasts with the university town and health-service hub that Lancaster has become. Situated on the edge of a wide, tidal bay, Morecambe is a seaside town, once a thriving working-class resort with a strong heritage of popular entertainment but now poor, struggling with a reputation as a dull and run-down place to live (see Jordison & Kieran, 2003). It hit the international headlines in 2004 when 23 illegal Chinese migrant workers were drowned in the quicksands of the bay while collecting shellfish for a company based in nearby Liverpool. A film and a novel were subsequently based on this disaster.

Like many other rundown seaside towns in the UK, Morecambe has been the focus of a multi-million pound regeneration project over the last 10 years, and has had some spectacular inward investment, especially in the renovation of the beautiful art-deco Midland Hotel (www.midlandhotel.org/). But at present, it is the kind of place that is hit hard by government austerity measures with

Revisiting *Local Literacies* **103**

BOX 7.1 Shirley's Original Pen Sketch

Shirley: how others see me

How do I think others see me? Who knows? I suppose it depends on who you ask. I would hope I haven't crossed anyone that they would wish me the worst they could, but I'm also no saint, and have ruffled a few feathers, mainly by not doing what others wanted, but I don't think I've hurt anyone to the extent that they feel any malice towards me.

The boys see me in different lights. I'm sure they think I'm mad, they know my sense of humour which they see as being a bit off sometimes. I may say something very seriously and its only when they see me grinning that they realise it's a joke. I do have to watch this sometimes though, I have almost hurt their feelings. It does boil down to moods at the time. Their view or opinion of me is quite important to me. I know people who have grown up hating their parents and resenting them for one reason or another. I hope my boys don't grow up feeling like that about me or Jack.

So from the boys – fun, loving, supportive and understanding. A friend.

From Jack – expressive, supportive, a partner and friend, an ally.

From others – think of me with dread in their hearts, a listener, a helper, a fighter of causes, someone who will go where they probably wouldn't have thought of, an advice giver, trouble shooter.

I hope.

---

fragile businesses that rely on a dwindling tourist industry and many people dependent on welfare benefits.

Since our original study, then, Shirley had made a small move in geographical terms, but one that was much more significant in terms of culture and economy. This made me reflect more deeply than before about the geographical location of Lancaster and Morecambe as active participants in the ethnographic account. The towns are transit points on mainline train and road routes to and from the North of England and Scotland, between the major metropolitan areas of Liverpool and Manchester. Morecambe Bay itself is an economic force: a shoreline with seaside resorts and a nature reserve for migratory birds. It has exploitable resources that include shellfish, a gas field, a nuclear power station, tidal and wind power, with their own seasonal and daily rhythms. I will return to this point later

104 Mary Hamilton

in the chapter when I discuss the ways in which it is possible to pick up threads of Shirley's experience and trace them far beyond the local everyday.

In personal and family terms, Shirley's first husband, Jack, had died since we interviewed her in 1992, and she had remarried and changed her name. Her two sons have grown up and one of them died 4 years ago. The other lives close by and has a two-year-old daughter—Shirley's only grandchild. For several years Shirley continued her interest in local politics and formalised this by becoming a local councillor in Morecambe between 1995 and 1999. During this time she was involved with the multimillion pound regeneration project, which she is proud of. She then stood unsuccessfully as a county councillor, and continued as secretary of the local Labour Party for several years, until she took paid employment (6 years ago) in a local foyer—a hostel and training centre run by a third-sector organisation for young homeless adults. She works full time as a project night worker and we talked a good deal during the interview about this work, her feelings about it, and how it links with the themes of literacy and change that were apparent in her interviews in the original *Local Literacies* project. Shirley's public profile has therefore waxed and waned over the last 20 years, and since taking on full-time work she has dropped out of formal politics.

How Does She Feel About Having Taken Part in the Original Local Literacies Research Project?

Although at the time Shirley was a full and helpful participant in the project, it seemed to have made little long-term impression on her. She vaguely remembered talking to Sarah, the research interviewer we worked with, and she was interested in the book we had written but had never seen it before or had any curiosity about what had happened to the data we collected from her. She has experience of other research projects too, which suggests that being asked to take part in interviews and filling questionnaires are more commonplace event in people's lives than perhaps researchers give credit for (Briggs, 2007).

When I took back her interview transcript this time, Shirley's reaction was different from before, when she fretted about the appearance of the transcript and the way it represented her use of language. This time she said 'I sound quite wise.'

Have Shirley's Literacy Practices Changed Since we Interviewed Her in 1992?

In the form and context through which they are expressed, Shirley's literacy practices have changed. However, in terms of the meanings and motivation for her, the original themes were still relevant, although I was aware that the way I structured the interview might have tended to emphasise continuities and overlook differences. When she looked at her pen-sketch she said: 'Yes, that's me, that is still me! I'm still a doer and I still hope people think that they can come to me if they need somebody to help.'

In talking about her involvement with dyslexia, which she picked up as the first thing to discuss in the interview she said:

> I now work as a night support worker for [a third-sector housing organization] and discovered that I have a number of dyslexics living there. I'm seeing it from a different perspective now . . . Yes, dyslexia is . . . I'm still discovering dyslexics.

One very striking thing about our discussions was her frequent reference to popular culture, especially music, which Shirley hardly mentioned in her earlier interviews, but also television. She pointed me to popular culture resources when I asked about a topic—for example, when I asked about the public image of the town of Morecambe where she now lives and when she was explaining her work in the foyer to me.

She shares an interest in music with her new husband, Geoff, who likes karaoke and listens to music a lot. Unlike her former husband with whom Shirley shared a lot of book-reading interests, Geoff is 'not a reader.' Shirley says she has always been interested in a wide range of music. She met Geoff through the karaoke evenings at a local pub run by her son, Toby. She said 'I have always liked music' so it is interesting that this never featured in the repeated interviews we carried out in the original *Local Literacies* project. Did it not arise because we didn't think to ask? Was it mentioned but not pursued? Is it now salient because of the change in Shirley's closest family relationships? Has she changed? Such examples made me strongly aware of how partial a picture ethnography can create and how little you can know of someone even after repeated interviews and observations. There are always more dimensions, more dispositions that might surface in different times and places. The story of a life is always too rich to do justice to in a single research study.

One continuity that surfaced was an interest in art. In the original interviews this had made only a minor appearance when Shirley described how she, Jack and their sons all enjoyed drawing and painting, and she talked about how they had painted a mural on the bathroom walls. Both her sons went on to develop their artistic talents, studying at the local art college and designing tattoos. Her older son, Toby, went on to work very successfully with a motorcycle retail company creating and painting customised airbrushed designs.

Another continuity was Shirley's interest in knitting and other textile crafts. I immediately spotted the basket of needles and craft materials in her living room, just as Sarah had documented Shirley's knitting machine in her original field notes. Shirley no longer does machine knitting but she talked at length about a craft project she is starting with the residents of the hostel where she works. I will return to this below.

How Has the Change Toward Computer-based Reading and Writing Affected Her?

Shirley says she loves computers 'absolutely.' She reported using digital technologies in a range of different areas of her life in ways that reflect her wider lifestyle and relationships. She appeared never to have had any formal training with computers and talked about her first trial and error experiences with using the computer in the council offices as a local councillor in the mid-1990s:

> at that point I didn't even know how to switch one on and I'm going 'whooo' and I was watching the Chief Revenue Officer with his and I said 'so can you do . . . ' I'm asking him questions and he's saying 'Shirley, I don't know, Shirley, I really don't know, I'm just learning this.' So he was learning and at the same time I was learning!
>
> My very first computer [given to her by her brother] . . . I think was steam driven . . . I had an office set up upstairs, with a desk and set it up on the desk. Yes . . . there wasn't even colour, it was just black and white, you know. And it was this huge bulking thing and I thought, oh my goodness me! But I did all sorts on it. And now I do it without even thinking about it.

She emails family and friends, downloads photographs, does some online shopping, is on Facebook and watches YouTube. These activities were not pointed out to me as special or significant but routinised just as print literacies were (and still are) discussed in her interviews. Of mobile [cell] phones she said:

> I resisted for years—I have a landline and an ansaphone—people know how to get hold of me. Only drug dealers use mobile phones in Morecambe! I succumbed partly for the kids. If they need me, I want to be there, if Toby wants to get in touch. My granddaughter, Kailee, has her own mobile even though she's only 2½ years, and she sometimes rings me!

Her use of a mobile and emails is circumscribed by her job as she has to be careful not to give out her contact details to the residents she works with. Her landline is still important and historically her number has been widely circulated locally through her involvements in community organisations and as a local councillor. It is still used by local people looking for her help. They also email and contact her by letter.

Does Shirley See Literacy Differently Now as a Result of Her Life Experiences?

Shirley's discussion about dyslexia and how it is just as important an issue for the young people she works with in the foyer shows continuities with her earlier views of the value of literacy and her commitment to working on it with individuals, especially the younger generation. She responded directly to this question by talking about everyday practices:

> I think it's just as important . . . because literacy is such a big part of everything, if you can't read how do you know if the tablets you've just bought from the chemist are not going to poison you? . . . there's not always somebody around who would advise you in a responsible way.

Her account of how she works informally with residents in the foyer mirrors her earlier involvement with the dyslexia association.

> Some of them will readily tell you, 'Shirley, I can't read this, can you read this for me?' Some of them will get a letter and they'll struggle to read it or they'll call somebody and say 'What does that say? Did I read that right?' and the ways of coping with it are still the same.
>
> We had a young man who had serious reading and writing difficulties, and he could read but very badly, and so on a one-to-one basis I started reading *Harry Potter* with him and he was getting on quite well with that and then he left us.

As well as the one-to-one support she gives to the residents of the hostel, she has started a reading group and encourages them to read books by linking them to films on DVDs, which they watch together:

> I do a DVD night but I'm also taking books, so I'm taking films of books and we're having a little reading group and I'm going to read to a group . . . and then we can discuss it afterwards and compare it to the movie. What I will do is offer the book to. . . . If my voice is going and I need a coffee, 'Does somebody want to take over this?' you know. I might let them do that as well.
>
> We've done a few movies. We did *The Woman in Black* and one of the girls said—and she's a real tough nut—she came in and she went 'What are you watching?' and I was like '*The Woman in Black.*' 'Oh, I read this in school' and she plonks herself down on the chair and I looked at her and said 'Did you?' and she sits there arms crossed. She's a really . . . she's a very angry young woman and I understand why she is an angry young woman because I'd be dammed annoyed as well. She came in about half an hour after it had started, and she sat and watched the rest of the movie and I said to her 'Well?' and she said 'What?' and I said 'How did it compare to the book?' and she said 'I think I'd need to see the film from the beginning,' but she said 'Yes, it stuck pretty well to the book.'

108 Mary Hamilton

As a project night-worker Shirley enjoys a much more informal relationship with the residents than the day staff are able to develop, and although she said it was difficult and sometimes depressing she also said:

> I enjoy doing the nights because I can have a more relaxed relationship with the residents because I'm not on their backs about, you know, 'you haven't been to training today, have you been to the City Council and sorted out your housing benefit? Have you been to the Job Centre and sorted out your Job Seeker's Allowance?' I'm not on their backs over things like that. I'll just go and 'Have you had a good day?' and they'll go 'Well . . .' and I'll say, 'So, we didn't go to the Job Centre then, did we?' and they'll go 'I never got there, I spent all day in bed, Shirley.' 'Oh.' So my relationship with the residents is totally different.

She described how she makes photo-collages with the hostel residents documenting fund-raising events they have been involved with such as Comic Relief and sponsored bike rides. One of her special talents is dreaming up humorous captions for the photos, and this reminded me of the editorials she used to write for the neighbourhood newsletters in Springside more than 20 years ago (see Barton & Hamilton, 2012, p. 110).

She said, 'I'm still an avid reader personally' and she likes the feel of a book in her hands. She has been tempted but hasn't succumbed to a Kindle yet. During the interview she obligingly focused on literacy-related activities, but it was clear that she uses a range of other popular media alongside books and print literacy and, in many respects, as shown above, she seems to have incorporated digital tools seamlessly into her repertoire.

This is illustrated in one further example of a craft project Shirley is developing in the hostel. She explained that she was going to introduce knitting to the residents. When I queried whether they would find this an attractive idea she explained that they would be making mobile phone cases using a design based on the video game 'Angry Birds' and also making figures of rock musicians starting with Freddie Mercury. She had searched on-line and downloaded the patterns using her mobile phone, and when I later looked for the patterns myself I discovered the vast world of 'Amigurami' (knitting and crocheting small figures, mainly of people and animals).[2]

What Can We Make of These Findings? Discussion of the Different Aspects of Shirley's Experience

Shirley's conversation in the interview constantly moves back and forth between wider issues, local relationships and popular culture. As well as being a style of narrative and story telling, I now see this as an important part of her sense-making of her everyday experiences—both for herself and to enlighten others. As an

Revisiting *Local Literacies* **109**

example, she explicitly linked her work in the homeless foyer with a book called *Generation F* (Smith, 2011) ('I bought that because that's my job, that tells everybody what my job is') and also linked the experiences of her residents with the *Jeremy Kyle Show* (see also Marsh & Bishop, 2014), which was on the television with the sound turned down during the interview. She explained how some of her ex-residents have appeared on the programme and gave the examples of a custody dispute involving a young man she knew, and of a disagreement between a young woman and her mother. The television show trades in highly emotionally charged personal relationships with a lot of conflict, and it is interesting that this kind of social interaction is what Shirley says she enjoyed about being in politics, too:

> I miss the thrust and the cutting of . . . being able to slice somebody down to size. I loved that, especially fellow politicians, well politicians from opposition parties. I used to love that. I became very caustic with my wit.

Always, as in the earlier interviews, Shirley acts as a 'go-between' and she is comfortable with the less formal role she plays with the young residents as a night-worker in the foyer, mediating the ways in which people are positioned by their institutional encounters—whether on- or off-line. However, as her roles have developed and become more formal (as local councillor and employed project worker in the foyer) she now speaks more fully from the institutional side of this interface and this is signalled in her narratives and in the way she explains the issues she cares about. For example, we see the younger people's literacies through her eyes as a project worker with particular agendas for them.

Through Shirley's narratives about her activities as a local councillor, parent, grandparent and her informal activities as a foyer night-worker, we can glimpse something of the communicative interfaces between public-facing institutions and the individuals who engage with them. These interfaces are more complex than perhaps is acknowledged in policy and practice. In her employment at the hostel, her work as a local councillor and her communications with family and friends, Shirley described lags in the use of new forms of communication, with institutions' continued use of the telephone, face-to-face meetings, individual emails and letters rather than the more impersonal digital interfaces now being rapidly developed by commercial and public organisations. The role of different employees and mediators is various and subtle, as are the ways in which they are used by citizens in search of solutions to their everyday problems. These interfaces are still hardly explored in the literacy studies research tradition (Taylor's 1997 work is one exception) but they are crucial for understanding how public participation and collective action can be supported, and how literacy practices might act as a barrier to such action.

The revisit interview has a strongly developmental aspect to it, as in Heath's revisit to the children and grandchildren of Trackton and Roadville. It reveals

110 Mary Hamilton

the intergenerational relationships within which literacy and other communication practices are progressively reconfigured and throws new light on historical family detail offered in the first interviews. We get to find out what happened to Shirley's younger son, Ben, whose dyslexia had featured so strongly in the earlier interviews and was one of the drivers for Shirley to get involved with local parent groups and eventually as a school governor. One of the most moving statements was when I asked how Ben got on in his later schooling career. Shirley replied:

> He did alright, eventually. What I found was, the higher up the education system he went . . . the support was better. . . . In the last two years at school they did a mentoring scheme for the younger ones that had started at senior school and [Ben] was a mentor for some of the young ones and he absolutely loved it and he used to come home and say, 'Was I like that Mum?' and I'd say 'Yes, you were.' So he recognised himself in some of these younger ones as well, you know, so it was quite good in that he saw both sides of it.

We also get to find out what happened to Ben's older brother, Toby. We meet his daughter, Shirley's only granddaughter, SueAnn, 'the apple of everybody's eye' and learn how the two-year-old is being incorporated into the worlds of popular music, dance and art, print and digital technologies. This happens through the karaoke sessions she listens to and when Shirley watches old musicals with her. She has her own mobile phone on which she rings her grandmother. Her father absorbs her into the world of vernacular design through his interest in tattoos and his work customising motorcycles; and SueAnn's godfather runs a local tattoo parlour. Reading books are bought for her by relatives. She is thus influenced not just by her parents but by the wider environment created by her extended family and friends, including her grandmother, her step-grandfather and her godfather.

I did not find it easy to directly explore Shirley's 'sense of place' with her, as I was curious to do. Shirley didn't comment on newcomers to the area, or suggest that digital technologies have brought the world to her doorstep. She responded to my question about how Morecambe is seen by outsiders by talking about a recent BBC film, which had reconstructed the lives of three families from the town's past using empty houses in the town as the settings. Perhaps this reflects the sense of a place marooned in the backwaters of globalisation, whose glories, such as they were, are still seen as 'past' with the stalling of hopes for regeneration. The retro attraction of the refurbished art-deco Midland Hotel also fits in with this image. As someone who has always been actively involved in politics Shirley is well aware of the wider issues and external forces that are at work in her local community. This is shown by her comments on the Morecambe regeneration project and her analysis of the issues facing the young people she works with. However, she and her family still live very locally, day to day, not being able to

Revisiting *Local Literacies* **111**

afford to travel much and when they do, revolving this around relatives who live in other parts of the UK.

Reassessing *Local Literacies*: What Would We Do Differently Now?

I commented at the beginning of this chapter that our original strategy of focusing in depth on literacy practices in one locality had its roots in traditional anthropological study, but many things have changed since we first designed the *Local Literacies* project. These changes are not just in the research site and the individual lives within it, but we ourselves have changed as researchers and the theory and methodologies of literacy studies have moved on too. Taken together, these changes make our original focus on the profiles of individual people, and the boundary we set around 'one community' a little uncomfortable for revisiting. Neither the physical site nor the individuals themselves any longer seem adequate as a focus for understanding the nature of locality and I would like to explore these discomforts a little further in this final section.

In Barton and Hamilton (2012), we note that theory and methodology are inextricably linked. The original theory and methodology we used in *Local Literacies*

> identified particular units of analysis: the concept of the *literacy event* (drawn from Heath) provided a starting-point for analyzing interactions, while the concept of *literacy practice* provided a way of relating these to broader cultural and structural formations. Concentrating on specific domains of life, the detailed, multi-method, collaborative and responsive methodologies provided practical models for carrying out research and identified key dimensions of practices such as physical settings and activities; material resources and artefacts; identities, values, feelings and motivations; roles played by other people and their institutional links, such as social networks, networks of support, mediators, sponsors. Juxtaposed with discourse analysis, these have proved to be powerful ways of researching and analyzing texts and practices.
>
> (p. xxvii)

However, although we began to talk about the interfaces of everyday practices with institutional literacies, much remained to be explored about how to work, both methodologically and conceptually, with the relationships between the everyday and faraway, the local and the global, without returning to old ideas about literacy as an autonomous set of universal skills. Since our original study, globalisation has become a key focus of interest for social theory (see Wellman, 2002, p. 3; Urry, 2003, p. 84). There is a growing interest in how issues such as travel and migration, changing patterns of employment, communication technologies and global consumption impact on people's everyday lives.

Further methodological issues include the increasing importance of multimodal analysis aided by social semiotic theory and the need for methodologies to consider the increasing presence of digital literacies in people's lives (as in Hine, 2005). These new concerns have 'stretched' literacy studies and prompted the development of new concepts, which can expand the reach of literacy research (see, for example, Brandt & Clinton, 2002; Scollon, 2001; and Kress, 2003). The notion of 'translocal literacies' focuses on tracing patterns of literacy across contexts in order to understand the dynamics of local global relationships and how literacy is changing within virtual worlds.

Concerns with globalisation and seeing local cultures within a world system have also led to developments in ethnography. Time is seen as a significant dimension of cultural understanding—change, movement, connections across timescales. Boundaries in field sites and interconnections between different local sites are seen to be constructed by the researcher through the lens of their research questions, rather than being 'found' as pre-existing units or relationships. In particular, Marcus's (1995) proposal of a multi-sited ethnography has been widely taken up (see, for example, Coleman & von Hellerman, 2009). Fortun (2009) explains this approach as the study of open systems which

> are continually being reconstituted through interaction of many scales, variables and forces. The ethnographer's task is to map an array of constitutive dynamics including, but not restricted to, the local. Fluency is required across sites, disciplines and languages in order to produce dense and complicated accounts of how the contemporary world works.
>
> (p. 74)

Analysis in multisite ethnography is an iterative process whereby the collection of successive waves of data is driven by the meanings and implications of data discovered through earlier observations and the enquiry so far.

A single locality is thus a starting place from which connections will be traced outwards, as in Scollon's (2001) notion of a 'nexus of practices' rather than a single isolated point. This leads to a strategy of following the trajectories of texts, people and activities—figuring out where they have come from, how they circulate and where they are headed.

Shirley's observations about Morecambe and my own comments earlier in this chapter about its geographical location on Morecambe Bay suggest something of how this could be done. The task is to explain how the local and the global are assembled through a variety of experiences and information about Morecambe, much of which is refracted through the media and through other people's accounts. Both global and local places are assembled rather than discovered, and there are many scales and perspectives through which Morecambe can be viewed.

In this process of assembly, as Smith (2005) recognises in her institutional ethnography framework, texts are pivotal for co-ordinating and aligning social action across sites and distance. Socio-material approaches, such as Actor Network Theory (ANT), similarly point out the crucial power of texts as they travel between locations, people and social domains (see Latour, 2007; Hamilton, 2012). Actor network theory is based on the very same methodological premises as multi-sited ethnography, asserting that the strategy of following the actors, stories, discourses and threads offers new insights into shifting formations of power relations. ANT explicitly adds the non-human actors as integral constituents of these networks (Krauss, 2009, p. 146). Both literacy studies and ANT maintain that cultural artefacts mediate moment-by-moment social interactions, acting as points of contact and fixity for developing shared meanings within the flow of social life. As Burgess (2006, p. 9) notes, the events within which these artefacts are embedded can be seen as "analytical doorways into an understanding of social systems."

In summary, the result of this attention to methodology is a convergence of critical approaches from a range of disciplines: anthropology, cultural psychology, social semiotics, sociology, and science and technology studies, which all recognise the significance of texts and the everyday practices around them, but also assert the openness and fluidity of social process and problematise the bounded nature of locality. As a result, if we were to begin now to explore local literacies, it is likely that we would assemble the account rather differently. We would focus less on developing profiles of individual people as the centrepieces of the study and shift our attention and research effort to tracing the threads of social actors, organisations, significant texts, locations and events outwards from them, using the concepts described above and the new framings of globalisation, multi-sited ethnography and socio-material theory.

Embryonic aspects of this strategy can be found in *Local Literacies*, but in the original study we didn't, for example, link our access points for literacy systematically with the individual participants or trace the threads of their lives outwards from Lancaster itself. We were too concerned to cover all bases in the quest to achieve a full and rich picture of the 'local community' of Lancaster.

We learned much from the detailed attention we paid to literacy in the physical routines of daily life in Lancaster. In revisiting this site, we have documented small, local examples of change which are not 'textbook' examples since individual lives never quite fit the generalisations, but they are still subject to the broader changes that concern us—communications, migration, employment, demographic change. The challenge for the researcher is to trace how they fit into, or give clues to, a bigger picture. This involves noticing the details, but also making the connections. Shirley's changing life experiences are of great interest in their own right from a longitudinal perspective. However, it is the threads that connect this life to other lives, times, events and issues—the web of meanings and relationships from which Shirley's stories are assembled—that now seem of most value to me in understanding literacies.

114 Mary Hamilton

Notes

1 All interviewee names have been anonymised.
2 Amigurami activities are supported by numerous online sites, which offer patterns but also blogs and forums for discussion. The Freddy Mercury pattern that Shirley had found was offered through the blog of an Indonesian woman living in North America who is dedicated to bringing knitting crafts to Indonesian society.

References

Barton, D. & Hamilton. M. ([1998] 2012). *Local literacies: Reading and writing in one community.* London: Routledge.

Brandt, D. & Clinton, K. (2002). Limits of the local: Expanding perspectives on literacy as a social practice. *Journal of Literacy Research, 34*(3), 337–56.

Briggs, C. L. (2007). Anthropology, interviewing, and communicability in contemporary society. *Current Anthropology, 48*(4), 551–580.

Burawoy, M. (2003). Revisits: An outline of a theory of reflexive ethnography. *American Sociological Review, 68*(5), 645–679.

Burgess, A. (2006). Linking the local to the global: The role of the ILP in mediating across timescales. Unpublished paper, Lancaster Literacy Research Centre, Lancaster University.

Coleman, S. & von Hellermann, P. (Eds.) (2009). *Multi-sited ethnography: Problems and possibilities in the translocation of research methods.* London: Routledge.

Fortun, K. (2009). Scaling and visualising multi-sited ethnography. In S. Coleman & P. von Hellermann (Eds.), *Multi-sited ethnography: Problems and possibilities in the translocation of research methods* (pp. 73–86). London: Routledge.

Graff, H. (1987). *The legacies of literacy: Continuities and contradictions in western culture and society.* Bloomington, IN: Indiana University Press.

Hamilton, M. (2012). *Literacy and the politics of representation.* London: Routledge.

Hamilton, M. & Barton, D. (1999). The texts of everyday life: Public and private identities in vernacular literacy practices. *Cuadernos Linguistics and Society, 3*, 45–71.

Heath, S. B. (1983). *Ways with words: Language, life and work in communities and classrooms.* Cambridge: Cambridge University Press.

Heath, S. B. (2012). *Words at work and play: Three decades in family and community life.* Cambridge: Cambridge University Press.

Hine, C. (ed.). (2005). *Virtual methods.* Oxford: Berg.

Jordison, S. & Kieran, D. (2003). *Crap towns: The 50 worst places to live in the UK.* London: Boxtree.

Krauss, W. (2009). Migratory birds, migratory scientists and shifting fields: The political economy of a northern coastline. In S. Coleman & P. von Hellermann (Eds.), *Multi-sited ethnography: Problems and possibilities in the translocation of research methods* (pp. 146–160). London: Routledge.

Kress, G. (2003). *Literacy in the new media age.* London: Routledge.

Latour, B. (2007). (2nd ed.). *Reassembling the social: An introduction to actor-network-theory.* Oxford University Press.

Lemke, J. (2000). Across the scales of time: Artifacts, activities, and meanings in ecosocial systems. *Mind, Culture, and Activity, 7*(4), 273–290.

Marcus, G. E. (1995). Ethnography in/of the world system: The emergence of multi-sited ethnography. *Annual Review of Anthropology, 24*, 95–117.

Marsh, J. & Bishop, J. (2014). We're playing Jeremy Kyle! Television talk shows in the playground. *Discourse: Studies in the Cultural Politics of Education, 35*(1),16–30.

Ofcom (2011). Communications market report. London: Office of Communications.

Scollon, R. (2001). *Mediated discourse: The nexus of practice.* London: Routledge.

Scribner, S. & Cole, M. (1981). *The psychology of literacy.* London: Harvard University Press.

Smith, D. (2005). *Institutional ethnography: A sociology for people.* Toronto: Altamira Press.

Smith, W. (2011). *Generation F.* Cheltenham: Monday Books.

Street, B. (1984). *Literacy in theory and practice.* Cambridge: Cambridge University Press.

Taylor, D. (1997). *Toxic literacies: Exposing the injustice of bureaucratic texts.* Heinemann Educational Books.

Urry, J. (2003). *Global complexity.* Cambridge: Polity Press.

Wellman, B. (2002). Little boxes, globalization, and networked individualism. In M. Tanabe, P. van den Besselaar & T. Ishida (Eds.), *Digital cities II: Computational and sociological approaches* (pp. 11–25). Berlin: Springer-Verlag.

8

ARTIFACTS OF RESILIENCE

Enduring Narratives, Texts, Practices Across Three Generations

Kate Pahl and Aliya Khan

Introduction

In the Ferham Families project we (Kate Pahl, Andrew Pollard and Zahir Rafiq) were exploring the artifacts of identity and narratives of migration of British Asian families from Pakistan who migrated to the UK in the 1950s (Pahl & Pollard, 2008, 2010; Pahl et al., 2009; Pahl, 2012). We wanted to celebrate the heritage of families in Rotherham and consider their achievements. We called the project 'Ferham Families' to signal the way in which the families were part of a local community, called Ferham, in Rotherham, and to celebrate that community. The project resulted in a museum exhibition and a website called *Every Object Tells a Story* (www.everyobjecttellsastory.org.uk). The website included images of objects from family members and traced their life stories through everyday objects. It also included a teaching pack for adult literacy tutors and a Flash presentation where the objects fell through the digital landscape, accompanied by the spoken word. This was accompanied by an exhibition, held in Rotherham Arts Centre in 2007, where the family objects were displayed alongside their stories. This exhibition was co-curated with family members and included display cases based on long ethnographic interviews about what objects were important to the family.

Our focal family was the Khan family—grandmother and four adult children, one female (Ravina) and her three brothers (Akram, Zafran and Jaan). All had young or teenaged children of their own. In the original study I (Kate) interviewed Ravina, and Andy and Zahir interviewed her grown-up brothers. One of the brothers, Akram, had a daughter, Aliya. As part of the project, the artist and web designer Zahir Rafiq worked with the children of the family who were involved, and co-curated a section of the website in which they placed their favourite objects in their bedrooms and talked about them. Zahir said that his inspiration came

Artifacts of Resilience 117

FIGURE 8.1 Image of Exhibition (Photo Taken by Steve Wright)

from the 'Barbie' website, which his own daughter loved, who was four at the time. Zahir wanted to explore the children's special objects with them, and they co-constructed the website. In this website, Aliya Khan (then aged ten) described how she loved Harry Potter, and also how she loved a pair of gold earrings given to her by her grandmother.

Aliya's family came from the Pathan regions of Pakistan and included her grandfather (now passed away) and her grandmother, still alive, her mother, father, brothers, uncles and cousins, all of whom contributed to the *Every Object Tells a Story* website and exhibition. One of the aspects the original team wrote about was the way in which some objects, such as gold, held family values and ideals, and were intangibly passed across generations (Pahl & Pollard, 2008). A substantial part of the original project consisted of in-depth ethnographic interviews with family members about their special objects.

I (Kate) interviewed Ravina (Aliya's aunt) back in 2006 about her special objects, memories and stories connected with her family. As part of the revisiting project, I have reinterviewed Ravina with a specific focus on literacy learning across generations. This has created a new set of thoughts and ideas about the value of literacy for women in different contexts.

I (Aliya) interviewed my grandmother, Ravina's mother in 2013, about her literacy learning. I also explore, with Kate, the family history. I intertwine my mother's story, and my story together with Ravina's story into the history of my family with a particular focus on literacy.

Here, we (Aliya and Kate) jointly explore the literacy lives of these women 6 years on and reflect on what endures, and what has changed since that time. We used these interviews as a heuristic to explore our changing interpretative schema, both of the original dataset but also of the new dataset. With a focus on literacy lives, we focus in on the concept of resilience across generations. This is drawing on Aliya's own understanding of resilience and is framed by her lens. We make this framework come alive as we co-create a shared epistemological framework to look at the data, both old (2006–2007) and new (2012–2013).

Our writing is also intertwined. We change voices as we switch between Aliya (now 19) and Kate (original researcher). We realise this might create a more complex experience as a reader, not only in relation to the subject matter, but also the way this is reflected in the writing. As the stories of the family are interwoven, our writing styles interweave. The writing of this chapter is intentionally multivoiced, reflecting the new collaboration that we have been in together. We call this collaboration co-production and below, describe our methodology.

Co-production as a Methodology for Revisiting

The original research process of the Ferham Families research project relied on traditional ethnographic methodologies. We conducted ethnographic interviews (Spradley, 1979) and engaged in a process of recursive coding where we checked with families our interpretative framework in a cyclical process of interpretation (Barton & Hamilton, 1998).

Now we would have done this very differently. We would have involved the families in the writing of the grant application, the framing of the research project,

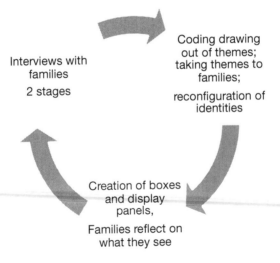

FIGURE 8.2 Cycle of Co-production

the research questions, the construction of the research, data collection, analysis and writing up, in a more open and democratic process by which the people involved in the study became the subjects, not the objects of research. Since doing that project I (Kate) have moved increasingly to involving community partners in the design and construction of research, a process I am calling co-production. This process is dialogic, led by communities and involves the production of multivocal texts and crucially involves community members in the production of research (see also Hart & Wolff, 2006; Armstrong & Banks, 2011; Campbell & Lassiter, 2010).

By involving Aliya in this process, we are decentring the stability of the academic expert who knows and who is authoritative about the dataset under discussion. Instead, the process of academic enquiry is more about the usefulness of the research to develop a framework that can make sense of literacy practices for the people involved in the research, not the researcher. Aliya observed that doing research in this way is more direct and more relevant, as well as being more powerful. For her, the ideas are linked to her first-hand experience of her grandmother.

Our focus here is on the processes and practices of co-producing the revisiting project, with a particular interest in the concept of intergenerational literacies and their potential for resilience. We revisit the Ferham Families project, with an interest in the literacy lives of the women in the family. We have adopted the methodology of co-production, drawing on the work of collaborative ethnographers Eric Lassiter and Elizabeth Campbell to guide our practice (Lassiter, 2005; Campbell & Lassiter, 2010). This way of working is about the close relationship between research subject and researcher in ethnographic research to create collaborations of enquiry. We pursue a very specific slant on the data. Rather than concentrating on the relationship between objects and stories, which was the original brief of the project, we consider ways in which literacy practices have shaped identities across the generations. We understand that literacy practices, such as prayer, poetry or stories, offer properties of resilience, held in different ways by different family members. We adopt a feminist stand-point, and concentrate on the women in the family, with a particular focus on Aliya, then age 10, now 19, her grandmother (78) and her aunt, Ravina (50). Through this lens we enquire how literacy plays out and has a different role across generations (Holland & Lave, 2009).

Our work is framed together and the thinking is entwined. We explore how this more collaborative methodology changes both the framing and the thinking reflected in this article. While I (Kate) reflect below that I might have taken this in a certain direction, Aliya influenced me to think differently and analyse the data differently. Below we present our joint thinking.

Co-production in research involves a process by which knowledge is co-created with a shared framework. This involves the co-creation of an analytic framework as well as joint data collection, construction of research questions and a research focus. If research informants construct and frame research, this shifts how research is constructed, analysed and presented. Eric Lassiter and Elizabeth Campbell were ethnographers who worked with community members to create a co-produced ethnographic text called "The Other Side of Middletown" (Lassiter et al., 2004). Members of the African American community in Muncie, Indiana, worked with university researchers and students to create a shared, co-constructed ethnographic text, which was produced by and for the community. In order to do this, they went through a process of "reciprocal analysis" to create shared multivocal texts that reflected community realities and concerns in their own words using chapter headings they jointly constructed (Campbell & Lassiter, 2010). This involved co-writing and co-interpreting ethnographic interview transcripts. Here, we (Aliya and Kate) adopt the same procedures to look at the literacy lives of three women within the Khan family, all of whom are passionate about literacy, education and the advancement, in particular, of women's education.

When I (Kate) initially wrote about the Ferham Families project, I co-wrote with Andrew Pollard and Zahir Rafiq, the artist, web designer and adviser to the project (Pahl & Pollard, 2008, 2010; Pahl et al., 2009). However, family members were not included in the writing process. This article is now co-written with Aliya, and explores, from her perspective, what revisiting means to her. Revisiting was emotionally complex. Aliya described the process of revisiting to me:

> It was incredibly—shocking—to go back on it after so long, and hear your own voice and how you have changed, and although those things remain the same, I am still dedicated to my family and my grandparents and I still love Harry Potter, like I said, on there, people are always changing and like I said people part with one another which is why my nursery school photo was still there.
>
> (17 July 2012)

Revisiting is about real lives and trajectories, which carry hope and transformation within them. It can also throw up surprising and new ways of seeing original data. For example, when I (Kate) first interviewed Ravina I focused on her love of gold and decoration (Pahl & Pollard, 2008). It was only on revisiting her house and talking to her again that I realised that she was much more interested in her job as an English as a second language teacher, and could have contributed to the teaching resource pack embedded in the *Every Object Tells a Story* website. I had not heard that part of her story fully.

When I (Kate) first did the study, the objects were the most important. Now, education, and lived experience of education, has become more important. Below we explore the intersections between stories, objects and literacy lives with a particular focus on the education of women.

Stories Across Generations: Exploring Literacy Lives

Revisiting for us became a process of reframing. Instead of using the term "artifactual literacies" from Pahl & Rowsell (2010) we have used the concept of 'artifacts of resilience' to describe the relationship between resilience and literacy practices. These might be objects, such as a candle, that are closely linked to poems or stories, and endure across generations in those stories. These artifacts become part of stories told and retold, until they become a "tale told by others" (Hymes, 1996). It is in this sense that we consider the artifactual nature of stories. We explore ways in which stories that have endured across the generations contribute to a 'resilient self.' We have then applied this concept of resilient artifacts to literacy. Here, we understand the 'self' to be something that is within a context of family, and is not framed individualistically but is a connected and family-defined concept (Hart et al., 2007). The connectivities between and across stories, objects and identities interest us with relation to literacy practices. These unspool across generations and create moments of resilience.

When we unpack the relationship of the self to stories, we understand the self to be layered through stories. The self is to do with nurture throughout our lives, and how we are conditioned to be this resilient person. Within the revisiting research project, the resilient self is linked and supported by a 'literacy life,' a trajectory of learning and growing in relation to literacy and identity that is particularly nurtured within the home space (Erstad et al., 2009). Holland and Lave (2009) talk about the interaction between 'enduring struggles' in this case, the quest by girls for education in Pakistan and then the consequence of migration to the UK and local practice as being embodied in everyday artifacts. Here we focus on these artifacts, but have developed the idea, from Hart et al. (2007) of *artifacts of resilience*—that is, particular narratives, sayings, texts and practices that have helped shape literate identities over time, in this case, of three generations of women. We construct this framework across the fields of literature on resilience, together with Lave and Holland's concept of the historical production of persons. We also draw on feminist theory of girls' identities in which 'Becoming is necessarily tied to the new and to the future, to the novelty that is involved in transformation and to the openness and uncertainty that this produces' (Coleman, 2008, p. 89). This helped us make sense of Aliya's future trajectories as they opened out in relation to her past experiences. They were mediated through narrative encounters with her mother, aunt and grandmother's own stories. For example, Aliya told a story about a candle that held her family's special feelings. She told this as a poem. She then used it as a protective story. Her engagement with this supported her resilience in life. We have observed that young people have agency as to how they construct resilient identities. Children and young people grow and are socialised but also have agency as to how they develop and become resilient (James, 2013). We therefore reframed our analytic framework to understand what literacy contributed to identity formation, with Aliya's own story at the forefront of our analysis.

Introducing Aliya

Aliya's literacy life was linked to a love of stories, reading and special poems. It rested on a valuing of education across the female generations in her family. These were powerful narratives of identity that describe better imagined futures within particular local contexts. First described by Aliya when she was ten, these narratives resurfaced when she was older and provided an insight into a powerfully resilient cultural space in which Aliya herself was nurtured and supported to achieve her goals in life.

Aliya constructed her literate identity through stories. When I (Kate) first met Aliya, she was just ten. She described listening to her grandmother, who told her oral stories. Her interview was conducted in a room where her grandmother was present. Aliya told me about her grandmother:

> She used to tell me stories about when she was at Pakistan to get me to speak with her and it takes me a long time to get to sleep because I'm not obviously sleeping so she used to tell me stories about when she was in Pakistan, the way she used to come to England and stuff, and I used to fall asleep with that.
>
> (12 September 2006)

We discussed this on 17 July 2012, when Aliya told me:

> I used to share a room with my grandmother before I moved here, and we used to bicker so she used to tell me stories to mellow me down a bit. She used to tell all sorts of stories, religious stories about my grandfather about relatives, and it would be like bedtime stories to get me asleep and she taught me a special prayer which I still read to this day three times so it protects the household, from any spirits or any things happening while we are sleeping, sleep peaceful, I was four years when I learned that, yeah, so for the past thirteen years I have been reading that [laughs].

Here, the thread of storytelling is described as enduring across time, both intergenerationally and across the two discussions, which are 6 years apart. The process of constructing these stories and then retelling them provides a source of resilience for Aliya.

Introducing Aliya's Grandmother

Aliya interviewed her grandmother and she found out the following about her early years in Pakistan:

There wasn't a girls' school. She would have schooling with her brothers and they would all be with her. They would drop her off and pick her up, she was only young, about 6 or 7. When the girls' school developed, the maid would take her and drop her off. Grandmother was taught to read and write—she learned with blackboards, little slates. The teacher had a big one, they had little ones. There were English ladies there who only spoke Urdu.

Ravina, in an interview with Kate, also commented about her mother's (Aliya's grandmother's) literacy practices and how she was able to use these when she came to the UK:

> Mum's 77 isn't she, and Aliya's mother is 43, so mum's time, it was kind of unheard of but my grandfather sent her to school. She used to go with a maid, she used to go with her and back—but in a burka. But he sent her and when she came to England she said I couldn't have prayed enough for him, for when I first arrived here there was no telephones no nothing the only contact was writing, I could write so I could write to them and then she had all the ladies in the area, when she went to school she learned Urdu that was the national language, Pakistani, even though where we were we were Pathan so she had all the other Asian ladies, there weren't that many at that time they used to come and they were illiterate, she used to get all the other ladies to write their letters for them.
>
> (Interview, November 2013)

Aliya said that her grandmother then learned English when she came to the UK. Aliya reflected that she had not realised how difficult it was for her grandmother coming to Rotherham, missing all those home comforts. I (Aliya) always knew she thought education was important, but this process highlighted it all the more. The process of getting to England, it all fitted together much more like a jigsaw.

Introducing Ravina

We now meet Ravina, Aliya's aunt. Ravina was interviewed by me (Kate) in 2006. In this interview, she discussed her love of gold, her passion for home decorating and sewing, and her business as a wedding designer. Ravina's passion for gold for its enduring powers and for its aesthetic qualities were quickly absorbed into the exhibition and much of the subsequent writing we did about the project (e.g. Pahl & Pollard, 2008), but one aspect I (Kate) did not focus on sufficiently was Ravina's identity as a teacher of English to adult women.

Looking back, Ravina's identity as an English as a Second Language (ESOL) teacher and the daughter of an educated woman defined her much more strongly than I realised. This woman was Aliya's grandmother, who taught her prayers and bestowed an understanding of prayer and religion. When I (Kate) reinterviewed Ravina in November 2013, we began with her identity as an ESOL teacher. In this interview, Ravina described the passion she had for teaching English to women who had made Rotherham their home and her teaching project with Afghan women. She recalled religious literacies of her mother, Aliya's grandmother:

> RAVINA: Mum, she brought all these little books of prayers that she brought from Pakistan, I remember she brought all these little books that had prayers in them and she would sit there and bind them and we were fascinated. She would use old newspaper and the covers were all—it was like an activity and we used to love mum doing it and we asked how she did it and she said she used to use chapatti flour.
> KATE: As a glue.
> RAVINA: Yes, to bind them. There were no religious materials at the time. It was 1962, there was nothing here. She brought them with her, prayers, even the Quran, she used to read them often, they used to get a bit tatty, she would bind them, whatever wallpaper dad put up, what was left over she would bind them with that [laughs].
> KATE: I love it!
> RAVINA: When I finished my Quran—I was eight, I started at six—it was really early age, she made a cover for my Quran, from fabric. . . . I made them their covers, we had a good laugh about it.
>
> (Interview, November 2013)

Here inscriptions are made material in particular ways that are tied to cultural practices in the home. Aliya saw this practice as being about how her grandmother entwined religion and literacy into objects, and this was how she was conditioned from an early age. She remembered the books, and her own Quran, also covered with fabric.

Education for Women as an Enduring Narrative

Aliya's mother and grandmother were, unusually, educated in an era when for women to acquire a good education was still relatively rare, especially for Pakistani women. Literacy, for Aliya's grandmother, as well as for her mother, was an essential tool for survival and a source of resilience across generations. Here is Aliya's mother talking about her education:

> I was one of the lucky ones—my father believed in education, my father let me drive and go to university, I fulfilled his dream. I didn't want to go university but it was his dream. I had to do that. I am like my father I believe in education, it is what I do now.
>
> (17 July 2012)

This links to the way in which Aliya's parents are now educators and continue to have a passion for education. The concept of being 'lucky' is an intangible one; embodied within a trajectory of resistance it is also contingent upon local practice. It is also dependent on the concept of having a 'dream' and going into a new world.

Aliya both transformed and acknowledged the enduring values she inherits. She acknowledged the 'inexorable links of rights and responsibilities that connect past to present (and future) generations' (Cwerner, 2000, p. 338) but also had a dialogue with those generations, so that 'the generations in question are in perpetual dialogue with each other' (p. 341). Below, we expand upon these ideas in more detail.

Narratives of Resilience

Narratives of resilience tell stories about ways of surviving. Through stories new meanings are made of the present and also the future. Aliya told many narratives of resilience. Her most powerful resilient narrative was that of Harry Potter:

> Harry Potter it was like something you could escape to but also something you could relate to like we discussed it was this new world and everything was exciting and it made you feel you were in there with them. I have always been fascinated by supernatural things and things like that.
>
> (17 July 2012)

When I (Kate) first worked with Aliya she talked about how she loved *Harry Potter* and how she read it in Pakistan. Aliya, like many young people, 'grew up' on *Harry Potter* but also, there was an element, within the story, that she related to, the idea of this 'other world.' Harry Potter experiences adversity, but overcomes it, and is someone specially selected to be a wizard. This narrative of identity offered a future self for many young people who experience some degree of adversity, and offers an important narrative of hope (Hart et al., 2007) to relate to. Aliya owed her love of reading to her mother: 'All because of my mum, she's the one who got me into literature, reading and things, when I was a child she used to read stories to me' (17 July 2012).

This love of reading is then linked to her passion for stories and literature. This is passed down and becomes something that carries forward into the future:

> Like I said, like about my mum getting me into reading because her father, she learned to read and write when she got to England at the age of six but her father he encouraged her to go into education, she got that from him, and I got that from her, and hopefully I will be able to pass that down as well.
>
> (17 July 2012)

Sedimented within everyday life were prayers and sayings that the family drew on in times of hardship but also within the everyday. Aliya learned a prayer from her grandmother:

> she taught me a special prayer which I still read to this day three times so it protects the household from any spirits or any things happening while we are sleeping, sleep peaceful, I was four years when I learned that, yeah, so for the past thirteen years I have been reading that [laughs].
>
> (Interview, 17 July 2012)

I (Kate) found the special prayer mounted in Ravina's house when I recently visited. Here it is as she pointed it out to me. She said her son also said the same prayer just before bedtime and it protected him too.

Here the special prayer follows Aliya through her growing up and its continued saying every day provides a talismanic presence, protecting Aliya from harm. In the Language as Talisman project,[1] we explored the ways in which language could be seen as a protective force, a source of resilience, and could be materialised in different ways (Pahl et al., 2013). What is powerfully present in Aliya's interview

FIGURE 8.3 Special Prayer in Ravina's House

is the feeling of how this particular message is inscribed into prayer and then endures in an embodied form over time (Rosowsky, 2008). A tangible message is held within and repeated internally. In this way, a written object becomes less visible as it is internalised. Language materialises and then dematerialises over time (Burnett et al., 2014). The sense of things changing and shifting in relation to a material status is also captured here by Aliya's mother, talking about the gold dowries that are handed down to women across generations:

> ALIYA'S MOTHER: You pass it down, my gold I don't wear it you pass it down, sentimental value.
> ALIYA: Her grandmother melted hers down.
> ALIYA'S MOTHER: New designs last time, when Thatcher was in, it was a very difficult time.
>
> (17 July 2012)

Rotherham, where this study was situated, experienced extreme hardship at the time of the miners' strike in the mid 1980s when many families did not have enough money to live on. Aliya's mother refers to this time as the last time when the gold was melted down, to celebrate Aliya's mother's marriage and then re-formed in new designs. Gold has both an enduring power and is associated with intangible values of family and continuity. Here, I associate it with resilience in the face of migration and the need to hold on to core values (Pahl & Pollard, 2008). In that sense it is also an 'artifact of resilience,' like Aliya's prayer. Ravina likewise associated gold with survival as well as with beauty:

> As regards gold, culturally a girl is always given gold when she gets married. As well as looking nice, because you wear the gold with your outfit, your wedding outfit, it is for a rainy day as well in case anything happens and you go, oh we'll sell the gold. Not only are you given gold, you are given other things in the dowry, and that is like your part of your inheritance from your parents so you kind of take your inheritance with you when you get married.
>
> (Interview, October 2006)

Gold as an artifact can be understood as enduring across generations and passed from mother to daughter. It transmutes and moves, changing in cultural value but subject to different interpretations and ways of knowing according to who is to make sense of it and where they are in history. The candle burns and wafts across the room, and the gold is melted down to become something different. This highlighted for us the intangible as well as tangible nature of meaning making across generations. Heritage can be touched, but it also dissolves. Resilient literacies have this quality of transmutation and transformation over time. This led us to the concept of intangible and tangible heritage, discussed below.

Intangible and Tangible Heritage

Heritage is also about change and the creation of new imagined worlds. Here, Aliya reflects on the way resilience is created through the process of going into another world. This going away and coming back provides resilience. Here, she talks about her poem:

> I remember in primary school I used to write a lot of poetry, rather embarrassingly looking back [laughs]. I remember this one poem that I had. I am not sure if it is upstairs actually or whether I threw it away as I was embarrassed about it. It is called 'A Candle for My Thoughts' um, and I wrote it with a learning mentor.
>
> (17 July 2012)

Here, Aliya describes a past literate identity, which is the self that wrote poetry. She attributed her ideas for the poem to her habit of going into different worlds:

> a train of thought would just come and like you said about going into another world, I would be in Aliya's world and Aliya's world could have anything it wanted to have in it, absolutely anything. That's obviously changed now as I have got older, I have got less imagination [laughs].
>
> (17 July 2012)

Like her love for Harry Potter, Aliya identified her literate life as a form of 'world making' that created opportunities for her to go into a space where anything could happen, a space that 'imagination seeks to change' (Leander & Sheehy, 2004, p. 4).

Aliya's poem was about the candle: 'A candle of my thoughts, how the wax melts, the smell the feel, everyone my family around . . .' She here articulated how the wax, like the gold in her family, melts, but that intangible melting also signifies the family, the core values that lie beyond the material world. These 'other worlds' provide links across the generations. Aliya's great-grandfather was also a poet, according to her mother:

> I do know he was a famous poet with the Pathans. A lot of them used to have like a gathering and with the Pathans they didn't use to write things down, they got passed from one to the other and my grandfather created poems around the stories that was told.
>
> (17 July 2012)

Likewise, Aliya's Uncle Jaan, described in the Ferham Families project, was also a poet and his description of his identity across the spaces of Pakistan and the UK was described in a famous quotation used in the museum exhibition:

Artifacts of Resilience **129**

I talk to my sister about this from time to time, and I said to her, I said last time, everything, you know, up everything in the stars, the sky, the atmosphere, the air, imagination, everything interesting right above, you get from my dad and then if you look down, everything in the soil, the grit, dirt, sweat, you know, plant, something foundational, hard work, you get all that from my mum, do you know what I mean, and we are in the middle here hovering really, in the strange world.

(Interview, 2006)

Aliya also negotiated the 'strange world' between Pakistan and the UK, but her world making is grounded in the female values she has inherited, in the gold that is melted and transformed, the candle wax that burns to signify family values, and the poems and stories that travel with her as artifacts of resilience over time. Aliya reflected that over the generations the resilience has carried through as well. The different generations interweave their values. This braiding includes Aliya's grandmother's religious knowledge, her mother's love of literature, her aunt's love of decoration and, as Aliya says, 'everything is plaited together in me.' Together, we identified the image of the plait, or braid, for the co-constructed knowledge within the family and how it works together to create strength.

When we originally wrote the first draft of this chapter in November 2012, we explored how the co-construction of a shared framework enabled new insights to occur. Below, we reproduce these original reflections. We then end with new considerations about the nature of the revisiting process. We recognise the way in which knowledge, in this article, also transmutes and is situated in a slightly different way from the conventional academic article. We here jointly consider the process of coming together with our shared framework and reflect on what the process of revisiting has enabled us to do.

Reflection from Kate (1 November 2012)

Co-producing knowledge involves acknowledging the ways in which lay or everyday knowledge as well as academic knowledge can entwine together.

When I met Aliya I was struck by her interest in, and fascination with, psychology, and to reflect that interest I began to read in that field. I was interested in the concept of resilience, from Angie Hart's resilience network (www. boingboing.org.uk/) and began to put together the work I did with Jennifer Rowsell on *Artifactual Literacies* (2010) and think about resilient artifacts. I realised, rereading Aliya's interview, that the prayer, the poem about the candle, the story of the gold, Harry Potter and the story about education being important from her mother, were resilient artifacts that were providing Aliya with the capacity to move ahead in her life and, while she had experienced some adversity, she was able to rise above it and respond to it with considerable resilience. This quality

130 Kate Pahl and Aliya Khan

was located partly within her literate life, shaped as it was by her mother and grandmother.

My aim in writing this chapter was to explore how Aliya has been constructing her literate life over the period of time since I last worked with her. In doing so, I have also linked to her school interests, and I have worked to unite the world of psychology with the world of English Literature, subjects Aliya is passionate about. I wanted to explore psychology as she was telling me about how much she loved that subject. Therefore, I have taken on Aliya's own epistemological space of practice, and developed an analytic framework from psychology—in this case, the literature on resilience. One aspect of the revisiting project is the framing that we as academics provide for the experience of living a 'literacy' life. I started by thinking about the relationship between lives lived, and history from Holland and Lave (2009). This brought me to Aliya's initial comments about the worlds she inhabited, across the generations and her grandmother's stories. Inspired by Aliya's mother's story of how she became empowered to become an educator, I read Coleman's work on the importance of notions of transformation in women's accounts of themselves through time (2008). I thought about the relationship between tradition, and memory and the need to revise and reimagine better futures in dialogue with the past, drawing on Cwerner (2000). Finally, I thought about the concept of 'learning lives' in relation to identity, literacy and meaning, using ideas from the 'learning lives' project (Erstad et al., 2009).

Aliya's Reflections (1 November 2012)

Kate and I have been working on this project for a few months now, following up the project we did together in 2006. I find her words in this piece like poetry, yet I enrobed within them many facts of my life as well as the themes within it. The theme of resilience is key to the piece; how it has been linked with artifacts of my life is astonishing. I believe, though, that we all go through some kind of toughness in our lives and the material we delve into during our childhood (in my case my love of reading, especially the world of J.K. Rowling) in which we are allowed to escape, even if only for a short period of time. Kate and I have revisited this throughout our meetings together. She shares my passion for reading and understands my and my family's appreciation of key artifacts such as gold, literature, the importance of education, and many other important factors in my life, which we discussed and not, as you may think, for materialistic reasons do I hold these in such high stature. However, due to the stories and the links behind these objects, I will hold these dear throughout my life and their associations will never be forgotten. I hope our project has shown you the way in which such little items in our lives shape it so expansively, showing how much they affect the people we are today, making and shaping us, and not forgetting how family is at the heart of it all.

Conclusion and Joint Final Reflections (3 January 2013)

We now present some subsequent thinking that we have done together. Our thinking has been in the field of stories, memory and daydreaming. These were themes that emerged from our second period of analysis. We begin with the concept of stories. We have been thinking about stories as a place of safety. Aliya highlighted this passage from the work of Lalitha Vasudevan (2011) who wrote about stories, and how "stories do not merely begin and end; they are spaces we inhabit, in which we dwell and seek solace, find comfort and peace and sometimes provocation" (p. 1168).

Stories open a door to allow us to escape from reality even if only for a short space of time and that is why they are important as we all face difficulties, but we must stay resilient. And in order to do so we must find solace in escapism through literature. The process of exploring the tangible and intangible heritages of Aliya's grandmother, aunt, mother and her own thoughts has led to a realisation of the braiding process of stories across generations and how they come together and then move apart over time, coalescing and re-forming in new ways.

Here we draw on the work of Paul Ricoeur (1980), in his article on 'Narrative Time,' where he talks about the process of creating memories as being "Itself the spiral movement that, through anecdotes and episodes, brings us back to the almost motionless constellation of potentialities that the narrative retrieves" (p. 186). Here, Ricoeur describes the process by which context cues trigger our memories, and how we go back to what we know, and this always involves going back to upbringing and family. This then links back to the process of socialisation and how we are nurtured when we are younger. James (2013) writes about the process of socialisation from children's perspectives. Her focus has been on "the twin ideas of the importance of the individual and of their social connectedness" (p. 178). James particularly stressed the way in which enduring relations with past and future generations become central to the children in her study's present activities. We could see this past in the present quality with many of Aliya's reflections on her heritage. However, part of this process involves what Aliya described as 'world-making' when we go into another world. When we daydream, we escape into a different world. We are conscious when daydreaming yet completely unaware of our surroundings. Yet this process is important for our development and for renewed hope (Bloch, 1986). This process of going into another world is important in order to create resilience and new ways of imagining. Within this process, reading, writing, dreaming, telling stories and prayers, are central.

ALIYA: The process of working with Kate was enjoyable but familiar. I like the fact we worked together on it. I am not a test subject I am actually entwined within what is going on.

KATE: I have found it really eye-opening working with Aliya and hearing her interpretations. She has made sense of her family in a very different way to how I encountered them in 2006. I realise now how extremely passionate they are in relation to literacy, but also the complexity of the generations over time, and their braided identities entwining and then coming apart to make meaning in new ways. To me, they are an amazing family who can teach me how my work can be valuable but also how they can provide a mode of transmission and heritage across generations.

We both realise that this way of thinking about resilience is different from the practice theories of New Literacy Studies and relies more on Aliya's insights and ways of knowing. However, we would like to argue for a way of writing, thinking and presenting data that fully includes the people in the data. This co-produced way of working also might lead us in new and interesting directions. Aliya feels that her family story and heritage, as described here, can be understood through these theoretical perspectives. Our multivocal writing reflects these complex ideas, and we too have braided our conceptual framework together in a joint piece of writing.

Note

1. Language as Talisman was an AHRC Connected Communities funded project. The team included Deborah Bullivant, Cassie Limb, Hugh Escott, Jane Hodson, David Hyatt, Steve Pool and Richard Steadman-Jones in collaboration with Marcus Hurcombe, Youth Worker, and two schools in Rotherham. It ran from February 2012 to November 2012.

References

Armstrong, A. & Banks, S. (2011). *Community-university participatory research partnerships: Co-inquiry and related approaches*. Newcastle: Beacon NE.

Barton, D. & Hamilton, M. (1998). *Local literacies: Reading and writing in one community*. London: Routledge.

Bloch, E. ([1954] 1986). *The principle of hope*. Oxford: Blackwell.

Burnett, C., Merchant, G., Pahl, K. & Rowsell, J. (2014). The (im)materiality of literacy: The significance of subjectivity to new literacies research. *Discourse: Studies in the Cultural Politics of Education*, *35*(1), 90–103.

Campbell, E. & Lassiter L.E. (2010). From collaborative ethnography to collaborative pedagogy: Reflections on the other side of middletown project and community-university research partnerships. *Anthropology and Education Quarterly*, *41*(4), 370–385.

Coleman, R. (2008). Things that stay: Feminist theory, duration and the future. *Time and Society*, *17*(1), 85–102.

Cwerner, S.B. (2000). The chronopolitan ideal: Time, belonging and globalization. *Time and Society*, *9*(2/3), 331–345.

Erstad, L., Oystein, G., Sefton-Green, J. & Vasbo, K. (2009). Exploring 'learning lives': Community, identity, literacy and meaning. *Literacy*, *43*(2), 11–106.

Hart, A. & Wolff, D. (2006). Developing communities of practice through community university partnerships. *Planning, Practice and Research, 21*(1), 121–138.

Hart, A., Blincow, D. & Thomas, H. (2007). *Resilient therapy: Working with children and families*. London: Routledge.

Holland, D. & Lave, J. (2009). Social practice theory and the historical production of persons. *Actio: An International Journal of Human Activity Theory, 2*, 1–15.

Hymes, D. (Ed.). (1996). *Ethnography, linguistics, narrative inequality: Towards an understanding of voice*. London: Routledge.

James, A. (2013). *Socialising children*. Basingstoke: Palgrave Macmillan.

Lassiter, L.E. (2005) *The Chicago guide to collaborative ethnography*. Chicago: Chicago University Press.

Lassiter, E. Goodall, H., Campbell E. & Johnson, N. (2004) *The other side of Middletown: Exploring Muncie's African American community*. Washington, DC: Altamira Press.

Leander, K. & Sheehy, M. (2004). *Spatialising literacy research and practice*. New York: Peter Lang.

Pahl, K. (2012). Every object tells a story: Intergenerational stories and objects in the homes of Pakistani heritage families in South Yorkshire. *Home Cultures, 9*(3), 303–328.

Pahl, K. & Pollard, A. (2008). 'Bling—the Asians introduced that to the country': Gold and its value within a group of families of South Asian origin in Yorkshire. *Visual Communication, 7*(2), 170.

Pahl, K. & Pollard, A. (2010). The case of the disappearing object: Narratives and artefacts in homes and a museum exhibition from Pakistani heritage families in South Yorkshire. *Museum and Society, 8*(1), 1–17.

Pahl, K. & Rowsell, J. (2010) *Artifactual literacies: Every object tells a story*. New York: Teachers College Press.

Pahl, K., Pollard, A. & Rafiq, Z. (2009). Changing identities, changing spaces: The Ferham Families exhibition in Rotherham. *Moving Worlds, 9*(2), 80–103.

Pahl, K., Bullivant, D., Escott, H., Hodson, J., Hyatt, D., Hurcombe, M., Pool S. & Steadman-Jones R. (2013). Language as talisman. AHRC Connected Communities Scoping Study. Available at: www.ahrc.ac.uk/Funding-Opportunities/Research-funding/Connected-Communities/Scoping-studies-and-reviews/Documents/Language%20as%20Talisman.pdf

Ricoeur, P. (1980). Narrative time. *Critical Inquiry, 7*(1), 169–190.

Rosowsky, A. (2008). *Heavenly readings: Liturgical literacy in a multilingual context*. Multilingual Matters: Clevedon.

Spradley, J. (1979). *The ethnographic interview*. Belmont, CA: Wadsworth.

Vasudevan, L. (2011). An invitation to unknowing. *Teachers College Record, 113*(6), 1154–1174.

9

REFRAMING READING YOUTH WRITING

Michael Hoechsmann and Naomi Lightman

Few people in this world realize just how powerful the words we use can be. The pen is mightier than the sword, yet few of us speak our minds . . . Next time someone goes on a rant about "those damn gays," consider standing up for those who aren't there to stand up for themselves . . . One thing is certain: By not standing up to be counted, you could be part of that volatile concoction that begins to destroy those around you. And when the flames begin to lick at your own feet, there might not be anyone left to lift you out of the fire.

(S. Trimble, 1998, Young People's Press)

Introduction

In practical terms, it is hard to measure the impact of a youth media experiment in the informal education sector[1] at the time of its occurrence. Most youth-serving media organizations dedicate themselves to the exigencies of the daily requirements for programming while struggling to sustain their funding. Consequently, limited resources are available to undertake a careful chronicling of outcomes, beyond what happens in a three-year funding cycle. This scenario was certainly the case at Young People's Press (YPP), a project that the two of us were involved with at the turn of the century, one as educator and editor, and the other as youth participant.

Yet youth media organizations must make claims about potential outcomes, such as capacity building and empowerment, in order to justify their existence to funders and other community organizations. Often, the primary evidence available is the material artifacts produced by participating youth. One such sampling of youth voice is the above quote from a former YPP author, which has all of the characteristics that are valued by mentors/educators in the youth-serving informal education sector: a critical, outspoken stance towards troubling social justice issues; a grounded sense of self in relation to others; an understanding of the social change potential of writing; and an insistence on ongoing civic engagement. Read statically, as a synchronic snapshot of a young journalist swept up in the euphoria of youth, this quote appears to prove that informal education projects in media and journalism provoke the results to which they lay claim. Yet questions remain, and they have plagued us in the intervening years since our involvement with YPP. Do projects that seek to enable and empower youth for a lifetime of citizenship engagement truly have a profound long-term impact on their participants?

Given the opportunity to revisit the YPP experience we shared many years ago, we decided to convene a small gathering of former YPP journalists to 'check in' with them. We hoped to see whether and how their involvement in YPP had influenced their varied life pathways. We also took the opportunity to review some research—mainly content and discourse analyses of YPP news articles—that Michael had conducted in the intervening years since his involvement at YPP and to test some of his claims on the group of former youth journalists. There are three points of departure to this chapter, one we will call *the backstory*, another *the reading*, and the third *the revisiting*.

1. *The backstory*—Young People's Press (YPP) was a non-profit Canadian national news agency for youth aged 14–24, that existed from 1995 to 2005 and was at its zenith in a two-year period between 1997 and 1999 when the organization provided roughly two pages of content on a weekly basis to 'young street,' a youth-oriented section of *The Toronto Star*, Canada's largest circulation newspaper. Naomi came to YPP in September 2000, as a sixteen-year-old work-study student from a local high school. Michael spent four postdoctoral years (1998–2002) working as YPP's Director of Education.

2. *The reading*—Reading Youth Writing is the title of a co-authored book (Hoechsmann & Low, 2008) that chronicles and analyzes youth 'voice' across a variety of media. In it, Michael makes some claims that are summarized in this chapter (below). The conceptual heuristic suggested by *Reading Youth Writing* was intended to tilt the literacy discussion from a focus on the technology of writing to an engagement with the editorial content of youth authorship across modalities. The other function of the heuristic, described above and drawn upon in this account, is to parse reading, youth and writing as discrete units of analysis: *reading* in terms of the content and voice of youth writing, *youth* in terms of the meaning of being a young person both then and now, as well as an analysis of the economic and societal factors that have shaped and altered the external conditions in which youth document their lived experiences, and *writing* in terms of the medium itself, deciphering how

youth cultural production has changed and evolved over the past two decades with the introduction or evolution of new technologies.

3. *The revisiting*—a small group of five former YPP journalists, all of whom had contributed several articles during their time with YPP, gathered in Fall 2013. Our revisiting involved a focused roundtable dialogue on youth journalism, the value of youth voice, the impact of the cultural and technological changes of the intervening period and the stories of the life pathways of the various participants. The meeting took place at the Centre for Social Innovation, a meeting space and café in Toronto's trendy Annex neighborhood. The intention of the revisit was to test the hypothesis that sustained participation in a project like YPP,[2] which promises capacity building and empowerment, leads to future citizenship engagement.

The Backstory

Young People's Press (YPP) was a small, grassroots, youth-serving non-profit organization, started in 1995 by the Canadian Center for Social Justice and inspired by *Children's Express*, an American and UK-based news agency that involved children and teenagers in the production of news content. During its tenure, YPP published copy written by youth, 14–24, in several major Canadian newspapers— including regular columns and features in the *Halifax Chronicle Herald* and *The Toronto Star*—and through newswire services such as Scripps Howard in the US and CanWest in Canada.

YPP was founded on the idealistic premise that if youth were given the means to have a voice in the public sphere, that an authentic outpouring of youth expression would result. The motto of YPP was 'What's on your mind?' and the mandate was to empower young people through capacity building and publication in mainstream newspapers. In practice, this meant that the organization was necessarily structured as a nontraditional newswire service, one that would recruit 'journalists' based on their access to a 'story' and then instruct and guide the youth on how to write within a news genre. Many of the writers whose stories were disseminated by YPP were one-timers who attended a workshop or responded to a call for publication. Others, including the individuals we assembled for this revisiting, took the opportunity to write several articles over a longer period of time. While an underlying goal of the organization was to contribute to the development of forms of participatory democracy for youth who otherwise might not have been able to find their 'voice,' at the time it was unclear if the underlying inequalities between the mostly white and male, adult editors and the young writers were substantially upended. Given the collaborative nature of workplace writing, YPP editors would sometimes substantially rewrite youth articles before publication, and, even if this were intended as a pedagogic intervention, the follow-through teachable moment was not always forthcoming.

The educational component of the organization included the creation of teaching materials, particularly the YPP Writer's Guide, the provision of writing workshops for young people, and just-in-time instruction and editing with youth in the process of researching or drafting a story.[3] Despite some reliance on 'middle-class kids with modems' to provide regular copy for the weekly columns and features, the majority of the outreach and education efforts of YPP were targeted to socially, culturally and economically marginalized youth. The targeted outreach was primarily the result of the desires and socio-political aspirations of YPP staff members who fashioned themselves as streetwise activists and who were not only willing to go the extra distance to make the project as inclusive as possible, but who ascribed much of the short- and long-term success of YPP to the number of marginalized young people who could be published and hence given a voice. These efforts brought YPP editors and educators to mainstream high schools, youth organizations and community centers during their recruitment and outreach, but also to insurgent spaces where they would work with inner city homeless youth, queer youth collectives, First Nations youth in urban and reserve contexts, Black youth in an Afrocentric summer camp in Toronto's suburbs, and incarcerated youth in a detention center.

According to the *Ryerson Review of Journalism (RRJ)*, "young street . . . represented a defining moment for YPP—an organization that was founded in late 1995 with the laudable aim of engaging young people in social and political issues" (Tam, 2002). The same article details how the use of YPP copy in the 'young street' section was curtailed in 2000 by a new editor at *The Star* due to a perceived lack of quality in the content. "It was . . . becoming difficult for YPP to provide copy every week because many of its writers were high school students, and it was becoming a burden for them. I also found that the stories were of a similar genre, of a similar idea, and were all starting to sound the same" (Lesley Ciarula Taylor, quoted in Tam, 2002).

YPP's final cover article prior to being terminated as the major provider of content for the 'young street' section was a critical feature story on HIV/AIDS education and support programs within Toronto's racialized minority communities. The following week's 'youth' feature was an adult staff writer's piece about the relative legitimacy of unauthorized Pokemon cards. Subsequent to this change, the 'young street' section, the name of which was changed six months later to *Boom!*, offered an eclectic and meandering range of articles primarily written by adult *Toronto Star* staff writers.

The argument that the quality of the youth-written copy was not up to par does not wash in the face of reader-response and audience research, which demonstrates that assumptions are made about authors based on their experiences and expertise. The *RRJ* quotes Hoechsmann, stating that 'people have a different perspective when they read articles written by young people.' In other words, the expectations made on youth authors are different from those made of older industry hacks. The space afforded by 'young street' to give youth a voice in a profound, far-reaching, and protracted manner remains an interesting social experiment that demonstrates a viable model for citizenship journalism in the era before participatory culture became mainstreamed. The totality of the youth views expressed, as described in the 'reading' section below, demonstrates some interesting patterns in regards to how young people represent themselves to a public audience when given the opportunity.

In regards to the rationale for the changes to 'young street' away from youth-written content, this likely had more to do with internal demands at *The Toronto Star* to return the pages to staff writers (Tam, 2002) than a discourse on the quality of youth journalism. Yet regardless of the true reason behind the demise of 'young street,' the funding model upon which YPP relied was not sustainable in the long run and the organization subsequently faltered and disbanded in 2005.

The Reading

With over 450,000 paid weekday subscriptions in the late 1990s, *The Toronto Star* had a readership of well over one million people per day. Given this broad audience, many youth were highly motivated to put pen to paper and contribute to the 'young street' section. Their output was expressive of a positive, public advocacy for change. It is difficult to quantify the results of public education, but the 'young street' writing experiment exposed literally millions of readers to youth views, and hundreds of young people were empowered to use newly developed literacy skills to actively participate in the discourses of the public sphere. Youth who had never dreamed they could publish a piece of writing in a major Canadian newspaper have now done so with YPP's help, and some were subsequently emboldened to pursue a life of writing.

A content analysis of the articles published in *The Toronto Star* over the almost two-year period in which YPP delivered the 'young street' content demonstrates two dominant themes: one related to personal growth and social change, and the other focusing on relationships with others. Over the 22-month period of direct collaboration with *The Toronto Star*, YPP published 297 youth-written articles in the 'young street' section, in addition to the weekly Very Cool (pop culture: events and 'stuff') and Confidentially Yours (advice) columns. A principal journalistic genre taught at YPP was first-person opinion-editorial writing, a style of expression that seemed to correspond well to how young people articulate their beliefs. These pieces were published in a weekly Youthbeat column in *The Toronto Star* and also on a series of e-zines published by the organization.

Given that YPP's motto for youth authorship was the wide-open phrase 'What's on your mind?' these findings present an interesting perspective of youth attitudes and views in diverse, multicultural Toronto at the turn of the last century. The main issues identified, examined, and recorded by youth at YPP were education (66), bias towards youth (63), activism (60), global and social consciousness (60), multiculturalism and diversity (59), racism (57), popular culture and mass media

(45), sexuality (41), body image (38), peers and peer pressure (31), and voluntarism (31). Of course, there is some reported overlap between these categories, particularly in the social change/consciousness and diversity/racism themes. But the results are significant in their generalized focus on the negotiations of self and group identity between self (body image, sexuality, education and voluntarism) and other (social change/consciousness, diversity/racism, voluntarism and inter-generational bias). Another overarching theme in YPP's copy was an analysis of the role of media/pop culture, education, and intergenerational misunder-standing in overdetermining youth experiences. The other themes that emerged in YPP content, albeit in smaller numbers, were the familiar ones commonly identified in efforts by adults to chronicle youth experiences: crime/law (24), home/family (21), youth subcultures (19), low-income realities (19), consumerism (17), drugs (16), and work (15). That these themes were registered by youth is not surprising, but their relatively lower prominence indicates that young people do not readily adopt the 'frames' through which adult journalists view their lived realities.

In order to make the representation of youth 'voice' as inclusive as possible, YPP put effort into reaching out to racialized minority, Aboriginal, street, and LGBT youth. Most significant was the participation of youth representing Canada's racial and cultural diversity in the cadre of writers. A full 47 percent of the bylines of YPP articles published in *The Toronto Star* during this period, for example, were from racialized minority and Aboriginal youth, a fact not lost on the Canadian Race Relations Foundation, which presented YPP with an Award of Distinction in 2001. These results were exemplary in a period when the Ryerson Department of Journalism found that the representation of minorities in Canadian newsrooms hovered at about 3.4 percent (Miller & Caron, 2004). YPP's achievements in this realm were, to an extent, the result of focused outreach. However, they also demonstrate that young people of racialized backgrounds were ready for social change; given the chance to shake the status quo and contribute to public discourse through mainstream media contribution, many seized the opportunity. A considerable number of the articles went far beyond simple platitudes of cross-cultural celebration; recurring themes included cultural hybridity, histories of race relations, and contradictions at the heart of Canadian multiculturalism.

The capacity building structured into the experience for youth contributors was one both of professional development in journalism and broader citizenship engagement in general. Of those who did not continue formally in the field of journalism, many left YPP with the knowledge that they could return to journal-istic writing as occasional contributors and use writing as a medium to impact the world around them. Yet like many non-profits, YPP organized its activities around funding opportunities from corporate and government agencies and foundations that normally focused on annual outcomes. This topsy-turvy method of administering an organization favored data-collection models predicated on publication output, not on writer empowerment. Unfortunately, the organization did not set up longitudinal forms of data mining that could monitor the activities of YPP writers once they had left the organization; only anecdotal evidence remains of how this experience affected the lives of the participating youth writers. The occasion of this revisiting allows us to catch a glimpse of how this early experience in citizenship journalism affected the lives of some of the participants, to explore whether YPP changed those who became deeply involved, or whether those participants were already on a predetermined path.

The Revisiting

In convening our small group of YPP writers, we settled on a selection process based on a convenience sample of former YPPers who had published at least three pieces in *The Toronto Star* and who still lived in or near Toronto. Our email query yielded a 33 percent response rate. We noted the likelihood that the individuals who self-selected to participate were motivated to contribute because they had had positive experiences at YPP, biasing our discussion towards those whose impressions were favorable. However, as the topics for reflection were situated firmly in the past, we were less concerned about barriers to participation or potential repercussions for respondents. While we initially considered doing in-depth individual interviews with each respondent, we ultimately settled on using a focus group format. We reasoned that despite any potential drawbacks in terms of anonymity or distinctiveness of responses, a more dialogic methodology would facilitate comparisons between participants and group reflection and enrich the overall data collected (Kvale, 1996).

The participants of our revisiting were Naomi (the co-author of this chapter and a doctoral student at the Ontario Institute for Studies in Education/University of Toronto [OISE/UT]), Shellene (a journalism graduate who is a Communications Specialist in the corporate sector and has occasionally maintained a blog), Kathy (an MFA graduate with a day job as an administrative assistant and a thriving vocation as a creative writer), Shaun (a school trustee with the Toronto District School Board and a doctoral student at OISE/UT), Kirk (a journalism graduate, and a B.Ed. and M.Ed. graduate who presently works as a high school history teacher), and Michael (co-author of this chapter, OISE/UT Ph.D., university professor and occasional op-ed writer).

Youth Voice

It is not surprising in a group of former youth journalists that strong opinions were expressed about the importance of youth voice and its generalized lack in public discourse. Kathy put it most starkly: 'No one really gives a sh*t about what youth have to say unless they are marketing something to them. They don't care about issues that youth are actually facing or giving them a forum to explore those issues.' Shellene pointed out that there is a common misconception embedded into journalistic practice, that interviewing youth, or members of racialized communities, functions as inclusion:

> A lot of people who are not youth believe that they can write from the youth perspective, just as a lot of people from outside of racialized communities feel they can write from that perspective. But this is ultimately not inclusive. They [outsiders] think that talking to someone [from a different community] is sufficient. But having people who are from these different communities actually participating in creating the content that goes in the newspaper is so different. It is so much more engaging to have a young black man write about the issues a young black man faces, rather than someone else ask this young black man what the issues are and write it from their own perspective.

There was also a consensus in our discussion that YPP had allowed participants to write from our own lived experiences. Shaun pointed out that youth involvement could be seen as volatile or even threatening to mainstream discourse, as opposed to relying on traditional journalists to portray youth from a so-called 'adult perspective':

> [YPP] was young people talking about issues that really mattered to them and that they could relate to and talk about. Maybe that's dangerous to the status quo because you are putting issues out there that make people uncomfortable and not necessarily the type of things that the dominant [groups] would like to hear about.

Kirk emphasized that YPP had provided him with a space to give voice to his existing critiques about society's treatment of young (and racialized) peoples:

> I felt that if I went directly into a mainstream media outlet, I would not have had the leeway or the freedom to discuss the ideas that I was able to at YPP. And also the manner in which I could discuss them would not have been possible at a mainstream news agency.

Shaun stated that he wasn't looking to be a writer when he was connected to YPP. Instead, he viewed journalism as a vehicle to give expression to his preexisting concerns about social justice issues and anti-racist activism and disseminate them to a broader audience in an accessible format. Shaun's most memorable article addressed the local debate within the Toronto School Board on formal anti-racist policy. He presented a perspective focusing on the intersectionalities of oppression,[4] or 'double-disadvantage' experienced by some young people, a forward-thinking concept at that time:

The piece that I was most proud of was called 'Toronto School Board equity policy on fire.' It was the first piece that came out at the time talking about the provincial policy that [Ontario] school boards had created focusing on equity. The equity policy was talking about race and culture in the absence of analysis of gender, class, sexuality and all those others things. I remember that piece coming out and the chair of the school board writing me a letter. I remember the change that came out of the conversation because they needed to reconceptualize [the policy]. And, of course, there were many challenges, like religious leaders saying 'no, you shouldn't be talking about sexuality.' So, in that context, it was a very big thing that we now all take for granted—the idea that equity doesn't just mean race. And I don't think many people would dispute that today.

Kirk recalled being drawn to YPP as a youth of colour with a desire to be heard and to have a social impact. He said that his primary identity centered on being a young, black male in a white dominant society, and that he had an urgency to speak his own truth. Among various pieces he wrote at YPP was a feature article entitled 'Stereotypes of black youth and the police.' While Kirk stated he wouldn't write the article in exactly the same way today, in his opinion, the underlying issue about a lack of understanding between Black youth and police has not changed. He illustrated the relevance of his article by drawing a parallel to a recent police shooting in the Greater Toronto area:

It was so tragic because I felt we had dealt with these issues in my article. We had had this conversation about Black youth and the police and the lack of relationship that we have. And now this incident happens when a young nineteen-year-old gets nine shots for no apparent reason. And so the question is, where is the young person's voice that can give testimony to the authenticity of the protest that erupted downtown? We don't see young people actually discussing these things in the manner that YPP did. And I felt that if YPP was around now it would be an amazing time for young people to echo the sentiments that they feel, not just the way they do it in the streets, but in the way they write about these things.

The participants emphasized that there is a value to enabling youth voice on the central issues of the day, but that this does not emerge from within a vacuum. Perhaps the failure of a major newspaper to recognize that generating youth voice requires an educational involvement and respectful dialogue with young people is reflective of the absence of an understanding of the public pedagogy of YPP. Shaun stated that he would not have been able to write journalistically without the mentorship of YPP editors:

I would not have had a clue how to start. They just guided me along, like 'maybe that opening paragraph needs some work' and I would not have understood that otherwise. Knowing I had to get x, y, z in the 600 word limit, I think those are the tips that helped me become a better writer ... with YPP I knew who I could talk to to get that guidance and mentorship.

Our interview group emphasized the unique nature of the YPP writing process: they recalled working with editors who were focused specifically on youth contributors and youth content, and who advocated creative forms of writing output through the 'youthbeat,' along with providing skills, guidance, and friendship along the way. Generally, our research participants agreed that working with YPP gave them a first taste of the thrill of seeing their name in print and allowed them to access audiences outside of their immediate community. Kathy put it this way:

> There is something legitimizing about an institution like *The Toronto Star* saying your voice matters and it is important to our readership. There is something about that. And I still probably get the same high that I got back then every time I publish a piece.

For our focus group participants, it was a surprise to learn that *The Toronto Star* had terminated its relationship with Young People's Press due to an assertion that the quality of the copy was not up to par. Kathy acknowledged that the newspaper may have internal standards on quality, but said that she thought it was 'narrow minded' not to recognize 'what it was that YPP was doing and the important role it was filling.' For Shaun, the particular role of YPP was to highlight the unique value of youth voice: 'For me, there was a certain sense of authenticity and I think that is what is attractive about this, because it was young people who are caring about these issues and writing about these issues themselves.'

Youth Voice 2.0?

There is an irony to the assertion that there may be less youth voice in the Web 2.0 era of digital literacies and cultural participation than in the yesteryear of top-down hegemonic and homogenous mass-media production. Our discussions subsequently shifted to an analysis of the changing technologies of communication, which have opened up new venues and forums for youth expression and the considerable hype about lowered barriers to writing and sharing content that has been attributed to forums such as blogs, podcasts, YouTube, Twitter, and so on.

144 Michael Hoechsmann and Naomi Lightman

Despite all these technological innovations, Naomi stated that the audience today for most youth content is much diminished without access to high circulation publication venues:

> I think the problem with youth publishing solely in blogs and specialized media outlets is that you are preaching to the choir. The people who are reading it are your friends or community members, that sort of thing. And what I see as being most powerful about YPP, both for the writers and the readers, was that it was read by the whole of Toronto—everyone reads *The Toronto Star*. So it was not just young people, it was not just white people, it was all different types of people. And I think that kind of discourse has been shut down from mainstream media sources under the excuse that now there are blogs, that you can go write a little thing on the Internet that no one will ever read.

Kirk echoed this sentiment, stating that the fragmenting of audiences has led to diminished social space for conversations between youth and adults, and other disparate groups about current events. He identified numerous current issues, including the corporatization of campuses and tuition increases across Canada, as well as the gentrification of low-income neighborhoods, as areas where a genuine youth perspective is missing from the dialogue:

> There are so many issues right now that I feel need to be in the conversation of [the] media that we would have had the opportunity to discuss with YPP . . . And I feel like online forums do not capture that conversation as well as a newspaper does—the broad range of content and how seriously people take newspapers.

Recognizing the new doors opened by prosumer and participatory culture, Shellene took a contrasting perspective and emphasized the possibilities for diverse authorship on issues related to specific communities inherent in Web 2.0:

> I think that is beneficial to young people today. They don't have to wait for the editor of *The Toronto Star* to say 'yes, your writing is good enough to be in our paper.' They can say 'screw *The Toronto Star*. If you don't want to put my stuff in your newspaper that is fine, I am going to start my own thing and I am going to promote writing online, promote my own podcast, whatever. I am going to try to build my own following that way . . .' You can just do your own thing now, which I think is extremely powerful for young people or anybody who wants to share what they have.

While the mainstream media may be increasingly closed off to youth perspectives, Shellene suggested that young people are now free to develop and disseminate the content they want without having to negotiate the boundaries of mainstream press outlets: 'You cannot discount the importance of controlling your own content and [using] your own media. And how that is becoming more and more accessible to youth.'

As a cautionary note on the free-wheeling blogosphere, Kathy emphasized that the process of receiving feedback and vetting from editors is something she values highly in her own writing, and that this often gets omitted in instantaneous production of Web media.

> I do think there is something [exciting] about people creating opportunities for themselves and having a computer to plug in and express themselves. [But] there is also something to be said about having writers and journalists that have a certain ethical professional responsibility to express themselves accurately and well. I am at that point where there is not much creative writing I would put out without an editor because I want it to be edited, I want to know that it is good before I have people read it . . . I do not want to put out a zine anymore; I really want somebody to be putting it through some sort of process. But there's room for both, there is space for both. And I think both are important.

Again, the absence of a pedagogical intervention to help shape youth voice was raised as a shortcoming in models of youth voice not supported and encouraged by more experienced adult educators and editors. These writers who had experienced the potentials of journalism to mass audiences prior to the blow-up of the blogosphere, and under the direct guidance and tutelage of more seasoned editors and educators, seemed to have a biased and uniform skepticism to the potential of the citizen blogger. That said, the editorial freedom afforded to them by YPP went unmatched in the professional journalism contexts that some of them engaged in after YPP.

Biographies and Life Pathways

In regards to the influence that the YPP experience had on our lives and whether it helped determine our life pathways, it was clear that writing remains part of the connective tissue of all the focus group participants' lives. Yet interestingly enough, while some YPP veterans dot the Canadian mediascape, none of the group we interviewed ended up working in formal journalism. While YPP was not set up to provide vocational training, it did promise 'capacity development' and, indeed, many participants developed admissions portfolios for post-secondary journalism programs while at YPP. That said, it is quite likely that many of those who only came to YPP to get some bylines for their portfolios were already on the road towards a career in journalism. Those who became directly involved in the organization as students, staff, or occasional workshop leaders had a broader, less vocational, experience that impacted their lives in terms of leaving a residual desire to seek out opportunities to have a voice and make a social impact, rather than landing a job in a highly conflicted newsroom. A case in point is that for Shellene, Kirk, and Naomi, who all spent time as interns and employees in professional newsrooms, there was a sense that YPP may have 'spoiled' them to the realities of 'real' news work in highly competitive environments, with transient working conditions and little agency to determine the subject matter of one's stories. Shellene made the decision to leave journalism after experiencing the siren-chasing realities of newsgathering at a major newspaper:

> I had a very idealized notion of what journalism would be, about writing great stories. When I started a job at the [newspaper], I realized it was not that at all. It was about spitting out who had been murdered, or the fire that happened that night. And that was it. They run you around the city, make you smell dead bodies, and call people about their children who have died. And you have to have a special personality or character to be able to do that for longer than a year, and that was not the personality or character that I had.

In Naomi's experience, working as an intern at an alternative weekly newspaper, she struggled with the growing trend towards lifestyle journalism, 'a focus on film, art, food, and not on news,' coupled with a stressful, highly controlled environment:

> I saw news as a vehicle for social justice and engagement, and that wasn't what it was about, so I kind of got jaded, I thought 'this is not what I want journalism to be.' And all the editors were extremely stressed out. I also got the sense that it was a very precarious lifestyle. All the writers were writing piece to piece and I guess had a realization that writing is important to me, but I don't want to be bossed around.

Of the three, Kirk had the most varied experiences in journalistic contexts, having worked in TV, radio, and print media. He too saw some of the industry limitations to involvement in 'quality journalism,' and upholding preexisting 'standards about how to cover or tell stories.' Ultimately, this led him back to seeing the value of the style of editorial writing practiced by YPP in the Youthbeat column, and to teaching his students to write and speak for publication or broadcast:

> I was unsettled by some of my [journalistic] experiences. But these led me towards looking back at editorial writing and for me today that is still and will always be a part of my life in terms of being able to echo, explain, and express experiences and ideas that I feel are important to me and to a lot of other people. In the meantime, I continue to teach students about writing

and writing structure, and also how they can become involved in ways that they may not have imagined before—having their voices heard and seeing/hearing themselves be published or broadcast. I feel that is what I can contribute to the idea of journalism even in the education field.

Kirk and Naomi continue to publish occasional articles in the alternative press. Shellene has had two blogs up and running at different times—one on current affairs and the other on Black hair.

Shaun, who works as a trustee for the Toronto District School Board while pursuing a doctorate in education, said that he never really saw himself becoming a professional writer. He wrote as a means to express himself about the social justice issues he was passionate about, and YPP was a critical asset in providing the skillset and confidence to write about those issues.

For me, it was never about being a writer. I did the writing because I was passionate about certain issues, social issues. YPP gave me the ability to use it as a vehicle to talk about those issues and I think what I took away from it . . . was that writing is a powerful vehicle. I knew that no matter what I ended up doing, it would be a skill that was developed through working with YPP. I am doing the same thing now, but I am doing it in a different venue. I may not be necessarily writing, but I am speaking out on things [that matter to me]. That ties back to the confidence that I got from writing through YPP and understanding that I could make change and reach out to other people.

Kathy, who is now a fiction author, stated that she 'was never somebody with a grand master plan. I wanted to do the kind of journalism like I was doing then and was interested in.' While journalistic writing is no longer her chosen vehicle of expression, the type of writing environment that was nurtured at YPP, through writing workshops and peer mentorships, is something she is pursuing in her professional life.

The process of revisiting the YPP experiment through the filter of these five participants' experiences paints a very rosy picture. What struck us most about this group of young adults is how profoundly impacted each of them had been by the YPP experience. Extrapolating from these findings is difficult, given that the scale of the project they were involved with was unusual. Even though YPP was a tiny non-profit organization, the publication vehicle of *The Toronto Star* disseminated the articles written by these former youth journalists to well over one million readers at a time and gave their words the authenticating seal of Canada's largest circulation daily newspaper. Given that the selection criteria we used to seek these participants to the revisiting was a minimum of three published articles in *The Toronto Star*, we drew on a select group of former youth journalists who had been blessed with an opportunity most youth will never get, so it is not surprising that they retain positive memories and that the experience had an

148 Michael Hoechsmann and Naomi Lightman

important impact on their lives. Nonetheless, what this revisiting demonstrates to us is that the YPP experiment had wings beyond our imagination, and that it did indeed leave an indelible mark on its participants that involved a mix of skill and will, a mix of learned techniques and practices, and an empowered sense of potential engagement as social actors. While some youth empowerment projects and initiatives will fall short of their proposed outcomes, our revisiting of the YPP project is a powerful reminder of the potential that these projects in the informal education sector can offer.

Notes

1. We use the phrase 'youth media experiment in the informal education sector' to describe a variety of community-based pedagogical projects oriented towards youth and media production that tend to be contextual and contingent. That we use the term 'experiment' refers to the unfortunate reality that many of these projects come and go based on funding windows and facilitators transitioning to other (often better paid) opportunities.
2. Young People's Press is now defunct, but this acronym has new life in the MacArthur Foundation's Youth Participatory Politics, available at: http://ypp.dmlcentral.net/, a project not dissimilar to our YPP in terms of youth voice and citizenship engagement.
3. An account of the pedagogical challenges faced, and strategies used, by YPP editors and educators can be found in M. Hoechsmann, *Teaching Media Writing* (2008), available at: http://newlits.wikispaces.com/Teaching+Media+Writing. The YPP Writer's Guide, a five-part curriculum for youth writers, is included as a series of attachments to this article.
4. Simian (2007) defines *intersectionality* as "an analytical tool that rejects the separability of identity categories, as it recognizes the heterogeneity of various race-sex groups" (p. 265).

References

Hoechsmann, M. (2008). From the classroom to the newsroom: Teaching media writing. *New literacies: A professional development wiki for educators*. Developed under the aegis of the Improving Teacher Quality Project (ITQP), a federally funded partnership between Montclair State University and East Orange School District, New Jersey.

Hoechsmann, M. & Low, B. E. (2008). *Reading youth writing: "New" literacies, cultural studies and education*. New York: Peter Lang.

Kvale, S. (1996). *InterViews: An introduction to qualitative reseach interviewing*. Thousand Oaks, CA: Sage Publications.

Miller, J. & Caron, C. (2004). Who's telling the news? Race and gender representation in Canada's daily newsrooms (online). *Diversity Watch*. Available at: www.diversitywatch. ryerson.ca/home_miller_2004report.htm#Intro

Simian, E. M. (2007). Doing intersectionality research: From conceptual issues to practical examples. *Politics & Gender, 3*, 264–271.

Tam, K. (2002). Growing pains: The scoop on Young People's Press, a wire service for kids that has dreams of playing with the big boys (online). *Ryerson Review of Journalism*. Available at: www.rrj.ca/m3760/

Trimble, Sarah (1998). Taking a stand isn't cool among teenagers. *The Toronto Star*, C 1–2.

10

A STEADFAST REVISIT

Keeping with Tradition, in a Different Space and Time

Jennifer Rowsell

Introduction

More than 10 years have passed since I first met Dorothy Rajaratnam in a *School and Society* class during her teacher preparation year. I remember Dorothy well; she sat at the front and side of a windowless room on the fourth floor of the OISE/UT building in Toronto looking alert and keen. This could well be how I cast my memory of her having got to know her over the years. To be sure, Dorothy stood out from the 70 other students as earnest and as an exemplary student—someone who arrived to class early, handed in assignments ahead of time, and helped others. But, again, that is a reality that I have crafted after getting to know her and her story.

During her second semester in the teacher education program, I selected her as a participant in a research study on how beginning teachers mediate their identities with pedagogy and educational theory. More specifically, I investigated how Dorothy embedded different parts of her identity, or drawing on Bourdieu (1991), her habitus, as an unfolding of her history and background, into pedagogic artifacts such as lesson plans, classroom designs, and planning documents. The modest study on teacher identity mediation was one of the first research studies that I conducted on my own as a newly minted Ph.D. Our small-scale study resulted in a chapter in an edited volume and part of a refereed journal article (Rowsell & Rajaratnam, 2005; Rowsell & Pahl, 2007).

I have kept in touch with Dorothy over the years, so as much as for practical reasons I thought of her when I started out on my revisit (see Introduction to this volume). Within the broader ambit of revisits, this particular revisit reveals some larger issues and tensions within education and teacher education. In the end, what became clear from my revisit experience with Dorothy is that for all

150 Jennifer Rowsell

of the inclusion work and radical aspirations[1] of teacher education research over the past decade—to incorporate and build on cultures, to differentiate instruction, to adopt inclusive approaches to student learning and backgrounds, there continues to be a resilience to schooling and education.

In this chapter, I take a life history approach (Goodson & Sikes, 2001) to Dorothy's revisit to analyze how Dorothy's account of her life and history disguise resilience and constancy of a teacher's philosophy and pedagogy. The chapter follows in four sections. The first section frames life history work and how I have applied it to my revisit with Dorothy Rajaratnam; the second section tells Dorothy's story; the third section provides interview and artifactual data to illustrate a life history approach; the fourth and final section steps back to broader implications of such work for research.

Adopting a Life History Perspective

Life history research rests on the notion that personal histories spill into different areas of our lives. As an approach to conducting research, a life history perspective (Goodson & Sikes, 2001) analyzes how past perceptions, memories, relationships inform the way that we conduct our lives. Life history researchers are attuned to the phrases, words, and thoughts that research participants use and how these linguistic and discursive choices relate to an overall life story. What clearly plays into a life history account is the reflexivity of the researcher who retells participant stories thereby inflecting their own history, perceptions, and discourses into the story. It therefore follows that any researcher who adopts a life history perspective would believe that there are always multiple realities in-play.

Another aspect of a life history perspective I find particularly compelling is the concept that there is a social script. By social script, I mean that we are born into particular circumstances and certain trajectories unfold from these circumstances as we come of age and become adults. Goodson and Sikes (2001) talk about the 'social script of expectations,' which can be played out quite differently for different people. As they eloquently phrase it,

> for the rich white male, the social script written before birth . . . may prove acceptable and will be lived and storied as planned. For those of other class, race, and gender, the script that is written by society will be more oppressive, and the life may be lived as an attempt to deconstruct the social script.
>
> (p. 61)

Applied to Dorothy's revisit, there is a social script embedded within her comments, sedimented within her artifacts (Rowsell & Pahl, 2007), inscribed in her life choices. By sedimented, I am referring to work with Kate Pahl in which we analyze parts of identity that become embedded into multimodal artifacts. Dorothy's social script harks back to a British schooling in Sri Lanka and to life choices and decisions that she has made along the way that have shaped her, quite formatively. Indeed, Goodson and Sikes speak of individuals who wittingly or unwittingly adopt a social script and equally, individuals who actively contradict or disrupt social scripts. It is precisely for this reason that Goodson and Sikes develop a distinction between life *stories* and life *histories* (my italics). The life story is "the story we narrate" (p. 62) and the life history is collaboratively constructed by a life storyteller and the researcher (p. 62). The distinction here rests on locating "a life story as it operates in particular historical circumstances" (p. 62). As a result, what frequently happens is that life histories reframe life stories—always bearing in mind that it is from a researcher optic (with all of her attendant subjectivities). In my efforts to tell Dorothy's life story, or at least parts of it, I implicate myself and my life story—that is, I realize looking back that I wanted and still want to tell a certain story about Dorothy based on the way that I see her and the kinds of pedagogy that I wanted to encourage, even promulgate in my teacher education work.

Individuals tell stories using narrative forms that are tacit, naturalized and that reveal ties to beliefs, values, and templates. Recounting events and stories carries with it complex interrelationships. Looking ahead to the Dorothy revisit, there is a resemblance between the routines and rites that she engaged in as a student many years ago in Sri Lanka and those that she appropriates now as a primary school teacher. In choosing to describe her contemporary classroom structures with similar phrases and concepts that she discussed when she talked about her childhood classroom, Dorothy closes off other interpretations. Through dialogues and emails with Dorothy over the past 2 years, she has emphasized certain experiences and not others. As Goodson and Sikes express it, "what is left out can be as significant and telling as what is included" (Goodson & Sikes, 2001, p. 46). Nonetheless, I should qualify that what I report on is by no means neutral because the telling of it involves aspects of my own life story. For example, there are choices and biases that I make in the following account. Foremost among these is the fact that I am very fond of Dorothy. I have met her family, I have witnessed her daughters become teenagers and I have watched from afar her make a home in Canada and these thoughts and sentiments filter into my retelling of the revisit. I have known three phases of Dorothy's story—the Dorothy before I met her, the Dorothy I met during her teacher preparation, and the Dorothy I revisited. This revisit documents the stories, discourses, and ideologies implicit to these three Dorothys, filtered through my interpretations and renderings of them.

Revisit Background

From my first interactions with Dorothy, what drew me to her and what continues to intrigue me, are the ways in which she steadfastly adheres to her pedagogical roots, despite significant training in 'new,' 'inclusive,' 'differentiated' methods of instruction, the strongest force in her teaching remains the more classic teaching methods that she experienced in Sri Lanka. Educated within a more traditional form of education, Dorothy learned through rote memorization, with basal readers, and by completing worksheets for arithmetic and writing skills.

To conduct the revisit, I met with Dorothy on two occasions and we spent a year emailing back and forth, and during that time she sent me what I call 'artifacts of her practice': lesson plans, newsletters, rubrics, and planning documents. In this way, there was regular correspondence and I became acquainted with her current story in more depth (as I did in 2003 when we conducted a study together and co-wrote a chapter).

Dorothy's Story

It took me a while to ask Dorothy about her childhood. I had a feeling that she moved to Canada under duress and that she was likely hesitant about discussing the move. When we discussed her story during our second interview, she went back to 1983, when there were riots in her hometown of Colombo, Sri Lanka. Dorothy is Tamil, which is a minority in Sri Lanka. In 1980, a civil war broke out in Sri Lanka between the Sinhalese and Tamils, resulting in around 800,000 Tamils leaving Sri Lanka. In 1983, Dorothy and her family were forced to leave their home and move to a refugee camp in the north of Sri Lanka. In November 1992, she moved to Montreal, Canada. Arriving as a young adult, Dorothy worked in a daycare center for a year and then worked part-time in a preschool and after this work experience she completed a Bachelor of Arts in Child Studies at Concordia University. In 1996, Dorothy returned to Sri Lanka, got married, and lived and taught there for 4 years, during which time she had two daughters (who are now grown up and who I met as children during my first fieldwork visit). Shortly after giving birth to Sarah, Dorothy taught grade 3 in a private international school for expatriates. Her daughters, Patricia and Sarah, were 5 and 3 respectively when I first met them and now they are young women.

Fast forward to the present day and Dorothy's story of fleeing a country under duress maps well onto the stories of students in her own classroom. Dorothy has taught in schools in the Toronto area. Known for the numbers of different languages spoken in a city, Toronto is highly multicultural. Presently, Dorothy teaches in a school with a high Sri Lankan population, so there is a great consonance between her childhood and the childhood of her students' parents. Although different because her students are second-generation refugees and immigrant families, Dorothy appreciates what it feels like to immigrate and to negotiate an identity in a new, quite different context.

Dorothy's Pedagogy Then

During our most recent interview, in May 2013, Dorothy spoke at length about her childhood memories of teaching and learning, more than she did during our earlier conversations. There is a nostalgic then-and-now (Comber, this volume) feel to her comments such as 'I grew up in an era and country when these skills [i.e. skills of speaking your mind and cooperative learning] were not cultivated because the main mode of teaching was direct instruction.' Dorothy frequently compares her own quite conservative education with that of her two daughters who experienced cooperative teaching models, student-centered teaching methods, and problem-solving models.

When speaking with her about her early learning memories, she describes vivid memories about learning and recitations from texts such as *Radiant Way*[2] basal readers. During our second interview and then emails after the conversation, Dorothy nostalgically recounted childhood memories of her education:

> I was educated in a Christian, private school and what I truly value are the spiritual teachings and core values of discipline that was instilled in me at a young age . . . A big chunk of my learning, at school, was through direct instruction. This consisted of the teacher explaining the lesson on a blackboard while we took down notes or the teacher would read a lesson from a book. We had workbooks for many subjects (e.g. Mathematics, English grammar) and we would work on many of these work sheets daily.
>
> (May 2013)

There is nothing particularly extraordinary about Dorothy's history in that many individuals have experienced traditional forms of instruction like this, but what piqued my curiosity is how she negotiates a conservative version of teaching with new trends like cooperative models. A second strong theme in Dorothy's teaching is storytelling and reading classic works aloud. When she talks about her secondary years of schooling, Dorothy highlights how much she prized reading classic works like *Great Expectations* and *Jane Eyre*. In her words:

> In hindsight, after having a taste of the educational system in Canada, I can say that the way literacy was taught may have not benefited all the children. For example, the teacher would read aloud a book with us and then give us a comprehension worksheet that contained open and closed questions. However, it was not modeled how to answer open-ended questions that contained inferring and reflective-type answers. In class we used the Radiant Way series and as we got older we read classics such as *Great Expectations* by Charles Dickens, *Jane Eyre* by Charlotte Bronte . . . etc. I clearly remember that some students were not avid readers in class. Perhaps this was because the genre of books chosen did not meet their interest. I wonder whether choosing a wider range of more contemporary authors and non-fiction books would have piqued their interest? Writing seemed a laborious task for some.
>
> (May 2013)

154 Jennifer Rowsell

Dorothy's recollections of her learning as a narrative trajectory relates to Ivor Goodson's conceptions about how individuals narrativize their life stories. In his work, Goodson (2012) speaks of 'describers' and 'elaborators.' Describers "describe what has happened to them in a kind of 'this is who I was way'" (Goodson, 2012, p. 5) and elaborators project stories and describe their life stories as "people who invent a persona and become it" (Goodson, 2012, p. 5). What is helpful about these conceptions of narrativizing stories is how describers and elaborators cast certain images of who one is in the world. To extend the motif of describers, Goodson speaks of 'multiple describers' who are individuals who move from country to country and these travels frame their narrativization or, as Goodson describes it, "their learning was most often focused on their life role but as they changed scripts so they flexibly embraced new learning strategies" (Goodson, 2012, p. 7). Premised on Goodson's definitions, Dorothy strikes me as a multiple describer rather than an elaborator, yet beneath the surface of her descriptive tales there are stubborn consistencies that manifest who she wants to be as a teacher. Reflecting back on the interview excerpt above, Dorothy recollects text genres that she read from primary and secondary school. In the reflection, Dorothy talks about how the canon, as in Shakespeare and Dickens, did not appeal to or interest all readers in her childhood classrooms and that it might have been more beneficial to use contemporary texts. Nevertheless, there is a tokenism about this comment that hints to me at teacher education discourse that she heard during her teacher preparation year at OISE (I know because I heard it too). Dorothy is aware that teaching the canon, on its own, cuts out students who prefer vernacular texts like comics or video games or texts that exhibit more cultural and racial diversity, and, as a result, she injects this discourse into her retrospection. Truth be told, Dorothy loves and prizes the classics, which is evident in informal comments and anecdotes she shared with me about her love of reading classics aloud to her students and further back, to her fond memories of teachers' oral recitations of classics. Here is an instance when I implicate myself in the revisit because, having studied English literature over the course of my undergraduate and graduate years, I have a bias for reading the canon and particularly hearing the canon read aloud—which, of course, plays into my account of Dorothy's story.

Returning to her life story, after attending a private school, Dorothy was refused entry into university because the Sri Lankan system limits entrance on a district basis. This means that a student from a lower income area with the same results will be admitted before a student from a more privileged situation. Dorothy's parents could afford to send her to the local private school, but they did not have the money to send her to a university. Her parents could not afford to send her overseas, and at the same time, Dorothy could not gain entrance into public universities, so Dorothy taught grade 3 in a private school.

Given this lack of formal training, Dorothy cobbled together an understanding of teaching by doing and she 'learned by observing the teacher teach in a very structured and disciplined environment' (June 2003). By structure and discipline, Dorothy learned how to project herself as an authority within pedagogic spaces through teacher talk and through rote methods. Clearly, these sorts of 'old school' practices go against the neoliberal agenda of contemporary teacher education. This teaching experience was foundational for Dorothy in that she forged a strong sense of what her teaching would be and in many ways it remains intact to this day. Even though she valued the 'core values and discipline' of her childhood, when I have observed Dorothy teach, she is not strict and demanding, but instead nurturing with children. Her teaching is a blend of old and new, of discipline thrown in with student-centered, cooperative methods. I think that what I remark today is the continuity of her teaching—that is, what Dorothy believed in 2003 is pretty much the same as she believes in 2013.

Of her own admission, Dorothy's childhood education was antiquated, and contrasted with more progressive theories and pedagogical models that she learned over the course of her teacher education year. Teacher education has attempted to stay ahead of the curve of change, over the past 40 years of scholars (Giroux, 1992; McLaren, 2000) and teacher educators have tried to liberate and emancipate pedagogy to make it more egalitarian, inclusive and differentiated (Freire, 1970). Resulting from such ideological work, there have been more inclusive and critical perspectives on how to teach and learn subjects like literacy. Within the OISE/UT teacher preparation program, Dorothy learned about cooperative learning models, inquiry methods, and community building activities, which she certainly partook in and enjoyed, but ultimately she always reverts back to more traditional methods that she experienced as a child.

Dorothy's Pedagogy Now

Dorothy's school is situated in northeastern Toronto, Clifton Public School (pseudonym), which has won awards over the years for being the most sustainable school in the province of Ontario and as such, it is rooted in its commitment to environmentalism and conservation. There are 700 students in the K-6 public school, 82 percent of whom speak a primary language other than English. Most of the children who go to the school were born in Canada, but their parents come from different countries with a large percentage from Sri Lanka and surrounding Asian countries.

When I reconnected with Dorothy to interview her in 2012 and then again in 2013, there were some notable changes in how she described her pedagogy. To be specific, Dorothy had enough autonomy in the classroom in 2013 to forge a definitive sense of *her* teaching methods and philosophies as opposed to the more contrived, didactic methods and philosophies that she learned during her teacher education year (that she felt beholden to display during our 2003 interview). In 2013, there was far more of a melding together of her childhood learning experiences with her experience teaching in primary classrooms, coupled

156 Jennifer Rowsell

with professional development and her OISE training. As well, Dorothy now feels far more at home in Canada. She is now a Canadian–Sri Lankan and when I met her she was a Sri Lankan living in Canada.

Dorothy's ideal classroom design, as seen in Figure 10.1 (which is modeled on her current classroom) exemplifies a conflation of old and new pedagogies, of cooperative models mixed in with small teacher and student-directed tables. I wanted to replicate parts of our research design from the 2003 study, so I asked Dorothy to draw her ideal classroom today. The interesting exercise for me is to juxtapose Dorothy's 2003 ideal classroom in Figure 10.2 flanked against her ideal classroom in Figure 10.1.

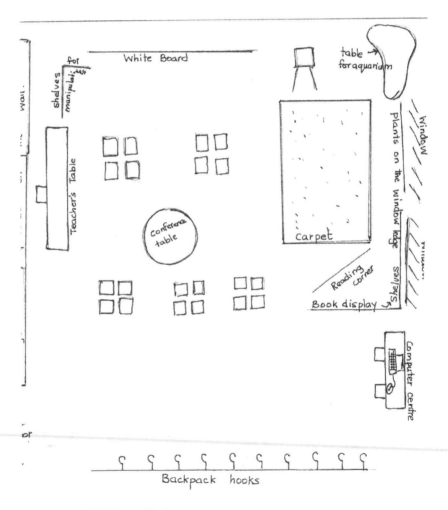

FIGURE 10.1 2013 Room Design

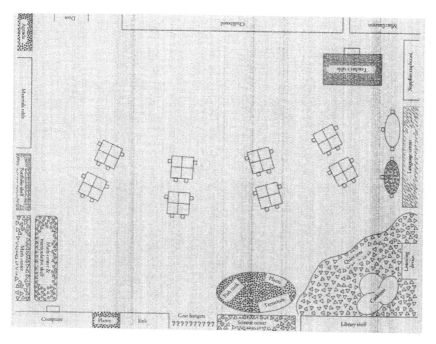

FIGURE 10.2 2003 Room Design

Within both classrooms there are desks in groups, there is a teacher's desk, there is an aquarium, there are shelves for math manipulatives and books, there is a carpeted area for storytime, and there are hooks for students' coats. The only real difference is the greater presence of technology with computers at the back of the room in the 2013 rendition. Both classroom layouts materialize a particular kind of teacher identity that does not really waver—despite major changes in the nature of teaching and learning over the past decade. Some areas have shifted somewhat, but the ethos of the 2003 space is retained in the 2013 space.

The two layouts maintain a continuity of pedagogy tied to authority, tradition, ritual, and the gaze of the teacher. Dorothy is not an authoritarian teacher, but she does adhere to a fairly traditional model of schooling. The location of the teacher's desk in a consistently central position in both layouts, and canonical books and textbooks on shelves beside her desk reinforce her commitment to her early memories of learning with teacher-centered instruction and recitations from the canon. Though she spoke at length about new pedagogies like differentiation and learning styles, the ethos of both spaces are rooted in a more traditional paradigm of teaching that she acquired as a child in Sri Lanka.

As well, the two classroom layouts enact what Jay Lemke describes in his seminal article *Across the Scales of Time* as *heterochrony*: "in which a long timescale process produces an effect in a much shorter timescale activity" (Lemke, 2000, p. 8).

158 Jennifer Rowsell

A decade has passed, actually 17 years have passed since Dorothy started teaching in Sri Lanka (in 1996), and the spatial patterning of her teaching methods are manifest within her idealized classroom design. Evidence of heterochrony can be seen with a longer timescale connected with a forum for storytelling (carpeted area with pillows and shelves of classic books); an aquarium connected to the fertile nature that she grew up with (and that she talked about in her 2003 interview and later in her 2012 interview); teacher-directed instruction through the white board and teacher's desk separated out from student groupings that directly impacts the social activities of learning and thinking. In fact, there are pieces of different timescales etched into these classroom designs.

Shifts in Dorothy's Teaching

With all of this said, there have been some changes over 10 years. A noted change in Dorothy's teaching is a steady realization that there is a difference between *performing* and *understanding*. What she has noticed over the years is that 'students perform well on direct questions, but they perform poorly on the open-ended, critical questions' (March 2012). The irony about this observation is that with the ascendance and continued popularity of inquiry-based learning in pedagogy, one would assume that students flourish with open-ended and critical questions, but Dorothy's 'steady realization' that students perform better on direct questions signals her own deeply felt convictions about more classic methods like direct questions and correct responses. It is precisely these types of responses that led me to conclude that longer timescales inflect her pedagogy.

Another shift in Dorothy's teaching over the years has been how much she foregrounds her culture, especially given the consonance between her culture and the cultural backgrounds of her students. Dorothy has always worked in multi-ethnic, multicultural schools in the Toronto area, but she has never had a teaching situation with quite as much similarity between her background and her students' backgrounds. In our 2012 and 2013 interviews, Dorothy talked about the strength of having the same background as many of her students. As an example, Dorothy talked about a classroom moment when she discussed primary and secondary colors with her students:

> for instance, I was teaching them primary colors [R: OK] and I told them, ok, the primary colors are blue, yellow, and red [R: OK], and I did an experiment with food coloring, you know, and so they did everything, and I said, 'in Canada you can go to a dollar store and get a pack of colors for a dollar and you would have 12 pencil crayons there, but' I said, 'when I was growing in Sri Lanka things were very expensive,' and I said, 'you wouldn't get, you know, crayons like in a dollar store just for a dollar, you'd have to spend a lot, so my parents would just go and get me the primary colors, and can you tell me how I would have created this?' and

they said, 'really?' and I said, 'yes, and I only had red, blue and yellow and then, you know, mix and mingle' [R: what a great example], so they know that they're also privileged in a country like Canada where they have so many resources.

(March 2012)

Growing up in Sri Lanka, she did not have access to things like dollar stores, and merchandise like food coloring was not easily accessible like it is for her students. Though almost all of her students are second-generation immigrants, their parents would be familiar with some of these experiences. Dorothy's move from Sri Lanka to Canada cannot be equated with her students' and their parents' stories of migration; they are different, obviously, but the fact that Dorothy shares their language and cultural practices lessens a gap between her own background and those of her students.

Adopting a Life History Perspective on Interview Data

Reflecting on interviews with Dorothy, she returned to pedagogical practices from her early learning, not as ideal by any means, but as formatively shaping the kind of educator that she became. Contrast these two excerpts from interviews:

In Sri Lanka it is so structured that the teacher is seen as the person who has all of the knowledge . . . *I learned by observing the teacher teach in a very structured and disciplined environment.*

(June 2003)

Students today perform well on direct questions, but they perform poorly on the open-ended, critical questions. One thing that I have noticed in my teaching over the years is that children, when they had to think, really dig deep into a story, predict, infer; students were not doing well as when I asked questions and probed content—*working directly with them, in a more structured and systematic way.*

(March 2012)

There is a consonance between the 2003 phrase 'I learned . . . in a very structured and disciplined environment' and Dorothy's reflections on her own students in 2012 when she says, 'I ask questions and probe content—working directly with them, in a more structured and systematic way.' Within a whole life or life history perspective there is the thread of structure, discipline and systemic thinking that runs through Dorothy's framing of her learning and teaching. This storyline of discipline and structure runs throughout dialogues with Dorothy about her teaching. In this next excerpt, in a later interview, Dorothy situates her practice

160 Jennifer Rowsell

within structures or what Goodson and Sikes call "already spoken words" (p. 75) which revert back to her childhood:

> I strongly believe that my students learn best by using most of their senses (seeing visuals, listening to eloquent explanations and instruction, and having direct hands-on experiences). I am a visual learner, so I usually make use of visual graphic organizers to simplify concepts and I use anchor charts that give success criteria for a specific concept. *Students also learn best when the teacher is able to articulate ideas using rich texts, handle robust discussions and use good vocabulary in day-to-day conversations.*
>
> (May 2013)

Embedded within this quote are social scripts that Dorothy grew up with that signal larger concepts such as classic literature as rich texts that invite 'robust conversations' and good vocabulary. As a child growing up in a middle-class household in Sri Lanka, Dorothy grew up with aspirations to be a professional and to live a productive life. This is a familiar script and one that I recognize, but certainly not from Dorothy's Sri Lankan optic. Dorothy's first memories of teaching and learning are firmly entrenched into her pedagogy. The following excerpt from my third interview with Dorothy illustrates an instance of a longer timescale vis-à-vis Dorothy's teaching:

> When I arrived in Canada first I didn't pay much attention to the teaching in Canada because I thought I would be an ECE educator working in a daycare. Soon I realized that children gravitated towards me when it was circle time, and I had a way of keeping them spellbound with my storytelling and read aloud activities. This mode of storytelling goes back to my childhood, hearing stories at school.
>
> (May 2013)

From a life history perspective, Dorothy's childhood fondness for storytelling recurred in our conversations about teaching language arts and literacy. This might not be particularly exceptional because all teachers to greater and lesser extents exhibit this very-same layering of timescales, which, through deeper analysis, expose some fundamental truths about not only one's life history, but also a wider cultural perspective on learning.

A Larger Story about Teacher Education

As with other revisits showcased in the book, there is a larger story to the Dorothy revisit. Dorothy has always thrived in school; why should she abandon an education that has done so well by her for a neoliberal agenda? From the 1970s onwards there has been a revisioning of pedagogy within teacher education to emancipate and to eschew failure and stratification (Freire, 1970), and to modernize and innovate it. Dorothy has a deep appreciation and understanding of the children in her classroom: she shares their Sri Lankan roots, she lives in their community, and she knows their parents. With the pendulum swings over the past 30 years and the infusion of technology and differentiated instruction, Dorothy appropriates some parts of it but ultimately adheres to her own life story as a learner and teacher.

The larger story here is about teacher education. Teacher education has entered an era of hyper-professionalism with extended teacher education programs in Canadian provinces like Ontario, with graduates from elite universities being recruited for jobs in inner-city schools with high underachievement, and with a proliferation of doctorate in education programs across North America to produce curriculum experts. This explosion of pedagogical and curriculum knowledge workers infiltrating schooling mirrors, in large part, programs in other countries such as Finland with high test scores and exemplary teacher training models where all teachers have a Master's in Education and many have Ph.D.s in Education.

A driving force behind all of this postgraduate education and professional development is building capacity in schools so that teachers can adapt to rapid change. Some of the rhetoric within teacher education pushes for data-driven, contextually grounded, and personalized teaching. David Berliner (2001, 2005) talks about stages of expertise in teaching through an iterative process whereby teachers get professional development as needs or demands arise, moving gradually from novice to expert (Berliner, 2001). Ultimately, what this increase in training and knowledge work does for teacher education is to create more expertise about a variety of dimensions of teaching and learning, thereby moving further and further away from Dorothy's felt sensibilities and habitus-led model of pedagogy.

The revisit experience featured in this chapter has revealed some paradoxes, at least to me, within teacher education. A paradox within teacher education remains—with all of our efforts to encourage differentiation and inclusion, there is a failure to appreciate that some people, even cultural practices, resist differentiation and inclusive approaches. Positioning stand-and-deliver methods or more structured, even rote learning as pedagogically inferior might run against felt connections and teaching preferences. A possible lesson from this revisit is that there is no single story to teaching and that teaching is about the actual people and communities in which we teach. With all of the rhetoric about teachers as knowledge workers, ultimately, teacher education should focus more on teachers who ground teaching in relationships, in community perspectives, and the lenses that individuals bring to their teaching.

Conclusion

The proposition of revisiting a learning life seemed daunting to me when Julian proposed the idea of the research symposium, subsequently followed by this edited collection. My mind went immediately to teenagers and young children whom I have worked with over the years, but these timescales did not strike me as long enough to write a meaningful revisit. Though I have been a researcher since 1998, the thought of going back in time seemed unrealistic and frankly, I did not think that I had the experience and wherewithal to do a revisit. To wax sentimental, what I realized in revisiting Dorothy is that when you conduct research with someone, you walk alongside them and your own story unfolds alongside their story. To draw on Wacquant (2005), knowledge and meaning in research is created by "the mindful *body of the analyst*" as "an indispensable tool for research" (Wacquant, 2005, p. 466). As Bourdieu et al. (1991) and others (Law, 2004) pointed out some time ago, our research practices generate the knowledge and meanings that we discover. Like other researchers in the collection, I realized something about myself and my work that I did not see before.

Thinking about Dorothy's story 10 years on, what benefit did 'teacher preparation' have for someone who is clearly equipped to teach young children? I went into the revisit imagining that Dorothy had become more Canadianized and had embraced differentiation, Tribes[3] training, and such, and although she maintains that she does, after many conversations, I have come to realize that Dorothy's teaching philosophy pre- and post-teacher education is pretty much the same. Dorothy endorsed and took up the norms, conventions, and values promulgated during that year, but did she do so because she is respectful of instruction, or because they actually work?

Within the community Dorothy teaches in, with many students from Sri Lanka and surrounding Asian countries, her traditional teaching with inflections of progressivism is simply more effective. Sustaining her conventional roots and bringing her childhood memories into her classroom is closer to what her students want than what her university thinks that they want. In this way, our revisit exposes a relationship between teaching theory and teacher identity, and while teacher education programs stress the importance of pedagogic theory, ultimately Dorothy's steadfast commitment to her ideals and values are the secret to her success as an educator in her community. I have therefore come full circle in this revisit. In 2003, Dorothy and I wrote a chapter about her pedagogic identity fully anticipating changes in the convening years as she begins a new chapter teaching in Canadian schools, but I am now faced with the same story at a different time and place.

Notes

1. By inclusion work and radical aspirations I am referring to efforts in teacher education to incorporate diverse cultures, linguistic systems, religious belief, values, etc. that tie in with an overall shift and neoliberal agenda.
2. *Radiant Way* readers are a set of British basal readers.
3. Tribes training (Gibbs & Bennett, 1994) is a professional development program that offers a series of activities to build cooperation and a caring environment within classrooms and communities.

References

Berliner, D. (2001). Learning about learning from expert teachers. *International Journal of Educational Research, 35*(5), 463–483.

Berliner, D. (2005). The near impossibility of testing for teacher quality. *Journal of Teacher Education, 56*(3), 205–13.

Bourdieu, P. (1991). *Language and symbolic power*. Cambridge: Harvard University Press.

Bourdieu, P., Chamboredon, J.C. & Passeron, J.C. (1991). *The craft of sociology*. Berlin: Walter de Gruyter.

Freire, P. (1970). *The pedagogy of the oppressed*. New York: Continuum.

Gibbs & Bennett, S. (1994). *Tribes: A new way of learning and being together*. Cloverdale, CA: Center Source.

Giroux, H. (1992). Literacy and the politics of difference. In C. Lankshear & P. L. McLaren (Eds.), *Critical literacy: Politics, praxis, and the postmodern* (pp. 367–377). Albany: SUNY Press.

Goodson, I. (2012). Investigating narrativity: An introductory talk by Ivor Goodson. In I. Goodson & P. Sikes (2001). *Life history research in educational settings*. London: Open University Press.

Law, J. (2004). *After method: Mess in social science research*. London: Routledge.

Lemke, J. (2000). Across the scales of time: Artifacts, activities, and meanings in ecosocial systems. *Mind, Culture, and Activity, 7*(4), 273–290.

McLaren, P. (2000). *Che guevara, Paulo Freire and the pedagogy of revolution*. Lanham, MD: Rowman & Littlefield.

Rowsell, J. & Pahl, K. (2007). Sedimented identities in texts: Instance of practice. *Reading Research Quarterly, 42*(3), 388–401.

Rowsell, J. & Rajaratnam, D. (2005). There is no place like home: A teacher perspective on literacies across educational contexts. In B. Street (Ed.), *Literacies across educational contexts*. Philadelphia, PA: Caslon Publishing.

Wacquant, L. (2005). Carnal connections: On embodiment, apprenticeship, and membership. *Qualitative Sociology, 28*(4), 445–474.

11

DRAMA AND THE LITERACY OF LIVES IN PROGRESS

Kathleen Gallagher

Introduction

In 1984 French-Canadian playwright Michel Tremblay wrote an ingenious little play called *Albertine in Five Times*. It is the story of one life, the life of Albertine, but told at five different times of her life, by five different Albertines: at 30, 40, 50, 60 and 70. The older Albertines know what the younger ones don't yet know. The younger ones remind the older ones of how different they were in their younger, less cynical and more passionate days. In the play, the five Albertines speak to each other and to their long-dead sister Madeleine. Each has 'her own story' but, together, they make a complex single person. It is a revisiting play. And it beautifully illustrates how memory both enlightens and confuses our sense of coherence as evolving individuals.

> ALBERTINE AT 50:
> You've got a short memory.
> ALBERTINE AT 60:
> What? I don't know what you mean.
> ALBERTINE AT 50:
> I've stopped complaining too . . . but I don't take pills . . .
> ALBERTINE AT 60:
> That won't last . . .
> ALBERTINE AT 50:
> Why shouldn't it?
> ALBERTINE AT 60:
> Because you're play-acting. You're going through a phase where you play at being happy and positive.

ALBERTINE AT 70:
  Oh, shut up!
ALBERTINE AT 60:
  You're no different! You've convinced yourself you'll be happy in your stinky little room, but the real you knows better.
ALBERTINE AT 70:
  At least I'm glad to be alive . . .
ALBERTINE AT 50:
  So am I . . . glad to be alive . . .
ALBERTINE AT 60:
  I don't believe you.
ALBERTINE AT 30:
  I'm young, I'm strong, I could do so much if it weren't for this rage, gnawing at me . . .
ALBERTINE AT 40:
  Sometimes I think it's all that keeps me alive . . .
ALBERTINE AT 30:
  It's true.
ALBERTINE AT 60:
  You'll get over that, too . . . Rage . . . Rebellion never solved a thing.
                                                                (pp. 45–46)

It takes the group of Albertines the entire play to gain a kind of unity and coherence. In the final pages we read:

ALBERTINE AT 50:
  Look . . .
ALBERTINE AT 40:
  What?
ALBERTINE AT 50:
  There she is . . . the moon.
  The five ALBERTINES look at the sky.
ALBERTINE AT 60:
  I can't see it . . . Where did I put my glasses . . . ?
  She finds them and puts them on.
ALBERTINE AT 70:
  It's beautiful.
ALBERTINE AT 40:
  Yes, beautiful . . . even from here.
ALBERTINE AT 30:
  It's so big.
ALBERTINE AT 60:
  . . . and red . . .

> *Silence.*
> ALBERTINE AT 50:
> You could almost reach out and touch it . . .
> ALBERTINE AT 60:
> She's alone, too.
> *The five ALBERTINES slowly raise their arms toward the moon.*
> ALBERTINE AT 70:
> Touch it . . . maybe it's the same one . . .
> ALL FIVE ALBERTINES: *as if they had made physical contact*
> Ahhhhh . . .
>> *The moon, solitary and blood red, rises.*
>> *Blackout.*

(pp. 75–76)

In the final moments of the play, the five Albertines come together, find a way to be, to manage the contradictions, the lack of continuity, the sense of rupture, the faulting memory. Not everything is resolved; answers still elude them, and us, the audience. Life, in progress, is messy. This chapter will explore what it means to conceive of research as a revisiting of a past from a present position marked by different or new perspectives. Like life itself, research that chronicles a life-in-the-making can be untidy. Inspired, then, both by Michel Tremblay's work, and by my own life's work in drama, I have settled upon one way to stay true to the collaboration at the heart of drama as literacy in my attempts here to approach longitudinal or revisiting research *relationally*.

Memory and Meaning

In his book *The Touch of the Past* (2005), my dear colleague, the late Roger Simon, eloquently articulates what it means to learn from the testimony of others:

> At stake in the touch of the past is the welcome given to the memories of others as a teaching—not simply in the didactic sense of an imparting of new information—but more fundamentally as that which brings me more than I can contain. To be brought more than one can contain is not a condition in which one becomes a symptom of a history one cannot possess, but rather a condition of possibility for true learning—one which bears the risk of being dispossessed of one's certainties.

(p. 10)

In the case of this revisiting project, the 'others' who teach 'us' are our younger selves, those of the research participants and myself as researcher. What is also especially important, to my work, about Simon's insight is that as long as we, as researchers, continue to believe it important to document our memories of our research experiences, those experiences remain in formation, their boundaries neither static nor stable. History is in formation as we tell it. A revisiting project is a bit about this idea of displacement in our own researching bodies, the experience of being stripped of certainties in attempting to accommodate both our own contradictions over time and the disobliging meanings of others. To excavate memory requires both an engagement with the past and a displacement of certainties that may have unwittingly gathered momentum over time passing.

In this chapter, I will share with readers my early conceptualizing of a particular research project and my collaborative planning with research participants with whom I first worked 19 years ago. In this revisiting project, I return to two women who were part of my dissertation research, one as a participant in one of the drama classes in the study (Sara[1]), the other as a videographer, helping me technically at the time but also as a 'key informant' (Connie[1]), someone who had a privileged retrospection on being a grade 10 girl, from her position at the time, as a grade 13 girl in the same school. The initial project was about gender, pedagogy and drama as a collaborative form of literacy; it is now also about deriving meaning over time in relation to the social actors of history and memory.

I chose these two women because they do not currently work in the arts and so how, if at all, drama is playing out in their current lives would be less obvious and would require a delving into lessons learned and their real world implications. This would offer, I hoped, the deeper pedagogical examination I was interested in. Further, after my initial contact by email, I realized that the very format of email was providing a productive reflective space that I thought could nicely serve the research. I made the decision, therefore, to continue our email conversation beyond the logistical to see what more our reciprocal communication through writing might afford.

Email communication allows time to pause and consider, to delete and reformulate. In person, interviewing is much more contingent upon its particular moment, much more an improvisation than is an email exchange. And the communication of an email exchange often interestingly registers somewhere in between formal and informal. Emails can also conceal and reveal how we are feeling all at once. And of course, they are open to minor, or more grave, experiences of misinterpretation. The semiotic world of email communication has the sense of immediacy (though responses can be hours, days apart) and the (often erroneous) sense of clarity and directness. Emails contain worlds of difference. Email exchange, then, is an interesting way to begin conceptualizing a research project because it signals, explicitly, that we are in the middle of our lives, in the middle of conversations, in the middle of relationships. Writing an email is a form of communication that allows us to be solitary while also in communication. The following, therefore, charts our email exchanges, which ultimately offered more than the organizational planning for our research. As we continued our conversations through email, it became clear to me that my research participants would become important conceptual collaborators, helping me to set

168 Kathleen Gallagher

the speculative perimeters for the study. The following charts our methodological development through email communication.

I began my first contact with my two research participants with the following email missive:

> *Hello to you both,*
>
> *I'm writing to you today with a request. I am trying to imagine what it might be like to revisit my doctoral research at St. Jude's [pseudonym] of many years ago, which you were both a part of. I'd like this revisiting to be more biographical than ethnographic, in the sense that I'm less interested in what drama at St. Jude's looks like now and more interested in what kinds of impacts, if any, studying drama then may have in your lives now.*
>
> *Neither of you currently works in the theatre or in the arts. That's good and what I want. I'm very interested in your recollections of the nature and quality of pedagogical work in the drama classroom; the things you learned about the theatre, of course, but equally significantly how learning generally in that context, and your understandings of social relations, have been affected by that time together those years ago. In what ways have models of working in drama, or that experience of drama class, prepared you for more deliberative and active participation in the public sphere? How have these understandings evolved into your current professional practices if at all? Or into your interests and outside professional lives?*
>
> *Please get back to me if this sounds like something you might want to explore with me.*
>
> *Thanks,*
>
> *Kathleen*

I had remained connected to each of these two young women since they had graduated from high school and I had followed their career developments with great interest. As I began to consider the project of speaking the lives of Sara and Connie, who I first knew as two teenage girls, I felt somewhat relieved of my previous roles as teacher and researcher, less tentative about how I might represent them through research as they are now 'successful' adults; I felt less worried about their futures than I did when they were teenagers.

Because we have remained in touch, although at some periods more closely than others, I also feel I have been informally 'observing' Sara and Connie for years. I was included in a group email in which Sara kept us informed of her medical school, internship, and residency experiences through her 20s and early 30s in New York City and Dominica. Similarly, I've been a confidante to Connie through several trials and life changes during her 20s and 30s, and most recently was seated at a table at her wedding with other artists, teachers and 'older friends' she's collected over the years.

So friendship, in both these instances, is central in the context of this new research and I will need to get over my hangovers of positivism that read proximity as invalidation. I am also aware that these two women have a very particular and thoughtful perspective on me. As former students, of course, they made a study of me every day. My research some 19 years ago, in drama classrooms with these two women, was the first and last time I made a study of my own practice. After all these intervening years, it is a little odd for me to return to that life as well.

What is the place of drama and drama learning in the lives of two women (now 38 and 36) who were in high school in the 1990s when I conducted my study of drama and adolescent identity construction in a publicly funded, Catholic, single-sex school for girls? The school where I conducted the research, and where I had taught as a drama teacher for 10 years, was a richly multicultural/ethnic/ linguistic school with over 48 different cultures represented in the overcrowded building of 1,200 students, built for 600. The drama classroom was in a dank basement where socially engaged art practices often lit the room on fire. A delicious irony of this revisiting project is that we will return through memories (individual and collective) to a past time of an "eternal present," in Martin Esslin's (1987, p.25) description of the special illusion that is drama.

A Conceptual Frame

Cultural theorist Richard Sennett (2012) in his book *Together: The Rituals, Pleasures and Politics of Cooperation* illustrates the power of cooperation and as I reflected back upon the pedagogy, I realized that this sense of collaboration I was trying to enact with my 'new' research participants was, in fact, the central and likely most important learning of any drama classroom—that is, the *literacy of collaboration*, of seeing oneself in a group and understanding that one's own desires and knowledge need to live in a dynamic relationship with the desires and knowledge of others. Sennett argues that there is an architecture of cooperation that serves to establish political togetherness in the wider public sphere, across gulfs of difference. Using the historical model of the Renaissance workshop, he argues that the nub of cooperation, "is active participation rather than passive presence" (p. 233) and this demanding sort of cooperation is not a given but *earned* in a rehearsal or theater-making process. It may also lay, he further argues, the groundwork for complex cooperation later in life (for a fuller examination of this aspect of Sennett's concept, see Gallagher, 2014).

The "rehearsal," as Sennett calls it, teaches everyday diplomacy rather than the zero-sum game, which may be more typical of high school classrooms. This kind of "re-pairing" (p. 229) or reformatting of ideas so that parties who disagree can continue to work together is the lifeblood of cooperation in the drama classroom, and is clearly about developing the kind negotiation and cooperation skills that come to have enormous social and personal benefit. In the current context of neoliberalism and the absolute value of 'the individual,' Sennett would speak instead of a kind of collaboration, or collaborative literacy as I prefer to call it, that I believe is the pedagogical core of drama. Literacy, in many parts of the Western world, is most often examined through standardized testing, written tests that should demonstrate the 'literacy skills' acquired by learners. I am interested instead in understanding what those rituals of collaboration have served in the adult lives of two women, well 'trained' in the rites and rituals of drama. Sennett argues that

> individualism names a social absence as well as a personal impulse: ritual is absent. Ritual's role in all human cultures is to relieve and resolve anxiety, by turning people outward in shared, symbolic acts; modern society has weakened those ritual ties.
>
> (p. 280)

I want to explore Sennett's idea that developing the skills to work with those who differ from you is the most pressing challenge facing civil society today. This is a claim worth examining if we take from this an expansive view of what it means to be a literate person in an age of cultural divisiveness. What literacies of collaboration did Sara and Connie learn through the rites and rituals of drama, and how do these understandings now serve them?

The Collaborative Literacies of Drama: A View from the Field

Literacy has been pulled into the service of many pro-social agendas, across a variety of educational and community contexts. Focusing on the classroom, Beach et al. (2010) position "dramatic inquiry" as a "literacy tool," defining dramatic inquiry as "embodied, collaborative, interactive, and sequenced improvised activities that young people engage alongside adults as they explore questions about a topic from multiple viewpoints by creating, experiencing, representing, and interpreting socially imagined events" (p. 73). Their notion of dramatic inquiry and collaborative pedagogy comes from a long tradition in drama education, which gained most prominence through the early work of Dorothy Heathcote and the later work of many of her disciples.

In *A Drama of Learning: Mantle of the Expert*, Heathcote and Herbert (1985) introduced the mantle of the expert approach to teaching and learning through the medium of dramatic inquiry. The approach itself inverts the positivist teacher–student model of teaching by prompting the students to direct their learning process through creative drama. The students, rather than the teacher, drive the pedagogical experience as constructors of knowledge rather than passive receivers—they are "endowed" as the expert (p. 173). *Mantle of the Expert* recasts the teacher and student in fictional roles where both are "living the experience" of being "in role." In this work was born, I would suggest, the idea of drama as a collaborative literacy although not named as such at the time. In *Mantle of the Expert*, the power of making meaning and communication is invested in the group. In this collaboration, the teacher is co-constructing rather than directing knowledge, driving towards an open-ended communicative network.

In an early article in the journal *Language Arts*, connections between the improvisational and collaborative nature of drama and literacy were well underway. Verriour (1990) defined storying in drama as a "shared learning experience in a dramatic context that requires thinking in the narrative mode and about narrative as a means of interpreting and verbalizing experience" (p. 144). Storytelling in the dramatic mode, according to Verriour, involves "students in the transmission and sharing of individual, personal stories, and also requires them to work together to create a collective story observing the mutually agreed-on rules and conventions of improvised drama" (p. 144).

Others have made the connection between drama and literacy more explicit still. In Baldwin and Fleming's (2002) book *Teaching Literacy through Drama: Creative Approaches*, they aim to provide a praxis framework for drama as a pedagogical tool to meet National Literacy Standards (NLS) in Australia. They argue that

> [d]rama is a shared and co-operative activity, which fires the individual and collective imagination. This can be channelled into forms of artistic expression, which may be written or spoken, individually or collectively expressed. Drama can provide these forms through which children's personal and interpersonal collective responses to literature can be explored and communicated.
>
> (p. 6)

The implicit aspect of 'togetherness' or a shared, common purpose in drama education work, illustrated in these various early examples, is interestingly related to another more contemporary classroom literacy practice: the spoken word. Kim's (2013) analysis extends beyond individual expression and empowerment, the more usual claims made for spoken word's efficacy. Instead, she positions literacy as facilitating social relationships and operating as a "technology of pedagogy that can reconfigure intertemporal relations with the historical (colonial) present and past, as well as interspatial relations" (p. 394). Kim adds, "when young people change the nature of conversation itself, we witness the fundamental practice of voice that is literacy" (p. 394).

The mistake to be made here is to assume that this "voice that is literacy" is some kind of consensual, harmonious voice. It was the case in my research 19 years ago and remains the case today in my most current research, that drama has the pedagogical potential to allow dissonant and discordant voices to co-exist in productive ways. In a recent publication, my co-authors and I have described drama and its pedagogies as a space

> where dreams of collaboration come up against the very real material differences diverse students bring to the teaching and learning encounter. The ability to discuss openly differing assumptions about the world remains key to working with, through, and across fundamental social differences; doing so also presents the possibility of unearthing a shared affective language.
>
> (Gallagher et al., 2013, p. 8)

This shared, affective language that can emerge in vibrant drama classrooms is key, I would think, to Sennett's sense that the negotiation and cooperation skills fundamental to a diverse community and exemplified in the historic model of the Renaissance workshop is also central to my proposal of a drama literacy of collaboration. Connie, in an email reply to my first set of questions aimed at helping us collaboratively conceptualize the research project, described it this way:

> *Drama forced collaboration. I had to learn/realize very quickly my relationship to the other people on the team . . . and my relationship to the project. There was no hiding in drama. Once I decided the role I wanted to play on the team, I had to play it because others had also chosen their role. So no one could upset that balance. And no one wanted to upset the balance; we were all comfortable in allowing each other to play the roles that we had chosen.*

In order to imagine how to articulate my idea of drama as a collaborative literacy, I needed first to see whether their memories of what togetherness looked and felt like matched my own or offered anything new or unsettling to my own. I asked Connie and Sara the following:

> *How did drama teach you about learning from/with other people? The 'group-y-ness' of it? What do people learn from that 'group' focus?*

In response to that initial prompt, Sara articulated the following:

> *Group assignments were a common exercise in many high school courses. In didactic classes like physics, group assignments often translated into a division of tasks that were individually performed, then quilted together into a submission that was deemed to be collectively authored. In drama class however, this was a completely different and much more challenging experience. Rather than be given a list of requisite items to submit, collaborative projects in drama were public expressions of concepts that we had been asked to collectively develop.*

Collaborative Conceptualizing

I have previously engaged, with research partners, in collaborative analysis through various innovative digital technologies (see Gallagher & Freeman, 2011) and written about the experience of collaboration with research participants (see Gallagher & Wessels, 2011) but I have never engaged in collaborative conceptualizing of a research project. For such a revisiting project, when researchers and participants plan to re-enter the past together and bring it into a productive relationship with present and evolving lives, it seems prudent to me to prepare together for such a sojourn. How will we engage with the past, with our different memories, with our present investments in seeing ourselves in particular ways? These are important questions to consider at the outset. The value of revisiting previous lives decades later, it seems to me, is not just in having hindsight or an interesting retrospective gaze, or finding things that may have been overlooked at the time, but in discovering how those presences and absences shed light on who we are, what we know, and what we value in the present.

To launch into the heart of the matter, and make this important relationship of past to present central, I asked in an early email to my research participants what role drama, or the learning they gleaned from drama, might play in their lives today. Here, Connie responds to my prompt about the place of her drama learning in her life now:

> *I began studying for certification exams in the financial sector and transitioned into a compliance role; again I excelled . . . why? Because it's all about PEOPLE . . . wanting to be heard.*

Story of Complaints

In the compliance departments I have worked in, I have always worked on complaints made by clients regarding unsuitable investments etc. I ask the clients and the advisors the same question when I am trying to determine the merit of the complaint: 'tell me the story from the beginning'. In hearing the story I create a skeleton timeline, the signed paperwork and trades become the evidence, I decipher intention in historical conversations between the client and the advisor through emails, I review handwritten notes sometimes taken 15 years ago. After I hear the versions of the story I look at the documents and try to piece it all together . . . it's a mystery (in every firm I've worked for they call me Nancy Drew because I have to solve the mystery . . . who's telling the truth?). There is a huge research component, much like in drama for a play: who are the characters, where does it all take place, what would that place look like, socio-economic characteristics, what is the mood of the place (in most complaint cases, it's the mood of the markets). There is also a major writing component in this position: timelines, executive summaries, writing to regulators in reply to their investigations, providing substantive responses to clients, errors and omissions insurers. There are a number of stakeholders that I communicate with (each differently). It's important to 'know my audience' throughout the process.

Sara took a similarly prosaic approach to the question:

There are two exercises that I remember as being incredibly insightful, and engaging, and have influenced my professional life on a regular basis. The first was that of improvisation. I remember it then to be an exercise in the ability to 'think on your feet', articulate one's thoughts fluently, and continue a conversation with coherence and confidence. What I have grown to realize is that those life rehearsals were equally important in teaching me how to LISTEN to what is being said, identify the salient points and subsequently use them as the launch point for the response. This is an invaluable skill, one that I could never have learned through lectures or texts.

Professionally, each interaction with a patient is an extension of those improv sessions, which are fundamentally different from the pre-scripted, systematic approaches to obtaining a 'patient's history' as taught in medical conventional education. Using the improv approach means that the conversations we have extend beyond listing symptoms and medical problems, and allow me to glean some insight into a patient's fears, expectations, goals of care and social support systems. It is this collection of information that forms the fundamental basis on which I base my decisions when devising a plan of care.

The second of these was the exercise in which we worked through 2 stories— one of a young slave girl who was with child sired by her owner, the second about a young man who refused to conform to his school's practices about expressions of patriotism. Through this exercise, I learned that multiple truths and multiple realities can coexist without hierarchy. This is contrary to the popular western ideal of medicine and its perceived inherent superiority and exclusivity. Furthermore, I realized that the importance of WHAT was said was directly linked to WHO said it (as defined by the intersections of gender, age, social status, etc.) and to HOW that message was delivered.

Both Sara and Connie articulated very clearly how the rituals of practice and the skills they attributed to drama serve them now professionally. It is unsurprising to me that both women make central their relationship to others, their ability to communicate clearly and work through potentially difficult, conflictual, or challenging circumstances by *listening* to others with care. In her philosophical reflection on listening, Fiumara (1990) mourns the fact that in the tradition of Western thought, we have, in effect, a system of thought that tends to ignore listening processes. A scan of the literature in drama education also reveals that the concept of listening has not been theorized, despite the fact that many accounts of practice seem to note its central importance in the process of theater-making. When we think about the literature on drama and additional language learning, or drama and literacy in particular, listening emerges certainly as one of the fundamental skills to be developed in such contexts. I have explored elsewhere this major lacuna in greater detail (see Gallagher & Yaman Ntelioglou, 2013). Yet, even without much theoretical probing, most research in drama concludes

Drama and the Literacy of Lives in Progress **175**

that healthy community building in drama processes asks participants to draw on their life experiences, as well as to listen to, and learn about, those of others.

Turning back to Richard Sennett (2012), he reflects refreshingly on the idea of listening:

> As in looking carefully, so a casual conversation requires skill to become a meaningful encounter; refraining from assertiveness is a discipline that makes a space for looking into another person's life, and for them, equally, to look into yours . . . Listening well is an interpretive activity which works best by focussing on the specifics of what one hears, as when we seek to fathom from those particulars what another person has taken for granted but not said.
>
> (pp. 23–24)

In addition to listening, one might also underscore the place of *story*, then, and the value of collaboration towards a common purpose or desirable outcome, as centerpieces of the very different, but clearly related, professional illustrations presented by Sara and Connie above.

In a subsequent email, and in the spirit of play, taking a leaf out of Michel Tremblay's script convention, I invited Sara and Connie to write a short letter to their fifteen-year-old self:

> *Can you write a few paragraphs (a brief letter) to that girl, from your vantage point now? What do you know now (about yourself, others, your world) that you wish she could have known then? What would you say to that girl, now?*

I wanted to begin to understand how they remembered their girlhood and in what ways it might congeal with, or diverge from, my own memories. If we were aiming to revisit the past together, it would make sense to explicitly visit each other's memories. That was my aim with the question. Sara wrote to me a few times, asking for an 'extension' and explaining that she was finding it hard to write the letter. She didn't explain why, in any detail, but told me she was having a 'hard time with it.' Obviously, this is something I would like to return to with Sara. Was the request challenging, or was imagining a conversation with her younger self difficult for other reasons? Might I still feel, to her, like a judge in her life? Ultimately, in Sara's playful letter, she addresses her younger self directly and plays with the idea of the 'assignment' I'd given her:

> *Like you, I have sat in front of a computer for days on end, with a (now on-line) thesaurus trying to craft something that is worthy of her high standards. I know what you're thinking: 'Why the heck are you voluntarily putting yourself through such an arduous process?' Two decades later, I still have the same initial instinct. Unlike you, however, I have the luxury of time and life experience to know that*

> *challenging yourself into doing something that's outside your comfort zone is one of the greatest ways to glean insight about yourself and your understanding of the world around you. Twenty years later, I find myself seeking out people and situations that allow me to contest my current perspectives. It's not like this process has gotten any easier though; it hasn't. The difference between you and me, however, is that I now work to embrace the objective, rather than be intimidated by it.*

Later in her letter to her younger self, Sara reveals more about her current self and helps me understand the person she is now, compared with the person I knew two decades ago. She also integrates her 'selves' and creates a clear story of enlightenment with age. As a researcher, this helps me understand how our research design should engage explicitly with the notion of a life trajectory. But what methods might we use to also challenge the continuity and developmental pull implicit in this description:

> *The version of our 'self' who left for medical school was confident in her decision, ambitious in her quest, but she seriously underestimated the psychological imprint that it would leave on her. She was not aware of how much that experience would challenge her core values; entrenching some, modifying most, and completely dismissing others. With her travels also came a greater appreciation for our cultural roots, specifically the music that captures the immigrant experience and a longing for the people and pleasures of home.*

Connie fully embraced the prudence of her older self and tried to bestow wisdom upon her younger one:

> *You're good at more than one subject. It's not the subject that will dictate who you will become. Review each subject that you excel in and find what parts of it you enjoy most. Do you like drama? Or do you really like the idea of stories, relationships, how one action can trigger multiple effects? Do you really enjoy the mystery of it all and figuring out whodunit? Try to find those feelings of excitement in other disciplines. For those subjects that you find more difficult, try harder!*
>
> *I know now that I took myself far too seriously. I didn't know how to filter the opinions and advice of those around me. I think travel would have helped me. Travel more, so that your world doesn't easily consume you and you can appreciate that there is far more to life than [name of the street the school is on] street. Travel so that the opinions of your usual group of people aren't your only sources of information.*
>
> *Decide on the life you want to live first, then decide what you want to do in order to fill your days in that life. Choosing the work/job first may not contribute to, or complement, the life you want to live.*

Once I had made some provisional sense of their responses, I again emailed my participants, about a month later, having decided to bring them more intimately into the process of research design.

Drama and the Literacy of Lives in Progress **177**

Hello Sara and Connie,

Thank you both for your responses to my previous questions. They've given me a lot to think about in terms of what it means to go back to the past, as the people we are now, and ask what else could be learned from that time together.

I have a further question for you: If we were designing this research together, rather than me 'researching' you, what methods do you think would help us design this project. Typically, with qualitative research, we think about interviews, although I tend to use all kinds of other interesting methods in my research (drama, writing, etc.). If we want to 'revisit' the past, from our current perspectives, what other methods do you think we could theoretically use to engage the three of us in a project of visiting our younger selves, at another time and place, that would ultimately offer us some new insights about that time and perhaps about our current time and thoughts.

It's a brainstorm session, in other words. How could we excavate that past from our current positions? What could we do? Together? Individually? How could we research that time?

Thanks so much for any thoughts you might have,

Kathleen

Sara replies:

Hi,

You're really asking me to push my limits with this line of questioning. I am so used to quantitative/scientific research methods that qualitative research approaches seem so foreign to me. OK. Here's an idea. Because there's always a soundtrack of music & lyrics floating around in my head, I thought that music would be a good vehicle for exploration. In my mind, there are 2 songs that are associated with high school drama. These are not linked to my participation as a student of the class, but rather as an audience member. One of the most poignant assemblies I experienced was one Remembrance Day. You skillfully crafted a tableau piece for these occasions, and although I don't remember the specifics of each piece, I can most certainly remember the musical scores and the emotions that they elicited. The two specific songs are 'Waltzing Matilda' and 'Mother's Pride'. I still experience a similar emotional surge that emerged the first time I heard these songs within the context of the tableau performances.

I specifically remember reflecting on the first Remembrance Day assembly I attended and thinking how powerful the tableau piece was, and how it was able to profoundly touch me, for I was not only a viewing audience member but also an emotional participant. I suspect that was the day I decided that I would choose drama for my requisite arts credit, as I too wanted to be part of something that could have such a far reaching impact.

> *Many years later when I was doing my rotation at the Veteran's Hospital in New York City, I was surprised to realize that the 'Waltzing Matilda' song played in my head while I walked through the hall and saw scores of amputated veterans. I guess the 'tableau' of wounded warriors in the halls and common rooms elicited a similar emotional connection to that drama piece of many years ago; it was like life was imitating art.*
>
> Sara

I remember the assembly well myself and I certainly remember the music. There is, of course, a world of research in multimodal literacy that speaks about this very kind of sensuous response to learning; research which centers on the body and its senses, as it explores learning and living processes. Rowsell (2008) writes:

> Art is a symbolic representation of one's internal world made external. Artefacts sediment moments as an expression of how an artist feels or thinks at a moment in time. Art and artistic creation thereby trace social practices used to express how one feels within a social context or social space.
>
> (p. 233)

Art not only sediments how an artist thinks or feels but also how an audience thinks or feels. Reception theory and those who have studied audiences for a very long time understand how potent the experience of spectatorship can be. Susan Bennett (1997), in her seminal text *Theatre Audiences: A theory of production and reception*, writes that what matters is "our willingness to engage with performances in ways that speak to the most intimate detail of our experience" (p. vii). It is clear to me that Connie, Sara and I will need to see a play together, enter a theater as individuals and exit as 'an audience.' As Eyre and Wright (2001, p. 1) describe it, "There's a sense of occasion in any theatre performance and of participation in a communal act: you go into a theatre as an individual and you emerge as an audience." As a future method, then, we will make such a trip in order to reflect on how we experience seeing theater, together, and what sensuous responses the shared event might provoke.

Also at play in Sara's response are emotions, or more precisely, her affective memory, which continues to reverberate in her present experience. "Through emotions, the past persists on the surface of bodies," says Ahmed (2004, p. 202). I realize Sara's idea to use music in our research design is a brilliant one. And clearly, the work of Sara Ahmed (2004) and her project that probes the cultural politics of emotion by asking what emotions do, will be especially important to engage. In fact, Sara's chosen example above, the Remembrance Day Assembly, provides an especially fertile ground upon which to explore what emotions do and, as importantly, how they might help us access a past and understand a present in this revisiting project. In Ahmed's book, she also turns to war as a concrete

Drama and the Literacy of Lives in Progress   **179**

example of the workings of emotion and their association with unjust social relations. In Sara's example, she is looking back to a performance that itself looked back to a time of war and loss. What did that looking and feeling do then (beyond encouraging Sara to take drama) and what does it do now, in a new cultural context of war and terror? In Ahmed's last chapter, she is asking what Butler (2002) has also asked: what makes a life grievable? Exploring what the emotions stirred from Sara's memory might tell us about her, that time, our times, is an interesting route to take, but what is even more instructive about Ahmed's work is that she considers emotions to produce "the effect of surfaces and boundaries of bodies" (p. 194). It is therefore not simply that we experience emotions (of empathy, disgust, release, etc.) but that we are shaped by the "contact zone in which others press upon us, as well as leave their impressions" (p. 194). These impressions also involve our investments in social norms. Emotions, in her theorizations, are not assigned to individuals or simply reflective of an interior state, but are instructive for how they work on and in relation to bodies. Emotions operate where we don't register their effects, she argues, in the form of signs and relations. As I read through the different compelling essays in Ahmed's book, I realized that in turning to emotion, as Sara's suggestion portends, we would be returning to the very notion of collaboration I began with. We would be considering the 'contact zones' of drama learning. How, then, to access the contact zones, the emotional terrain, of communities of drama learners, the fond and difficult memories, through the singular memories or experiences of the individual? Ahmed's work helps us understand emotions as other than individual possessions.

Connie's response was different. She wasn't sure when she might get to a reply because Connie's life is filled with chronic pain and her ability to engage, and even sometimes to work, is severely compromised. This is one of the perhaps foreseeable but no less difficult problems with 'revisiting research.' We are not who we were 20 years ago. Life marches on in its unpredictable way and when our health is fragile, everything else pales. Her email ended: 'Its officially true . . . if you don't have your health . . . you got nothin.'

Ah. A return to the ellipses of Michel Tremblay:

> **Ellipsis** (plural ellipses; from the Ancient Greek: ἔλλειψις, *élleipsis*, "omission" or "falling short") is a series of dots that usually indicates an intentional omission of a word, sentence, or whole section from a text without altering its original meaning.[1] Depending on their context and placement in a sentence, ellipses can also indicate an unfinished thought, a slight pause, and nervous or awkward silence. Aposiopesis is the use of an ellipsis to trail off into silence—for example: "But I thought he was . . ." When placed at the beginning or end of a sentence, the ellipsis can also inspire a feeling of melancholy or longing.
>
> (Wikipedia)

180 Kathleen Gallagher

Why, I thought, in typing out the script from the play at the opening of this chapter, are there so many ellipses? Interminably unending, unfinished.

> ALBERTINE AT 70:
> At least I'm glad to be alive . . .
> ALBERTINE AT 50:
> So am I . . . glad to be alive . . .
> ALBERTINE AT 60:
> I don't believe you.
> ALBERTINE AT 30:
> I'm young, I'm strong, I could do so much if it weren't for this rage, gnawing at me . . .
> ALBERTINE AT 40:
> Sometimes I think it's all that keeps me alive . . .

A revisiting project, as these preliminary, collaborative investigations have taught me, is fraught. Not only for the reasons I was expecting (how might we relate all these years later? what subjects will be desirable or undesirable to return to? what might be worth learning?) but also for those reasons I was not anticipating. Using life-historical methods and extending the life cycle of ethnography through an emergent meta-ethnography, researchers are bound to find themselves in the messy 'lives in progress' of research participants. These lives may have taken turns that are difficult to reconcile. Illness and changed life circumstances of all kinds need to find their place in the unfolding stories. Everyone must reconcile time passing and memories of other (better) times for some may make current life challenges all the more stark.

Theoretical work on memory, as well as intellectual work on emotions and affect, may provide some distance and intellectual rigour to make the potentially difficult journey worth taking. Further, making explicit the desire for the collaborative production of knowledge means taking account of which stories participants and researchers wish to expose to the light of analysis and which will remain in the fog. In the best cases, this puts researcher and participants in relations of mutuality and reciprocity that need to be negotiated in philosophical as well as in pragmatic terms.

As for where I personally stand now, these years later, revisiting my own young researcher self, I will reconsider Nancy Lesko's theorizing of adolescence, which challenges the developmental pull of that body of literature. Instead, Lesko (2001) argues for a recursive rather than a developmental look at adolescence, that time of in-between-ness, the not yet, the becoming. She suggests that educators can learn from adolescents just as adolescents can learn from educators and that is certainly also the case for researchers and participants. Rather than seeing ourselves progress through the evolutionary chain, instead of assuming our enlightenment through ageing, I will take a recursive look at our data/

conversations without thinking of the past, present, and future as unassailable stages of a linear progression. In future analyses, I will need to think of the possibilities of being simultaneously mature and immature, evolved and naive, in order to escape the notion that time is linear and cumulative, and we are, at present, better and more mature versions of our younger selves. In my participants' return to their pasts evidenced in this chapter, and in my own reflection on my earlier researcher self, it is tempting to cast a light of naiveté on those earlier selves and see our current lives as better, wiser versions of who we are. My efforts in future analyses will stay alert to this compulsion so that a developmental pull does not cloud the messiness of lives progressing and the eccentric and informative relationship between past and present.

My first attempt here at collaborative conceptualizing in revisiting research suggests to me that researchers and participants must leave themselves available to the uncertain and improvisational character of a trip to the past, taking in more than we can contain, perhaps, and being dispossessed of our certainties. I look ahead with interest and trepidation.

Note

1. All interviewee names have been anonymised.

References

Ahmed, S. (2004). *The cultural politics of emotion*. New York: Routledge.

Baldwin, P. & Fleming, K. (2002). *Teaching literacy through drama: Creative approaches*. London: RoutledgeFalmer.

Beach, R., Campano, G. & Edmiston, B. (2010). *Literacy tools in the classroom: Teaching through critical inquiry, grades 5–12*. New York: Teachers College Press.

Bennett, S. (1997). *Theatre audiences: A theory of production and reception*. Abingdon, Oxon: Routledge.

Butler, J. (2002). Violence, mourning, politics. Feminist Theory Address, University College London, 8 March.

Esslin, M. (1987). *The field of drama: How the signs of drama create meaning on stage and screen*. London: Methuen.

Eyre, R. & Wright, N. (2001). *Changing stages: A view of British theatre in the* twentieth *century*. Milton Keynes: Bloomsbury Publishing.

Fiumara, G. C. (1990). *The other side of language: A philosophy of listening*. London: Routledge.

Gallagher, K. (2014). *Why theatre matters: Urban youth, engagement, and a pedagogy of the real*. Toronto, London, Buffalo: University of Toronto Press.

Gallagher, K. & Freeman, B. (2011). Multi-site ethnography, hypermedia, and the productive hazards of digital methods: A struggle for liveness. *Ethnography and Education, 6*(3), 357–373.

Gallagher, K. & Wessels, A. (2011). Emergent pedagogy and affect in collaborative research: A metho-pedagogical paradigm. *Pedagogy, Culture and Society, 19*(2), 239–258.

Gallagher, K. & Yaman Ntelioglou, B. (2013). On the pedagogical importance of (not) knowing the other: Listening, risk, drama and difference. In M. Anderson & J. Dunn (Eds.) *How drama activates learning: Contemporary research and practice* (pp. 94–108). London: Continuum, Bloomsbury Academic.

Gallagher, K., Wessels, A. & Yaman Ntelioglou, B. (2013). Listening to the affective life of injustice: Drama pedagogy, race, identity and learning. *Youth Theatre Journal, 27*, 7–19.

Heathcote, D. & Herbert, P. (1985). A drama of learning: Mantle of the expert. *Theory into Practice, 24*(3), 173–180.

Kim, R. H. (2013). Never knew literacy could get at my soul: On how words matter for youth, or notes towards decolonizing literacy. *The Review of Education, Pedagogy, and Cultural Studies, 35*(5), 392–407.

Lesko, N. (2001). *Act your age!: A cultural construction of adolescence.* New York: Routledge Falmer.

Rowsell, J. (2008). Improvising on artistic habitus: Sedimenting identity into art. In J. Albright & A. Luke (Eds.), *Pierre Bourdieu and literacy education* (pp. 233 –251). London: Routledge.

Sennett, R. (2012). *Together: The rituals, pleasures and politics of cooperation.* New Haven, CT and London: Yale University Press.

Simon, R. (2005). *The touch of the past: Remembrance, learning, and ethics.* New York: Palgrave Macmillan.

Tremblay, M. (1986). *Albertine in five times.* Vancouver: Talonbooks.

Verriour, P. (1990). Storying and storytelling in drama. *Language Arts, 67*(2), 144–151.

Wikipedia. Available at: http://en.wikipedia.org/wiki/Elipses. Accessed 15 January 2014.

12

LIFE IN RHYME

Art, Literacy, and Survival[1]

Glynda A. Hull
Photographs by Randolph Young

> *This goes out to my Oakland people.*
> (RelixStylz, *Hard*, 2010)

Introduction

Police helicopters, flying low and buzzing loud, are a common part of the aerial landscape of Oakland, California, punctuating many an evening sky and reminding residents of the city's long experience with civil unrest and economic discontent. October 2012, for example, was the anniversary of the international Occupy Movement as it played out in Oakland, and on that date, police, activists, and the curious filled the streets, as searchlights and helicopters filled the air. Residents of Oakland, along with those of the surrounding Bay Area, have a history of activism and protest around social, political, economic, racial, and gender inequalities, and they are all too aware of living in a powder keg. Oakland is a medium-sized city, yet in 2010 it registered more than 500 separate shootings, 199 of whom were juveniles. In 2011, three children under the age of five were struck and killed by stray bullets, within a four and one-half month period, one in a baby stroller being pushed by his mother down the sidewalk of a busy street. Oakland is remembered as the home of the Black Panther movement from the 1960s, and as having had a prominent place at the table in the history of the US civil rights movement. Such history, a point of pride to many, has arguably faded of late in public perception, overwritten by stark statistics and the even harsher everyday life of too many residents in relation to crime, murders, gangs, drugs, unemployment, foreclosures, and police misconduct. To live in certain

FIGURE 12.1 Mural Photograph

Located on International Avenue between 103rd and 104th Streets in East Oakland, this Plan Bee Mural was painted by well-known graffiti artist Mike 'Dream' Francisco to memorialize Plan Bee, aka Jesse Rahim Hall, a founding member of the Oakland rap group, Hobo Junction. Bee was gunned down in 1992, sitting next to the intended target, as was his little brother Bobby in 2008. Dream was gunned down in 2000 on San Pablo Avenue in Oakland, the victim of a random street robbery.

parts of this city, to be young, and especially to be Black but also to be any young person of color, is right now to be embattled and to do battle, quite literally, and also as we shall see, symbolically, in a fight to survive.

There are sociological and historical accounts of urban political conflict in Oakland, notably Rhomberg's recent book *No There There: Race, Class, and Political Community in Oakland* (2004), which details both how diverse communities have mobilized and also how they have fragmented during the last half century, and the implications of such struggles for contemporary American democracy and debates about civic engagement. There are celebrations of the city's multicultural achievements and autobiographical forays that pay homage as well as cast blame, such as novelist and poet Ishmael Reed's *Blues City: A Walk in Oakland* (2003). There are numerous critiques of Oakland's school systems and classrooms, sometimes taken to task for unwitting contributions to the construction of youthful identities that fail to position or equip young people for hopeful and productive futures. Ann Ferguson's *Bad Boys: Public Schools in the Making of Black*

Masculinity (2001) is the sine qua non of this category. And so it is that a variety of scholars, in a range of disciplines, have attempted to come to terms, in some measure, with the complex racial, cultural, and political milieu that is Oakland, sorting out the possibilities but mostly the challenges that it signifies, here at the beginning of our new millennium for urban dwellers in the US and sometimes beyond.

In that general sense, this chapter is a modest attempt to add to an ongoing and broad conversation and debate—one that is played out not only in the academic literature but digitally in the blogosphere and the media, as well as face-to-face in families and neighborhoods. However, our focus here will not be on social movements, institutions, and cultures writ abstractly or painted large, though these will figure as backdrop, but rather on the lived, everyday experience of one young African American man and his boldly tenacious, yet tenuous, and to date successful drive to survive the streets of Oakland. What makes his life as lived in current times especially apropos in relation to the topic of this volume, 'revisiting learning lives,' with a focus on literacy research, is the semiotic agency he exerts, within the socio-historical constraints of his life in these times, through sustained and serious engagement with what I will call, following Paul Willis (1990), 'symbolic creativity' and the creation of a 'grounded aesthetics.' I am especially interested in the exercise of such agency as it intersects with space— material and symbolic, local and global—and with modalities or semiotics—music, print, and image, especially for the light these conjunctions shed on the new communicative affordances and demands of a digital and global world.

History

> *And it just took me off the street and gave me a chance to tell my story.*
> (Randy Young, interview, October 3, 2013)

Around 15 years ago federal grants became briefly available in the US to found community technology centers in low-income neighborhoods, the hope being that such centers would close opportunity gaps, preparing adults for new kinds of jobs and giving youth a leg up on school success. One such center in Oakland, California, taught digital storytelling. It offered a space, tools, and support for elders, adults, and children to create brief movies that coupled a spoken narrative with images and background music (e.g. Hull et al., 2006). Such opportunities were then rare, and hundreds of children, youth, and adults eventually participated in the classes and workshops offered at the center, including a young man named Randy, also known through his nom de plume as 'RelixStylz.' His artistry as a digital storyteller became part of the academic literature on literacy through publications exploring his compositions (e.g. Hull & Katz, 2006; Hull & Nelson, 2005; Nelson et al., 2012). He created multiple, remarkable digital stories over a period of years, and still creates them on occasion, long after the specific technology programs in which he participated ended in concert with the sun-setting of their funding streams. Randy expertly blended original music and lyrics with photography, much of it imagery of local neighborhoods: kids sitting on stoops, a clerk in a liquor store, a schoolyard viewed through a prison-like gate, and community murals, billboards, and scenes. His work had particular hallmarks: a striking aesthetics of the everyday, the articulation of his subjectivity as a young African American man, and the desire to offer social and political critique.

I have been witness to and beneficiary of Randy's artistic life over the years. Staying in touch mainly through text messaging but also through occasional meetings and social events, we developed a history and a connection and became friends, and my documentation of Randy's life as an artist gradually became a collaboration. It is Randy and his creative oeuvre as RelixStylz that I 'revisit' in this chapter, seeking to understand its nature and its continuities and discontinuities in the challenging context of the urban space that is Oakland. I have found this revisiting also requires thinking anew about the nature and conduct of scholarship that stretches across time and space in a digital age (see the Introduction to this volume).

My research over 10 years ago that took Randy's creative work as its focus centered on understanding the aesthetic power of multimodality. I had seen the dramatic effects of his digital stories, especially his very first effort called 'Lyfe-n-Rhyme,' on local and global audiences. What made his digital stories such compelling viewing, I wanted to know, and how was this multimodal meaning making accomplished textually? In this early research (e.g. Hull & Nelson, 2005), my co-authors and I focused exclusively on Randy's digital stories, and within those stories, on the conjunction of image and word. We took this focus despite the fact that sound tracks formed the musical background for each of the stories, and that all of this music (except for the Miles Davis tune that he had chosen for his initial digital story, 'Lyfe-n-Rhyme'), Randy had composed himself. Despite his talent for photography and the visual and his knack for wedding image and word with music, Randy's primary artistic identity was and remains that of a rapper. And, despite my knowledge that he wrote lyrics by the dozen and a then hazy understanding that he also created beats through digital sampling, my primary interest in his work remained for many years, until the revisiting project, the juxtaposition of image and word in digital stories, not the creation of beats and rhymes, even when that music was illustrated visually. In so focusing, as this paper will reveal, I had missed the full import for Randy of his engagement with symbolic creativity and what I could learn from it.

I contacted Randy during September of 2012 to ask if he would be interested in the 'revisiting' project—that is, in meeting with me to talk about his early work as a digital story artist and how that work and the world of digital composing have changed. He wondered in turn whether this project could not focus on his music in addition to his digital stories. Ultimately, we agreed upon a project in which we could jointly be invested, one that would have not only digital stories, but also his music, as the heart of his art, at center. We conducted audiotaped retrospective, informal interviews that juxtaposed his creative activities, both digital stories and music, then and now. I also thematically coded the lyrics of approximately 30 songs that Randy created and produced between 2008 and 2012. After I drafted this chapter he provided comments, and he also provided the photographs that accompany the words. We intend the photographs, not so much as illustrations, but as an additional layer of meaning, similar to if simpler than the multiple layers of meaning in digital stories, where image, word, voice, and music expand and modify each other.

Theorizations

> *Nightmares, can't get no sleep*
> *It's kinda bad, I guess it's my past that's catching up with me.*
> *Yeah I got a heavy heart, a lot of things on my mind*
> *So I spit in a rhyme, I call it black ice.*
>
> (RelixStylz, 'Black Ice,' *Hard*, 2010)

> *"To know the cultural world, our relationship to it, and to know ourselves, it is necessary not merely to be in it but to change— however minutely—that cultural world."*
>
> (Willis, 1990, p. 22)

Over the last 10 years Randy has composed (both beats and rhymes), performed, and recorded over 500 rap songs, created some 15 digital stories, and drawn upon during the process a variety of representational, compositional, and technical means, such as writing, oral composing, photography, videography, and a range of sound and recording equipment and software. This is an extraordinary output and signifies an extraordinary commitment to sustained artistic and literate practice. Because Randy identifies first and foremost as an artist, I have drawn upon Willis's (1990) ideas about symbolic creativity and a grounded aesthetics to theorize his life and work. Reporting his and his colleagues' ethnographic research on British youth's engagement with popular culture, Willis pointed out that "young people are all the time expressing or attempting to express something about their actual or potential *cultural significance*" (p. 1), through active intersections with media, through the articulation of personal styles, through choices and uses of music, and so on. Such pursuits, rather than being superficial or inconsequential, are at heart, Willis believes, attempts to create and sustain individual and group identities especially in the face of widespread economic, cultural, and ideological alienation in our late modern world. While many theorists would now readily agree with Willis that popular cultural engagement is a central site for youthful identity develop-ment, and even that such engagement is not merely passive consumption, what sets Willis's theorization apart is his insistent characterization of youth's popular cultural work as symbolic work— that is, the use and control of symbol systems in service of making a life, crafting an identity, and claiming a cultural space, and

188 Glynda A. Hull and Randolph Young

in doing so creatively, playfully, aesthetically, and sensually. This abstract human capacity he labels "symbolic creativity," and for its deployment in concrete contexts and situations, he offers the term "grounded aesthetic":

> This is the creative element in a process whereby meanings are attributed to symbols and practices and where symbols and practices are selected, reselected, highlighted and recomposed to resonate further appropriated and particularized meanings. Such dynamics are emotional as well as cognitive.
>
> (Willis, 1990, p. 21)

Willis warns against the reification of the external forms in this process—the symbols, texts, and artifacts—preferring instead to focus on the human activities of making meaning. "The aesthetic effect is not in the text or artifact," he writes; "it is part of the sensuous/emotive/cognitive creativities of human receivers" (p. 24). He offers the possibility that grounded aesthetics may have uses that are particularly powerful for groups and individuals who confront structural constraints that seem impossible to alter (or what Freire, 1970, called "limit situations"). To be sure, taking satisfaction in acts of symbolic creativity, to exercise our human capacities to create meanings and thereby to make our symbolic marks on the world, may seem thin gruel when set against the great inequalities and injustices of life that so many face. But the import of Willis's work is that we would do well not to underestimate this most human of symbolic capacities, or, I would add, to ignore the cultural sites, institutional spaces, and textual forms in which it flourishes. While literacy in the shape of academic essays and print-centric texts as composed in many school contexts certainly can and should be a vehicle for symbolic creativity, I would wager that for many US students at this historical juncture, they are not, and that such forms in such venues have in practice indeed been shorn of or disassociated from that creative capacity.

As a rap artist, Randy is part of the now global popular cultural movement of hip hop, and Willis would certainly consider hip hop to be the major contemporary example of a youthful grounded aesthetics and the exercise of symbolic creativity. Some scholarly commentators, parents, and spokespersons still decry the negative influence of rap through the racial stereotypes, anti-social behavior, materialism, and sexist and otherwise offensive language that it is claimed to exhibit and promote, but there is little doubt that the cultural tide has turned. This movement has not only gone global, feeding a worldwide entertainment industry as well as being appropriated by youth around the world, but it has received considerable scholarly attention for the past 20 years as well. In fact, a vast and energetic academic literature exists on hip hop (see, for a comprehensive set of examples, Forman & Neal's *Hip-Hop Studies Reader*, 2004). Some of this scholarship has made useful, explicit connections to the literacy classroom (e.g. Morrell, 2004; Morrell & Duncan-Andrade, 2002), recognizing

FIGURE 12.2 Shoreline Photograph

Oakland shoreline at Martin Luther King Park, Hegenberger Road, Oakland, CA, February 12, 2014. 'When you mention Oakland, most would automatically think urban city grunge, but there is a lot of unexpected natural beauty in Oakland.'

hip hop as a fund of knowledge (Moll et al., 1992) on which teachers can helpfully draw in order to build conventional literacies. Other researchers (e.g. Pennycook, 2007) have celebrated the multilingual diversity and ingenuity that characterizes current-day rap, turning young people's perceived difficulty with literacy on its head. Alim (2011), notably, has offered the term "ill-literacy," appropriating the inversion of "ill" in hip-hop discourse to suggest "good," which of course means the opposite of its conventional denotation. He thereby emphasizes the verbal and literate dexterity of hip-hop practitioners and implies the ethical and conceptual flat feet of widespread assumptions regarding literacy and certain youth.

The scholarship on hip hop thus forms a related backdrop, as an example of symbolic creativity, for understanding Randy's work, and it remains helpful for its insights on particular cultural histories, youthful discourses, and artistic genres and practices. I have framed hip hop as an instance of symbolic creativity, however, to keep our eyes on the prize of this larger construct. If hip-hop discourses can usefully be linked to literate practice, then literacy theory can likewise be animated via reference to art and performance, especially in a digital, multimodal age. Arts practices and aesthetic principles might, in fact, help us to reimagine literacy studies so as to foreground the role of a grounded aesthetics in acts of meaning making (Hull & Nelson, 2009). Dewey (1934/2005) reminds us that artworks can be focal points for making sense of the world, the nexus at which we synthesize and reconcile experiences. Eisner (2002) has similarly emphasized that the arts "help us to notice the world" and "provide permission to engage the imagination as a means for exploring new possibilities" (p. 10). Literacy studies, with its increasingly elastic focus on multiple forms of symbolization, might be further enriched through an examination of the artistic functions of awareness and imagination. Such a focus could shed light on how meaning is made in and sense derived from new kinds of texts, not only through the juxtaposition of modes, but through textual echoes, borrowings, and blendings, as will be the case for Randy's music. This focus will illuminate as well the contexts within which this meaning making is deployed.

Reflections

Survival through Art

> *'Giving up is hard to do,' I know, but I ain't giving up though,*
> *I'mma keep pushing, 'cuz I rap Oakland like Biggie rap Brooklyn.*
> (RelixStylz, *Hard*, 2010)

> *I'm rapping from the perspective of actually living through and surviving where most don't.*
> (Randy Young, interview, October 27, 2012)

Popular music is a major site for identity construction among young people; that much is beyond a doubt, as is the pride of place given to rap and hip hop around the world. While the consumption and sharing of music has been a familiar popular cultural practice for a long time, production has now come to the fore in music as well as other forms of symbolic creativity, just as it has in literacy per se, as writing or composing takes center stage from reading (Brandt, 2009; see also recent examples from the 'Maker Movement,' such as the Educator Innovator Network, educatorinnovator.org). Many youth routinely make their own beats and rhymes, especially since rap requires neither singing nor the ownership or mastery of musical instruments, so musicianship has been democratized, in a sense. But most never acquire, over a long period of study and apprenticeship, the facility with making raps that Randy has. When we met in the year 2000, Randy was already rapping and had been filling notebooks with his lyrics for years, but he had just begun learning and mastering the software program Reason (a music recording and production studio for writing, recording, remixing, and producing tracks). Speaking about himself during this pivotal period, he noted, 'That's where you see Randy making a transition from an average Joe artist.'[2] This transition, which he also described as the movement from being a rapper to being an artist, required two things: time and tools. As he put it, 'It's just an evolution over time and being able to have the instruments to translate what was going on in my head, you know, actually to come out of the speaker.' Getting access to technology was one of the most important benefits he took from being part of our community technology project. He pointed out that he had recorded his first digital story, the famous 'Lyfe-n-Rhyme' (www.youtube.com/watch?v=yfFg8zNkXZM), at the community center because he hadn't otherwise had access to a microphone. He likened such access to crucial incentives and essential nourishment: 'it's just like watering a plant.' Randy noted that, in contrast to raps, for which he has now assembled the needed tools, he hasn't yet created his best digital story, 'because I haven't had the best tools to make it.' Given access to the tools, Randy learns to master them, a process he characterizes as acquiring 'control,' and figures out how to 'make them do what I hear in my head.' It is noteworthy that his learning has been largely self-sponsored and that it has occurred over an expanse of time, a period of years.

Many of the themes and characteristic tropes that I identified in Randy's recent albums were present in his first digital stories and presumably in his early lyrics as well, and many are characteristic, in broad strokes, of rap in general. I even noticed on occasion the exact repetition of a few apt turns of phrase. The phrases 'life in rhyme' and 'poverty's concrete,' for example, occur in his work early and late. What has shifted over time, and to dramatic effect, is his complex skill-set as a rapper: his vocal range and expression, his use of metaphor and figurative language, his control over the multiple subgenres of rap, his facility at balancing hypnotic beats with lyrics that carry a message, and his ability to sample both beats and lyrics, making his work complexly and, to the student of his music, very satisfyingly intertextual. So, although the basic themes in Randy's music, and indeed his *raison d'être* as an artist, were largely formed when I first met him over 10 years ago, their expression now seems quite different and suggests intense, sustained practice and artistic growth. Randy is an unsigned artist, and he promotes his music on independent websites.[3] The hip-hop aficionados with whom I have shared his music note his talent and skill, and say they wouldn't be surprised if he were picked up by a label.

Randy consciously works within West Coast hip-hop traditions, and he also traces important influences on his work back to an uncle he considers an 'OG,' an original gangsta who did time in prison. He hangs out with the 'older town guys' and films 'old-school players' in order to 'just soak up a lot of gang.' Although he is often labeled a gangsta rapper, he believes that you only need to listen to his lyrics to know that this glove doesn't fit. His work makes frequent reference to other rappers (Tupac, of course, but also Oakland-origin rappers like Mac Dre), which he terms paying 'homage,' even as he strives to make his own sound. He is steeped in various additional genres of popular music, such as funk and rhythm and blues, and demonstrates that considerable historical knowledge through his sampling. Although he is grounded in what is called 'the Oakland sound,' he now makes no bones about seeking an audience that is national and global, explaining: 'I always thought of myself as an artist bigger than Oakland.' Randy is confident about his ability, with good reason, and at various times, he has tried to gain the sponsorship of famous artists and labels. Several years ago when I was living in New York City, he asked me to visit Fifty Cent's studio in lower Manhattan and drop off one of his mix tapes in an effort to attract the attention of this rap superstar. Randy has begun, to his surprise, to get local attention from unexpected fans. He recently went into an Oakland drugstore, where he stood in line to pay for some blank CDs, when he noticed that the cashier was staring at him, much to his irritation. The cashier then asked Randy if he intended to make more music, saying he recognized him from the World Star website. 'Get . . . outta here!' was Randy's delighted response.

Despite his pleasure in being recognized and his desire to be signed and to be compensated, Randy emphatically states that his art is not about money, and that he doesn't intend to 'comply,' to dilute his art and its message in order to create the sounds that are desired on the radio and by large record companies. He would 'rather kick the truth than tell a lie' ('The Bad Guy,' *MC. King*). Randy's characteristic gesture is geographic, as he asks his audience to walk with him, to traverse his community today or its past, to see with his vision. In so doing he raps about drugs, gangs, violence, betrayals, hustling, greed, evictions, police brutality, poverty—not in general, but specified, all from the local Oakland scene, drawing on his experiences and those of his circle and in his community. 'You can kill me on camera, that's plain to see/And get off with murder in the second degree' ('Mirror, Mirror,' *Hard*). Thus, Randy references the 2009 New Year's Day shooting in Oakland of an African American man by a policeman, in full view of dozens of people, judged to be accidental. He worries in his songs about children and women whose fathers and partners have been killed, and sometimes he extends his concerns to the global, intermixing references to Darfur and the Middle East with those of local tragedies and injustices. He is joyful, too, especially in his sampling of old school beats and lyrics, and often he is hopeful, looking toward 'a brighter day, a bigger faith.'

What I believe drives Randy, in continuing to build a remarkable and extensive body of work, what has compelled him to persist in making music, and honing and developing his skill all of these years, and what I did not properly understand prior to becoming immersed in and analyzing his music for this revisiting project, is the need to engage in 'necessary symbolic work,' to return to Willis's concept.[4] That is, he has been driven by wanting to impact, to change his social world by making and circulating his own tangible meanings within it; to do so creatively, aesthetically, intellectually, and ethically; and in so doing, to sustain an identity in the face of grave cultural, political, and economic alienation.

Literate Practices

With Relixstylz I can go into different perspectives and speak in third person. Because it's a lot of stuff that I go through, but it's a lot of stuff that I don't go through but have a knowledge of, just like Darfur. I'm not there, but I care enough to speak on it. I hear and I care, and just use RelixStylz as that voice to be able to speak.

(Randy Young, interview, October 27, 2012)

One of what I experience as Randy's most powerful songs is 'Black Ice,' from his *MC. King* album. In recounting how he created 'Black Ice,' he said he first made the beat by sampling the music of the older generation rhythm and blues singer Alexander O'Neal, whom he admired for his strong vocals. Listening to the beats, he came up with an organizing concept, the use of 'black ice' as a metaphor, or what he calls a 'theology.' Because black ice is both beautiful and dangerous, he felt it was an appropriate trope for signifying Oakland, where ugly things regularly happen, but sometimes beauty or good can come from them. Instead of writing the lyrics, he free-styled, stopping to record when he was satisfied with what he had composed orally. When I first met Randy, he wrote his lyrics in a notebook, but his compositional style now includes a reliance on the oral, probably as he has developed more expertise at rapping as well as a deep reservoir of images, phrases, rhythms, and themes. It is interesting to note, too, where digital stories are concerned, that he has long experimented with using different modalities as starting points, beginning sometimes with images, sometimes with words, sometimes with beats. His compositional repertoire, shifting among modes, demonstrates a great deal more flexibility than the term 'literacy' typically connotes, with one mode able to exchange places with another as need or inspiration demands.

A related, similarly flexible compositional strategy, the demonstration of which might be called 'transfer' in psychological literatures, was part of Randy's repertoire at the very beginning of his composing of digital stories. When Randy chose images to accompany his words and music, he in effect de-centered those images from other contexts and re-centered them in his own creative universe. As Bauman and Briggs (1990) would say, offering their "agent-centered" authorial framework, he "decontextualized" and then "recontextualized" these texts, which is a powerful compositional strategy indeed. And thus, in 'Lyfe-n-Rhyme' Randy decentered a photograph of Malcolm X from the US Civil Rights movement and recentered it in his digital story, using the resonance from that image to expand and animate the meanings of his own story as an African American man (Hull & Katz, 2006). I had been amazed right from the start at Randy's ability to create such powerful digital stories; he seemed to grasp the idea of a multimodal text intuitively. As I now understand, having immersed myself in his music, Randy was adapting the strategy of sampling that he had already developed to a high degree in rapping. Here is how Randy now describes that pivotal moment

194 Glynda A. Hull and Randolph Young

in which his set of representational means, and his understanding of it, suddenly expanded:

> I was able to take to the art of visual story-making automatically. I had no idea about it. . . . I had no idea about digital stories. But as I began to, you know, going through a new voice. . . . I could take images, use my mentality of how I was already doing music before this, and I see I have an avenue or a platform to actually translate image to the music. That's why 'Lyfe-n-Rhyme' came out like it did and had the effect that it did.

The process of recontextualizing has now become a commonplace literate strategy in a digital world where still and moving images are regularly repurposed, mashed up, altered, and otherwise appropriated, and where intertextuality (Kristeva, 1980) can be considered an interpretive habit of the late-modern mind. Randy was primed to excel at recontextualization and intertextuality by virtue of his musical expertise, and he continues to exploit these strategies in new ways. On two of his recent albums, he intersperses songs with excerpts from movies, raps, and television shows, excerpts that frame subsequent songs, layering significance and meaning. For example, 'Black Ice' is preceded by a brief sound clip of a woman crisply announcing the discovery of the latest endangered species, the young African American male. This clip Randy sampled from American rapper Ice Cube's first album, *AmeriKKKa's Most Wanted* (1990), and he intended it to jolt the listener into hearing 'Black Ice' and to pay attention to the lyrics, and not just the beat, through a particular interpretive frame. It is interesting to consider whether there might be other kinds of literate strategies, ones that perhaps apply across modes, that have emerged or been transformed through the coming of digital multimodality.

One literate practice that emerged anew for Randy is the radically increased capacity to circulate his music and digital stories on the Internet and for his work thereby to reach a much larger audience. Although the Internet was well established in 2000, social media reached prevalence only at mid-decade, including sites like YouTube that allowed the widespread sharing of video on the Internet for the first time. Twelve years ago Randy circulated his music by making mix tapes and selling them at markets, and he still does that today. However, he also now has a Web presence, initiated by his sister who uploaded some of his early digital stories, which Randy maintained and added to, including now albums of his raps and short videos on a range of topics, including his 'muscle car.' He appreciates knowing that his work is heard and viewed: 'I check online and you just see the responses and it's cool with me. It feels good to have people listening to it. And it feels good to know that I just made it from the heart.' His Internet presence, however, is sporadic; he will sometimes go for weeks without checking his music and media sites and channels, and he infrequently uses email, relying instead on text messaging and social media. Randy explained, 'gangster individuals,

FIGURE 12.3 Broken Telephone Photograph
47th and International Boulevard, Oakland, CA, March 15, 2014

they ain't really into all that Internet. No, we live action.' He's developed a Web presence because he needed to in order to promote his music and also because 'it makes no sense to have "Lyfe-n-Rhyme" if people can't see it. Look how many people it inspired.'

When asked how large his audience is, Randy noted that his digital story audience is larger than his music audience. Indeed, one of his digital stories, *Absolute* (www.youtube.com/watch?v=HeTHFHTd_xA), has had 250,000 views on YouTube. Compare this audience and reach with the year 2000 when his first digital story was viewed by a few dozen people locally and shown at a few academic conferences. On the other hand, Randy's music has rarely generated as much commentary or as many hits online. He sees his music as being 'harsher' and as allowing more topical scope and freedom than digital stories ('with music, I could do anything'), which he views as a narrower genre necessitating a more 'thought-provoking' treatment. The audiences that Randy imagines similarly require distinctive personae:

> In the hustler's realm, you got to have some balls. You can't build nothing and have somebody come take what you build, so you gotta be willing to push. So I can do that here, because that's what the gangsters gonna ride to.

I understand the significantly larger interest online in Randy's digital stories, in comparison with his music, as one more signal of the power in our current digital age of the visual and the multimodal as opposed to the verbal text. But this observation begs the question of what dimensions are added via the visual and the multimodal. In theorizing popular cultural texts, Willis (1990) suggested that part of their appeal is that their meanings are not overly determined and that they allow audiences to participate creatively instead of being "simply sent a 'message,' the meaning of which is pre-formed and pre-given" (p. 25). In something of the same vein, Eco (1979) proposed the notion of an "open text" as one that encourages a multiplicity of readings and positions readers to work alongside authors, imagining interpretations aligned with their own meaning-making histories. Thus, while open texts of course provide textual cues and features that guide readers toward particular paths, they also remain malleable enough to encompass a range of interpretations. It is intriguing to consider, in our multimodal age, how images and video, layered with sound and language, function within different genres and for different audiences to open rather than constrain interpretation (Hull et al., 2013). I believe that Randy's digital stories in contrast to his raps, in addition to being more 'thought-provoking' in their linguistic narratives and 'softer' in their beats as he aptly observed, have the added scaffolding of visuals that function to open interpretive pathways through the layering of meanings.

Research, Symbolic Creativity, and Relationships

> *It was hard to take all of these feelings and actually put them into audio and be this honest with you. How do I know you are gonna give a fuck? You could not care, and I'm telling you what's really happening with me.*
>
> *I give my sister a knife, a little knife. I give my wife a knife, you feel me? I can't be here all the time. I care for you all. Stand up for yourself.*
>
> (Randy Young, interview, October 27, 2012)

The process of 'revisiting' my early research on Randy's digital stories, in light of his music production, taught me that I had missed an important issue regarding transfer across modalities in digital multimodal composing, and that is the particular compositional practice related to "recontextualization" (Bauman & Briggs, 1990) or "remediation" (Prior & Hengst, 2010). In addition to these new insights about old understandings, the revisit outlined, in high relief, some discernible and dramatic shifts in meaning-making practices in our digital and global world. Randy's art has gradually been technologized (cf. Ong, [1982] 2002), via the increasing use of music software and also an increasing circulation on the Internet, and thus he is emblematic of many in our digital age.

Further, and more importantly, the revisit deepened my understanding of the enduring importance of what Willis calls "necessary symbolic work" (1990,

p. 11), whereby people "seek creatively to establish their presence, identity and meaning" (1990, p. 1). Initially, I had missed the full import for Randy of his engagement with symbolic creativity, and I knew little of the scope and virtuosity of his meaning-making practices. I could never have known, except through long-term longitudinal research or a revisiting, how his symbolic work was sustained and how it remained the creative centerpiece of his life. Randy's life as an artist and a social critic was what Willis called "necessary symbolic work," "that which has to be done every day, that which is not extra but essential to ensure the daily production and reproduction of human existence" (p. 9). Putting aesthetically formed and politically alert meanings into the world and circulating them, making material his human consciousness, was not Randy's pastime but his necessary work, a productive activity that altered the social world and that allowed him symbolically to survive.

It is commonplace to think of economic work as essential to survival, but it is instructive to ponder how symbolic work is necessary too, certainly for Randy, but also more generally for literacy education. To be sure, Randy would like to conjoin his symbolic work with his economic livelihood, provided such a conjoining did not require a compromise of his art. However, as his biography attests, he will engage creatively through symbolization regardless of whether this activity ever pays the bills. Willis claims that there is often a serious pleasure to be had and always a serious need to be satisfied through the exercise of symbolic work. The need has partly to do with establishing and enacting an identity and also to setting forth into the social surround one's own meanings, interpretations, and points of view, as well as feeling authorized to make known what the world looks like from one's own particular situated vantage point. For Randy such symbolic work parallels, echoes, and inscribes his literal struggle to survive ('It's body after body after body all the time/Can't tell nobody, but I'm dying inside,' *Absolute*). The pleasure has partly to do with engaging in necessary symbolic work creatively, aesthetically, and playfully. What might literacy education be, were it to concern itself with such existential and aesthetic issues, rather than reduce itself to questions of rhetoric or expression? What if our sights were set on enabling young people to experience the pleasure and satisfaction of necessary symbolic work?

Jackson (2013) has written recently about the African Hebrew Israelites of Jerusalem, describing the unexpected dilemmas that attended his ethnographic research with these people, dilemmas occasioned by the compression and reordering of time and space, and the wider distribution of information via the Internet, and also by research participants who were themselves able and even likely to look up his publications and perhaps to take issue with them. It is certainly the case that no longer can an ethnographer expect to spend months 'in the field' and then to come home to write in protected isolation. In an interconnected world, the researcher and the researched are potentially linked as never before, and with that joining, the roles they can expect to assume in relation to one another have shifted. A revisiting project has the potential to similarly shift such roles, and that was surely the case for Randy and me. Although we had never lost touch and had, in fact, collaborated around his work during the intervening years, my official request to juxtapose our work together, examining the then and the now, set in motion a new dynamic whereby Randy was able to successfully assert his desire to bring his music center stage, and I was able to hear him. We were also positioned to engage more reciprocally in the representation of the research—to wit, the photographs that layer this chapter's words with complementary but expanded meanings. The new dynamic was built in part, I believe, on the passage of time and the maturing of our relationship over the years as well as Randy's confidence and expertise as an artist, grown strong and sure. A significant benefit, then, of a revisiting project might be an adjustment or realignment of social relations, however perfectly balanced or imbalanced the researcher or participant had imagined these relations previously to be, such that new foci for the project, new understandings, and new and deeper social relationships can emerge.

There is a special responsibility and a special opportunity around research projects that involve acts of symbolic creativity in which an individual is deeply invested. If those acts also involve the assertion of an identity in a hostile world,

FIGURE 12.4 Street Sign.

'So many disappointments, you could see it in my eyes/In the streets of Oakland, Cali, I'm just tryna survive.' (RelixStylz, 'Black Ice,' *Hard*, 2010)

the burden of responsibility to hear and to respond is greater still. Over 50 years ago Ralph Ellison's *Invisible Man* revealed the invisibility of being African American in the United States. "I am invisible," Ellison's narrator explained, "simply because people refuse to see me. . . . When they approach me they see only my surroundings, themselves, or figments of their imagination—indeed, everything and anything except me." Petitt (2012), in a recent book on mass incarceration in the US, makes us realize how much still remains the same. She demonstrated how social science research over the last half century has itself contributed to rendering African American men invisible by systematically undercounting incarcerated persons, and thereby concealing the true extent of continuing decades and repeated generations of racial inequality. From the beginning Randy's artistic project, his long engagement with the creation of a grounded aesthetics, has been about making himself and his context visible. It has been about, that is, offering images and scenes and social commentary from Oakland, depicted vividly in words and sensually in sound and image as he asks his audience to 'Take a walk with me/Step by step' (RelixStylz, 'Walk with me,' 2011) through a landscape that is then transformed as his audience begins to see it through his eyes to 'See what I see.' What an intrepid endeavor, how daring in this way to reveal one's life in rhyme. The parallel challenge for the researcher, perhaps aided by the conceptual and methodological shifts made possible through revisiting, is similarly to clearly see and persuasively reveal.

Acknowledgement

Photography by Randolph Young.

Notes

1. Sincere thanks are due to Julian Sefton-Green and Jennifer Rowsell for their helpful comments on this chapter and to Adrienne Herd and John Scott for their long-term assistance with the research.
2. Unless otherwise noted, interview excerpts come from an interview conducted with Randy on October 27, 2012.
3. See for example, ReverbNation (www.reverbnation.com/relixstylz/songs), and for his digital stories, which feature his raps, he has a YouTube channel (www.youtube.com/user/Relixstylz).
4. It no doubt goes without saying that the full impact of Randy's grounded aesthetics of life as a young African American man in Oakland, California, cannot be experienced by reading a summary of the themes in his lyrics, or even by reading the lyrics themselves, but only through hearing them rapped, and also by seeing them interpreted through image, as occurs in digital stories.

References

Alim, H.S. (2011). Global ill-literacies: Hip hop cultures, youth identities, and the politics of literacy. *Review of Research in Education, 35,* 120–146.

Bauman, R. & Briggs, C.L. (1990). Poetics and performance as critical perspectives on language and social life. *Annual Review of Anthropology, 19,* 59–88.

Brandt, D. (2009). *Literacy and learning: Reflections on writing, reading and society.* San Francisco, CA: John Wiley.

Dewey, J. (1934/2005). *Art as experience.* New York: Perigree Books.

Eco, U. (1979). *The role of the reader.* Bloomington, IN: Indiana University Press.

Eisner, E. (2002). *The arts and the creation of mind.* New Haven, CT: Yale University Press.

Ellison, R. (1952). *Invisible man.* New York: Random House.

Ferguson, A. (2001). *Bad boys: Public schools in the making of black masculinity.* Ann Arbor, MI: University of Michigan Press.

Forman, M. & Neal, M.A. (Eds.). (2004). *That's the joint! The hip-hop studies readers.* New York: Routledge.

Freire, P. (1970/2000). *Pedagogy of the oppressed.* 30th Anniversary Edition. New York: Continuum.

Hull, G. & Katz, M. (2006). Crafting an agentive self: Case studies on digital storytelling. *Research in the Teaching of English, 41*(1), 43–81.

Hull, G. & Nelson, M. (2005). Locating the semiotic power of multimodality. *Written Communication, 22*(2), 224–262.

Hull, G. & Nelson, M. (2009). Literacy, media, and morality: Making the case for an aesthetic turn. In M. Prinsloo & M. Baynham (Eds.), *The future of literacy studies* (pp. 199–227). Houndmills: Palgrave Macmillan.

Hull, G., Stornaiuolo, A. & Sterponi, L. (2013). Imagined readers and hospitable texts: Global youth connect online. In D. Alvermann, N. Unrau, & R. Ruddell (Eds.), *Theoretical models and processes of reading* (6th ed.). International Reading Association.

Hull, G., Kenney, N., Marple, S. & Forsman-Schneider, A. (2006). *Many versions of masculine: Explorations of boys' identity formation through multimodal composing in an after-school program.* The Robert F. Bowne Foundation's Occasional Papers Series. New York: Robert F. Bowne Foundation.

Jackson, J. (2013). *Thin description: Ethnography and the African Hebrew Israelites of Jerusalem.* Cambridge, MA: Harvard University Press.

Kristeva, J. (1980). *Desire in language: A semiotic approach to literature and art.* New York: Columbia University Press.

Moll, L., Amanti, C., Bneff, D. & Gonzales, N. (1992). Funds of knowledge for teaching: Using a qualitative approach to connect homes and classrooms. *Theory into Practice, 3*(2), 132–141.

Morrell, E. (2004). *Linking literacy and popular culture.* Norwood, MA: Christopher Gordon.

Morrell, E. & Duncan-Andrade, J. (2002). Toward a critical classroom discourse: Promoting academic literacy through engaging hip-hop culture with urban youth. *English Journal, 91*(6), 88–94.

Nelson, M., Hull, G. & Young, R. (2012). Portrait of the artist as a younger adult: Multimedia literacy and "effective surprise." In O. Erstad & J. Sefton-Green (Eds.), *Identity, community, and learning lives in the digital age* (pp. 215–232). Cambridge: Cambridge University Press.

Ong, W. ([1982] 2002). *Orality and literacy: The technologizing of the word.* New York: Routledge.

Pennycook, A. (2007). Language, localization, and the real: Hip-hop and the global spread of authenticity. *Journal of Language, Identity & Education, 6*(2), 101–115.

Petitt, B. (2012). *Invisible men: Mass incarceration and the myth of Black progress.* New York: Russell Sage Foundation.

Prior, P.A. & Hengst, J.A. (2010). Introduction: Exploring semiotic remediation. In P.A. Brior & J.A. Hengst (Eds.), *Exploring semiotic remediation as discourse practice* (pp. 1–23). New York: Palgrave Macmillan.

Reed, I. (2003). *Blues city: A walk in Oakland.* New York: Random House.

Rhomberg, C. (2004). *No there there: Race, class, and political community in Oakland.* Berkeley, CA: University of California Press.

Willis, P. (1990). *Common culture: Symbolic work at play in the everyday cultures of the young.* Buckingham: Open University Press.

ABOUT THE CONTRIBUTORS

Barbara Comber is a Professor in the Faculty of Education at Queensland University of Technology. She is particularly interested in literacy education and social justice. She has conducted longitudinal ethnographic studies and collaborative action research with teachers working in high poverty and culturally diverse communities. Her research examines what kinds of teaching make a difference to young people's literacy learning trajectories. Her recent work explored the affordances of place-based pedagogies for the development of critical and creative literacies. She is currently undertaking an ethnography on educational leadership and turnaround literacy pedagogies and collaborative inquiry on ethical leadership in an era of high-stakes accountability. Recent publications include *Literacy in the middle years: Learning from collaborative classroom research* (Morgan, Comber, Freebody & Nixon et al., 2014), *International handbook of research in children's literacy, learning and culture* (Hall, Cremin, Comber & Moll, 2013) and *Turn-around pedagogies: Literacy interventions for at-risk students* (Comber & Kamler, 2005).

Catherine Compton-Lilly is an Associate Professor in Curriculum and Instruction at the University of Wisconsin Madison. She is the author of several books and has published articles in the *Reading Research Quarterly*, *Research in the Teaching of English*, *The Reading Teacher*, *The Journal of Early Childhood Literacy*, *The Reading Teacher*, and *Language Arts*. Dr. Compton-Lilly engages in longitudinal research projects that last over long periods of time. She followed a group of eight inner-city students from grade 1 through grade 11. She is now exploring literacy and identity construction for a group of children from immigrant families and plans to follow those children for 10 years. Her interests include examining how time operates as a contextual factor in children's lives as they progress through school and construct their identities as students and readers.

About the Contributors **203**

Kathleen Gallagher is Professor and Canada Research Chair in *Theatre, Youth, and Research in Urban Schools* at the University of Toronto. Dr. Gallagher's award-winning books include *The Theatre of Urban: Youth and Schooling in Dangerous Times* (University of Toronto Press, 2007) and *Drama Education in the Lives of Girls: Imagining Possibilities* (University of Toronto Press, 2000). Her upcoming book (University of Toronto Press, 2014) is titled *Why Theatre Matters: Urban Youth, Engagement, and a Pedagogy of the Real*. Her two edited collections are: *How Theatre Educates: Convergences and Counterpoints with Artists, Scholars, and Advocates* (University of Toronto Press, 2003) and *The Methodological Dilemma: Creative, Critical and Collaborative Approaches to Qualitative Research* (Routledge, 2008). Dr. Gallagher has published many articles on theatre, youth, pedagogy, methodology and gender, and travels widely giving international addresses and workshops for practitioners. Her research continues to focus on questions of youth civic engagement and artistic practice, as well as the pedagogical and methodological possibilities of learning and researching with theatre.

Mary Hamilton is Professor of Adult Learning and Literacy at Lancaster University where she co-directs the Centre for Technology Enhanced Learning. Her funded research projects have included literacy in the workplace (Leverhulme Trust); literacy practices in the local community; an oral history of adult basic education (both funded by the ESRC); Open Learning in Adult Basic Education (Universities Funding Council); Public Images of Literacy in the Press (Nuffield, Leverhulme) as well as a range of policy oriented and evaluation projects funded by UK government sources, local and national. She has co-coordinated a DfES/ESF funded network of Practitioner-led Research Projects for the National Research and Development Centre for Adult Literacy and Numeracy. Her books include *Literacy and the Politics of Representation* (2012), *Local Literacies* (1998, 2012), co-written with David Barton, which has just been reissued as a Routledge Linguistics Classic; and an edited book called *More Powerful Literacies* co-edited with Lyn Tett and Jim Crowther, University of Edinburgh.

Michael Hoechsmann is the Chair of Education Programs at Lakehead University, Orillia. His work and teaching resides at the intersections of media education, digital literacies and cultural studies. He is the co-author of *Media Literacies: A Critical Introduction* (2012, Blackwell) and *Reading Youth Writing: "New" Literacies, Cultural Studies and Education* (2008, Peter Lang). From 1998 to 2002, he was the Director of Education at Young People's Press, a national news service for youth, 14–24 years.

Glynda A. Hull is a Professor in the Graduate School of Education at the University of California, Berkeley, and the Elizabeth H. and Eugene A. Shurtleff Chair in Undergraduate Education. She recently collaborated with educators in several countries, with support from the Spencer Foundation, to create and study

204 About the Contributors

an international social networking project for youth. In California over the last 10 years, with support from the US Department of Education and other agencies, she has created and studied after school programs for K-12 youth that emphasize digital media. Her current research focuses on designing innovative online spaces for learning and exploring the burgeoning phenomenon of global schools.

Aliya Khan is studying Psychology, Sociology and Religious Studies for her A-levels at Thomas Rotherham College and is hoping to pursue a career in the Police. Her current interest is finishing her Duke of Edinburgh Award.

Naomi Lightman is a Ph.D. candidate at the Ontario Institute for Studies in Education at the University of Toronto and holds an M.A. in Political Science from McGill University. Her academic research centres on the intersections of schooling and transnationalism in Canada; her work in informal education focuses on bridge-building leadership activities with youth, working on Israel/Palestine coexistence and within Canada's first nation communities. Her academic work has been published in *Canadian Ethnic Studies* and the *Transnational Social Review— A Social Work Journal*. From the age of 16–19, Naomi was an active contributor to Young People's Press.

Claudia Mitchell is a James McGill Professor in the Department of Integrated Studies in the Faculty of Education, McGill University, and an Honorary Professor in the Faculty of Education, University of KwaZulu-Natal in Durban, South Africa, where she established the Centre for Visual Methodologies for Social Change. Her research interests span work in schools with teachers and young people, particularly in the context of gender and HIV&AIDS, through to work in Higher Education in the study of mainstreaming issues of gender and HIV&AIDS, to girlhood studies and in particular work related to gender-based violence, and to media studies and participatory visual methodologies. She is the co-founder and co-editor of *Girlhood Studies: An Interdisciplinary Journal*.

Kate Pahl is a Reader in Literacies in Education in the University of Sheffield. She is the author, with Jennifer Rowsell, of *Artifactual Literacies: Every object tells a story* (2010) and *Literacy and Education: The New Literacy Studies in the Classroom* (2nd edition, 2012). She is also the author of numerous chapters and articles in the field of literacy studies, participatory methodologies, arts practice and home cultures. Her research projects have included 'Imagine,' 'Writing in the Home and in the Street,' 'Language as Talisman' and 'Making Meaning Differently'— all funded through the Arts and Humanities Research Council's Connected Communities Programme. These projects have involved the co-production of research with community groups and artists. Her book *Materializing Literacies in Communities* will be published by Continuum Press in October 2014 and looks at literacy as embodied, sensory, and in place.

About the Contributors 205

Jennifer Rowsell is Professor and Canada Research Chair in Multiliteracies at Brock University's Faculty of Education where she directs the Centre for Multiliteracies. She has co-written and written several books in the areas of New Literacy Studies, multimodality, and multiliteracies. Her current research interests include children's digital and immersive worlds; adopting and applying multimodal epistemologies with adolescents and teenagers; and ecological work in communities examining everyday literacy practices. Her most recent books include *New Literacies Around the Globe* with Cathy Burnett, Julia Davies, and Guy Merchant and the *Routledge Handbook of Contemporary Literacy Studies* with Kate Pahl.

Julian Sefton-Green is an independent scholar working in Education and the Cultural and Creative Industries. He is currently Principal Research Fellow at the Department of Media & Communication, LSE and a research associate at the University of Oslo. He is an Honorary Professor of Education at the University of Nottingham, UK, and the Institute of Education, Hong Kong. He has researched and written widely on many aspects of media education, new technologies, creativity and informal learning. Recent volumes include: joint editing of *The International Handbook of Creative Learning* (2011) and *Researching Creative Learning: Methods and Approaches* (2010), both with Routledge; *Learning at Not-School* (2013, MIT Press); and co-editing *Learning Lives: Transactions, Digital culture and Learner Identity* (2013, Cambridge University Press).

Saskia Stille recently completed her Ph.D. in Curriculum, Teaching and Learning at OISE/University of Toronto, and her research program focuses on language in education, digital literacies, and participatory, collaborative research methodologies. She is currently a Senior Research Coordinator for the Literacy and Numeracy Secretariat in the Ontario Ministry of Education where she coordinates data collection, analysis, and evaluation of system-level education data to address issues relating to equity and student achievement in Ontario schools. Publications from her recent work appear in several edited books and refereed journals, including *Language Assessment Quarterly*, *TESL Canada Journal*, *European Journal of Teacher Education*, and *TESOL Quarterly*.

Randolph Young is a hip-hop artist living in Oakland, California. In his creative work he translates perspectives on urban life into the verbal, visual, and musical languages of hip-hop culture, producing critical understandings of social, political, and aesthetic experience. He is especially interested in the intersection of music and narrative, and how hip hop, more than any other music since the blues, celebrates the creation of stories that can appear merely incredible, transgressive, or violent, but are made convincing and meaningful by the teller. Young's mixtapes can be downloaded at www.datpiff.com/; his music is found on reverbnation.com/relixstylz; and his videos appear on YouTube under RELIXSTYLZ.

INDEX

activism 33–43, 137, 183
Actor Network Theory (ANT) 113
adolescence *see* youth
adulthood 25–29, 41
aesthetics, grounded 187–190, 197–199
agency 56–57
Ahmed, S. 178–179
AIDS 33–42
Albertine in Five Times 164–166
Alim, H.S. 189
Aliya 122–132
anthropology 3; *see also* ethnography
art 105, 178, 186, 189–190; survival and
    190–192; *see also* symbolic creativity
artifacts 116, 121, 150
audience 47
autoethnography 40–42; *see also* ethnography

Baldwin, P. 171
Barton, D. 99, 111
Bauman, R. 193
Beach, R. et al. 170
becoming 93
benchmarks 67
Bennett, S. 178
Berliner, D. 161
biographies 145–148
bodies 178–179
Bourdieu, P. 49, 51–52, 149; Bourdieu,
    P. et al. 162
Bowker, S. 101–111

Braidotti, R. 93
Briggs, C.L. 193
Buckingham, D. 46, 52
Burawoy, M. 4, 6, 32, 79, 83, 92, 100
Butler, J. 179

camera, digital 87–92; *see also* video
    camera
Campbell, E. 119–120
Canada 80, 136, 138–139, 152
change, theory of 6–7
civic participation 101, 138–140, 184
Clark, B.R. 71
class, social 6–7, 50–52, 137
classroom 156–157
co-construction 5–6, 129
Cole, M. 98
Coleman, R. 130
collaborative: conceptualizing 173–181;
    ethnography 99; literacy 169–172
Comber, B. 10
communication practices 99–100,
    109–110, 143–145; email 167
community 82–87, 101–102; technology
    and 191
Compton-Lilly, C. 11
computer-based reading 106
conceptual issues 38–42
contingency 92–95
cooperative teaching 153–156
co-production 118–120, 129–132

Cortazzi, M. 5
creativity 90–92
critical becomings 85–92
critical consciousness 51–52
cross-case analysis 62–63
cultural capital 23
cultural production 84–92
cultural studies *see* media studies
Cultural Studies Goes to School 46–47, 50
culture 158–159
curriculum 58
Cwerner, S.B. 130

data 40, 159–160
Dewey, J. 190
differentiation 161
digital camera 87–92
digital culture 53–55
digital literacy 79–84, 106, 112, 185–186;
    as cultural production 84–95; stories
    194–196
Dimitriadis, G. 5
discourse: analysis 62–64, 75–77;
    mainstream 141; temporal
    manifestations of 65–74
drag 37
drama 170–181
dramatic inquiry 170–171
DVDs 107
dyslexia 106–107, 110

Eco, U. 196
education 55–57; female 124–125;
    memories of 153–154; as social
    mobility 50; teacher 149–150,
    154–155, 160–161
Eisner, E. 190
Eliot, G. 7
ellipsis 179–180
Ellis, C. 39
Ellison, R. 199
email 106, 167
emotions 179
equity 141–142
ESOL 123–124
Esslin, M. 169
ethics 41–42, 95
ethnography 4–6, 82–84, 92–93, 95;
    collaborative 99; co-production and
    118–120; limits to 105; multi-site 112;
    researcher relationships 197–198; *see
    also* autoethnography
Eyre, R. 178

Facebook 47, 55
fan culture 48
feminism 119
Ferguson, A. 184–185
Ferham Families project 116–118
field, concept of the 82–84
film 85–87
Fiumara, C. 174
Fleming, K. 171
funding 139–140

Gallagher, K. 13
garden 86–87
generations *see* intergenerational
    relationships
geography 103
globalization 111–112
gold 127
Goodson, I. 150–151, 154, 159–160
Google Earth 85
Graff, H. 98
Grosz, E. 93

Hamilton, M. 11–12, 111
Harry Potter 125
Hart, A. et al. 121
Heath, S.B. 2–3, 5–6, 98, 100, 109
Heathcote, D. 170
Herbert, P. 170
heritage 128–129
heterochrony 157–158
Hinton, S.E. 16, 48
hip hop 188–191
history: life 2–3, 129–130, 150–151,
    159–160; social 68–70
HIV 33–42
Hoechsmann, M. 12–13
Holland, D. 121
hooks, b. 40
Hull, G. 13–14

identity 20–23, 51–54, 74–77, 187–188;
    digital 55, 82–85; literate 122–125,
    128–129; nomadic 93–94; political
    48; racial 184–185; teacher 149–150,
    157, 162
identity-construction 196–197; music and
    190, 192
iMovie 86
In My Life 33–34
inclusion 141, 161
inquiry-based learning 158
institutions 98, 109

208 Index

interfaces 109, 111
intergenerational relationships 110, 121–125, 131
internet 25–26, 41, 99–100, 143–145, 194–195
intertextuality 193–194
interview data 159–160

Jackson, J. 197
James, A. 131
Jemkins, H. 48
Jin, L. 5
journalism 139–140, 145–148
judgement 51–52

Khan, A. 12
Kim, R.H. 171
knowledge production 83–84, 88–91, 180

Lancaster 99, 103, 113
language 65–68; digital literacy and 81–82; materialization of 126–127
Lassiter, E. 119–120
Lave, J. 121
Leander, K. 87
learner identities 22
learning: alternative pathways 28–29; inquiry-based 158
Learning to Labour 7
Lemke, J. 100, 157
Lesko, N. 180
Levinson, B. et al. 51
life history 2–3, 129–130, 150–151, 159–160
life pathways 145–148, 176
life story 151, 154
Lightman, N. 12–13
listening 174–175
literacy 1–3; of collaboration 169–172; hip hop and 189–190; meaning of 100; as survival 69–70; *see also* digital literacy
literacy canon154
literacy learning 23–24; theories 17
literacy practices 94–95, 104–105, 193–196; in post-school life 20, 23–25; research and 119; social use of 27–29, 98–99
literate identity 122–125, 128–129
local cultures 112
Local Literacies project 98–100, 104–105, 111–113
Lolwana, P. 40

longitudinal perspective 2–4, 7, 17; *see also* temporal discourse analysis
Luke, A. 47

MacLeod, J. 5
mantle of the expert approach 170–171
Marcus, G.E. 6, 112
Massachusetts 73–74
materialization 126–127
meaning 7, 92, 162, 166–169; multimodality and 190, 196–197
media 143–145; consumption 51–52; digital 84–92; *see also* youth media
media studies 46–50, 54–58; effect of 51–54
memories 41, 93, 166–169, 175–176; senses and 178–179
methodologies 38–42, 99, 101, 111–113; co-production as 118–120; memory and 180; of Young People's Press 140
Miller, J. 40
minorities 94–95
Mitchell, C. 10
mobile phones 106, 108
Moletsane, R. 40
Morecambe 102–104, 112
multi-sited ethnography 112–113; *see also* ethnography
multimodality 186, 193–194, 196
multivocal texts 120
music 105, 186–187; *see also* hip hop

narrative 108–109, 121–127, 131; in drama 171; of life stories 154
Neale, B. 36
neoliberalism 6, 160–161, 170
new audience studies 47
newspaper *see* Young People's Press
nomadic theory 92–94
Norquay, N. 40

Oakland 183–199

Pahl, K. 12, 121, 150
participation 87–90
pedagogy 29, 56–57, 142–143, 151–158; drama and 170–172; radical 52
personal qualities 56
Petitt, B. 199
place 54–55, 101, 110
poetry 128–129
police 71–73, 183–184, 192
political engagement 137–139

political identities 48
popular culture 47, 105; as symbolic work 187–188; texts of 196
power relationships 98
prayer 126–127
process 87–92
professional development 160–161
public-facing institutions 109

qualitative research 62–63

race 54–55, 141–142; in Oakland 183–185, 192; in US 68–69, 198–199
radical pedagogy 52
rap 188–191; *see also* hip hop
Re/constructing Literate Identities 79–84
reading: antipathy to 21–22; computer-based 106; group 107
reading back 39–41
reconnecting 48–50
recontextualizing 193–194, 196
Reed, I. 184
reflexivity 5–6, 51–54, 92–93, 95; and life history 150
RelixStylz 185–186, 190–199
research 161–162, 196–199; collaborative 173–181
research questions 8–10
resilience, narratives of 121, 125–130
Rethinking Schools 61
revisit 2–9, 83–84, 92–95; co-production and 118–121, 129–132, 173; of *Fire+Hope* 33–39; memories and 166–169; and reconnection 48–50; social relations and 198–199; teacher education 151–161; and temporal discourse analysis 62, 77; of Young People's Press 140–148
Rhomberg, C. 184
Ricoeur, P. 131
Riggins, S. 40
rituals of collaboration 169–170, 174
Rowe, D.W. 87
Rowsell, J. 1, 13, 121, 178

school 2, 55–57; garden project 86–87; popular culture and 47
schooling 19, 67–68
Scribner, S. 98
Sefton-Green, J. 10–11
self 121, 138–139; *see also* identity
Sennett, R. 4, 13, 169–170, 172, 175
sexuality 36–37

Sikes, P. 150–151, 159–160
Simon, R. 166
Smith, D. 29, 112–113
social: change 7, 141–142; class 51–52, 137; histories 68–70; institutions 98, 109; knowledge 48, 92–93; mobility 50, 54–55; script 150–151, 160; space 93–94, 144
social reproduction theory 51
social research 38–42, 92–93; and race 199
socialization, of children 131
socio-material approaches 113
socio-semiotic readings 40–41
Soep, L. 5–6
Soft Cover group 32–42
South Africa 32–42
spoken word 171
Sri Lanka 152
Stille, S. 11
stories 71–74, 121–127, 131, 175; in drama 171; life 151
Street, B. 98
student participation 87–92
subjectivity 6–7, 51, 55–57
survival 190–192
symbolic creativity 187–189, 192, 196–199

taste 51–52
Taylor, S. 54
teachers 67–68, 75–76; education 160–161; identity 149–150, 157, 162; judgments 22
teaching trends 153–157
technology 84, 88–89; communication 99–100, 143–145; music 190–191
temporal discourse analysis 62–64, 75–77; manifestations 65–74
temporal language 65–68
textual practices 39–41, 113
theater 178
theory of learning 47
time 6–7, 36, 93–94, 112, 180–181; *see also* heterochrony; temporal discourse analysis
Toronto Star, The 138–140
Tottenham 46, 49–50, 54–55
'translocal literacies' 112
travel 24–25
Tremblay, M. 164–166, 175, 179–180

university 22
US 184–185, 199

Vasudevan, L. 131
vernacular 100, 154
Verriour, P. 171
video camera 87–92
voice 171–172; of minorities 94–95;
   of youth 138–145

Wacquant, L. 162
Walsh, S. 42
Ways with Words 100
Weis, L. 6–7

Willis, P. 7, 13, 185, 187–188, 192,
   196–197
working class 50; *see also* class, social
Wright, N. 178

Young People's Press (YPP) 134–140;
   revisiting of 140–148
Young, R. 13–14
youth 181–182, 187; voice of 138–145
youth media 134–135